Praise for *How to Differentiate Your Math Instruction*...

How to Differentiate Your Math Instruction is truly an educator's dream. The math tasks are relevant and effective for the era of Common Core State Standards. An educator, using this resource, can certainly be confident about meeting the instructional needs of a wide range of students.

> —*Dionn N. Brown, Assistant Director of Curriculum and*
> *Professional Development for Math and Science, Urban Teacher*
> *Center, Baltimore, Maryland*

This research-based resource, complete with video, provides a glimpse into how effective student-centered classrooms might look. The diversity of students in the classrooms supports the research that indicates that all students, given the opportunity, can and do engage in mathematical discourse and reflect on their own learning. The examples in the text and the video provide a lens through which all teachers can best meet the needs of all their students.

> —*Dr. Anne Collins, NCTM Board of Directors*

Teachers will recognize themselves and the challenges they face in this thoughtful, practical, and provocative resource. Through the use of real examples, video clips, teacher reflections, and practical tips, the very knowledgeable authors show classroom teachers how to make strides toward what often feels like an impossible goal. The vignettes are ones any classroom teacher could identify with and the videos bring to life the text. The tone and empathy of the authors transform the daunting task of meeting every student's needs into a manageable, even rewarding endeavor. This is a book all elementary mathematics teachers would benefit from reading.

> —*Lucy West, founder, Metamorphosis Teaching Learning*
> *Communities and author,* Content-Focused Coaching:
> Transforming Mathematics Lessons

Fabulous videos! Viewing young learners grappling with big math ideas is truly inspiring. The "math talk" in these classrooms gave me more ideas about how I might frame differentiated lessons for use with my own students.

> —*Barbara Allen-Lyall, mathematics director (grades 3 and 4*
> *School, Stamford, Connecticut*

(c

D1472096

As a teacher, it is great to have a resource that I can pick up and immediately get practical ideas to use in my classroom. The CCSS lesson plans are easy to use and share with colleagues. The *Take Action!* callouts are quick reminders of the important ideas that I can read over and over. A special thank-you to the teachers in the videos for opening up their classrooms so that we can learn together how to differentiate learning for all students.

> —*Marcia Witthus, kindergarten teacher, Kyrene School District, Phoenix, Arizona*

Teachers seeking resources to differentiate for a wide range of learners in their classrooms will find this to be a much-referenced addition to their shelves. Balancing theory and practice along with an understanding of the many demands on a teacher's time, the authors provide creative, interesting, and challenging mathematics for students at all levels in the classroom. The engaging video clips provide excellent modeling for implementation of activities.

> —*Christy Lyle, math coordinator, Kodiak Island Borough School District, Alaska*

The focus of this resource is right on target. It is important that teachers realize that attending to tasks chosen and the richness of mathematics available through well-chosen tasks forms the basis for differentiation. Vignettes throughout the book highlight application of ideas in real classrooms and teacher reflections give readers insights into how educators think about their instructional decisions. Also, the videos are great. This is a "must have" for anyone teaching mathematics.

> —*Dr. Susan Friel, professor, University of North Carolina*

How to Differentiate Your Math Instruction

LESSONS, IDEAS, AND VIDEOS WITH COMMON CORE SUPPORT

A MULTIMEDIA PROFESSIONAL
LEARNING RESOURCE

Linda Dacey • Jayne Bamford Lynch • Rebeka Eston Salemi

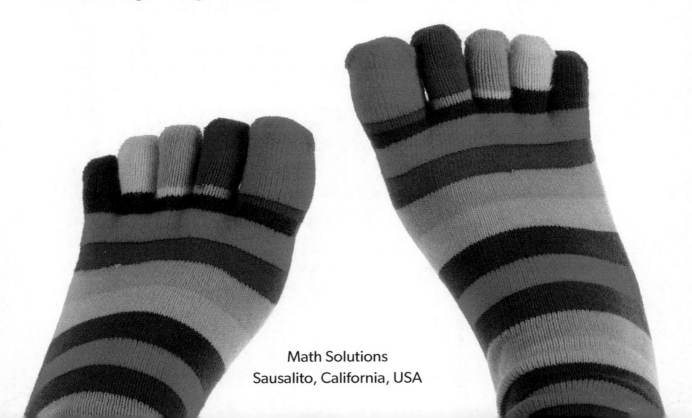

Math Solutions
Sausalito, California, USA

Math Solutions
One Harbor Drive, Suite 101
Sausalito, California, USA 94965
www.mathsolutions.com

ISBN-13: 978-1-935099-40-6
ISBN-10: 1-935099-40-X

Editor: Jamie Ann Cross
Production: Denise A. Botelho
Cover and interior design: Lisa Delgado, Delgado and Company & Susan Barclay,
    Barclay Design
Cover photo (bottom): Dusica Paripovi/Flickr Open/Getty Images
Composition: Publishers' Design and Production Services, Inc.
Interior images: Cambridge Public Schools, Cambridge, Massachusetts
Videographer: Friday's Films, www.fridaysfilms.com

1   2   3   4   5   6   7   8   9   10   31   22   21   20   19   18   17   16   15   14   13

A Message from Math Solutions

We at Math Solutions believe that teaching math well calls for increasing our understanding of the math we teach, seeking deeper insights into how students learn mathematics, and refining our lessons to best promote students' learning.

Math Solutions shares classroom-tested lessons and teaching expertise from our faculty of professional development consultants as well as from other respected math educators. Our publications are part of the nationwide effort we've made since 1984 that now includes

- more than five hundred face-to-face professional development programs each year for teachers and administrators in districts across the country;
- professional development books that span all math topics taught in kindergarten through high school;
- videos for teachers and for parents that show math lessons taught in actual classrooms;
- on-site visits to schools to help refine teaching strategies and assess student learning; and
- free online support, including grade-level lessons, book reviews, inservice information, and district feedback, all in our Math Solutions Online Newsletter.

For information about all of the products and services we have available, please visit our website at *www.mathsolutions.com.* You can also contact us to discuss math professional development needs by calling (800) 868-9092 or by sending an email to *info@mathsolutions.com.*

We're always eager for your feedback and interested in learning about your particular needs. We look forward to hearing from you.

Brief Contents

Contents

Part 2   Tools for Differentiation

Lesson Ideas
(including Common Core Correlations)

The lessons listed here are called out because they include detailed, step-by-step directions at the end of their corresponding chapter. For a complete list of lesson ideas featured in this resource see the "Teaching with the Common Core" table on page xxix.

Reproducibles

(continued)

Acknowledgments

This resource features stories and student work from many classrooms. Numerous colleagues, workshop participants, children, and parents informed our work. We are profoundly thankful for their insights, time, and contributions. We are particularly grateful to the teachers and administrators from the Cambridge Public Schools in Massachusetts who opened their classrooms and schools to us for filming. In addition to Eileen Gagnon, who helped to organize the filming and to edit the video, we thank Karla Anderson, Jessica Cocuzzo, Tori Corpas, Ben Geiger, Fiona Healy, Mark Healy, Monica Leon, Deborah Logiudice, Summer Thompson, and Meaghan Miller.

We are indebted to our editor, Jamie Cross, who gave us this opportunity to refine and update our work that originated in the Math for All series. We have been graced by her support for this project and her amazing editorial wisdom. Many thanks also to Carolyn Felux, who helped oversee the filming and connect the video segments to the text. Also, much appreciation to our production manager, Denise Botelho, who guided the text through its transformation to a professional publication.

We also express gratitude for Perry Pickert and his crew at Friday's Films for so expertly capturing the intent of this resource on video.

Last, we are thankful for the opportunity to work together again, to share ideas, to challenge one another, and to be nourished by our collaboration.

About This Resource

Why This Resource?

How can teachers meet the growing diversity of learning needs in their class-room? Furthermore, how do teachers meet this challenge in the midst of increasing pressures to master specified content? Differentiated instruction—instruction designed to meet differing learners' needs—is clearly required. By adapting classroom practices to help more students be successful, teachers are able to honor individual students and to increase the likelihood that curricular outcomes are met. This resource will help you to begin or deepen your use of differentiation strategies.

Trends and buzzwords come and go in education, but the need for differentiated intruction is constant. Our students deserve to have their individual needs met in their classrooms. Learning how to meet such needs is a career-long process, a major part of our professional journey. We know that this has been true for us and we are eager to share our current thinking.

Meeting the Growing Diversity of Learning Needs

Variations in student learning have always existed in classrooms, but some have only been given recent attention. Many educators are also rethinking what it means to learn and teach in this digital age. With information a click away, critical thinking, making connections, and decision making become key to success (Siemens 2005). The rapid development of new knowledge makes it essential that our students know how to learn and how to make choices. Increased access to social networks increases the need for our students to learn from their interactions with others; to contribute to theory-building within a learning community, and to negotiate among diverse thinkers.

Brain research has given us additional insight into the learning process; for example, it has shown us that there is an explicit link between our emotional states and our ability to learn (Sprenger 2008, Zull 2002, Jensen 2005). Having a sense of control and being able to make choices typically contributes to increased interest and positive attitudes. So we can think of providing choice, and thus control, as creating a healthier learning environment.

> Differentiated instruction—instruction designed to meet differing learners' needs—is clearly required. By adapting classroom practices to help more students be successful, teachers are able to honor individual students and to increase the likelihood that curricular outcomes are met.

At the same time that we are gaining these insights, the diversity of learning needs in classrooms is growing. The number of English language learners in our schools is increasing dramatically. Classroom teachers need to know ways to help these students learn content while they also learn English. Different values and cultures create different learning patterns among children and different expectations for classroom interactions. Also, our inclusive classrooms contain a broader spectrum of special education needs, and the number of children with identified or perceived special learning needs is growing.

This increase in diversity is happening at a time when our national agenda is clear—all students must meet standards and we must reduce the number of students referred to special education services. As stated in the introduction to the Common Core State Standards for Mathematics, "The Standards should be read as allowing for the widest possible range of students to participate fully from the outset, along with appropriate accommodations to ensure maximum participation of students with special education needs" (National Governors Association Center for Best Practices and the Council of Chief State School Officers 2010, 4). With the testing associated with the Common Core State Standards and the universal screeners associated with Response to Intervention, we are identifying more students who are not meeting benchmarks. It therefore behooves all educators to do whatever they can to increase their abilities to meet a greater range of individual needs found in today's classrooms.

> As stated in the introduction to the Common Core State Standards for Mathematics, "The Standards should be read as allowing for the widest possible range of students to participate fully from the outset, along with appropriate accommodations to ensure maximum participation of students with special education needs" (National Governors Association Center for Best Practices and the Council of Chief State School Officers 2010, 4).

Do I Have to Differentiate in Math, Too?

Many teachers find that thinking about ways to differentiate literacy instruction comes somewhat naturally whereas differentiation in mathematics seems more demanding or challenging. As one teacher put it, "Do we have to differentiate in math, too? I can do this in reading, but it's too hard in math! I mean, in reading, there are so many books to choose from that focus on different interests and that are written for a variety of reading levels." Although we recognize that many teachers may feel this way, there are important reasons to differentiate in mathematics.

There are several indications that we are not yet teaching mathematics in an effective manner, in a way designed to meet a variety of needs. Results of international tests show U.S. students do not perform as well as students in many other countries at a time

> Many teachers find that thinking about ways to differentiate literacy instruction comes somewhat naturally whereas differentiation in mathematics seems more demanding or challenging.

when more mathematical skill is needed for professional success and economic security. There continues to be a gap in achievement for our black, Native American, and Latino students. Gaps exist as well for our English language learners and our students who live in poverty. Many educators believe these gaps are a result of not having access to the curriculum. Last, we are a country in which many people describe themselves as math phobic, and others have no problem announcing publicly that they failed mathematics in high school.

In response to these indicators, educators continue to wrestle with the development and implementation of approaches for teaching mathematics more effectively. For example, current trends stress the importance of a focused and coherent curriculum, clearly identifying the standards that students must meet at each grade level. The way we teach math has changed, requiring students to communicate their mathematical thinking, to solve more complex problems, and to understand conceptually the mathematical procedures they perform. So how might we differentiate the way math is taught?

What's New in This Edition?

This resource is an updated version of *Math for All: Differentiating Instruction, K–2* and *Math for All: Differentiating Instruction, 3–5*. Five significant changes have been made:

1. Integration of *Math for All, K–2* and *Math for All, 3–5*
   The two books are now integrated. We decided to combine aspects of both books so that readers have a fuller vision of differentiation across grade levels. We believe the wider lens supports teachers in meeting the broad range of learners in today's classrooms, and better serves colleagues from different grade levels who want to explore these ideas together.

2. Common Core Correlations
   Suggestions are aligned with the Common Core State Standards. During the integrative process, we made sure to choose examples that reflect the Common Core State Standards for Mathematics. We also added sections to address key components of the Common Core, such as the Standards for Mathematical Practice.

3. Video Clips
   To help readers conceptualize more fully how the ideas in this book might play out in the classroom, video clips are included. These authentic examples also provide opportunities for readers to reflect on their own practice.

4. Updated Research

   Numerous new references are included for those who wish to read more about particular differentiation issues or techniques.

5. Friendly Format

   We included new design features in this edition to help you to focus on ideas of particular interest. For example, the *Lesson Ideas!* features allow you to implement a lesson idea easily from a vignette. Lesson plan callouts help you to find connections to the Common Core; *Take Action!* callouts highlight specific differentiation strategies.

Three Steps to Getting the Most out of This Resource

1. Decide where you are on your journey of meeting individual needs. Although this book is intended to be read front to back, you can address your own interests and wishes by creating your own pathway. For example, if a particular chapter fits your needs right now, start there.

2. Set yourself up to read the text with simultaneous access to the video clips. These clips are intended to be viewed alongside the book. Together, they give you a more complete vision of how differentiated instruction works in the classroom.

3. Identify one or more colleagues to explore this resource with you or to talk with you about its ideas. Although not essential, this collaborative process can deepen your understanding of the content in this resource as well as your awareness of your own practice.

Video Clips by Chapter

CHAPTER	VIDEO CLIP	LENGTH	TEACHER AND GRADE	DESCRIPTION
1	1.1 What Does Differentiation Look Like?	3:46	Mixed Grades	In this introductory clip, we get glimpses of classrooms in which differentiated instruction is happening, as well as thoughts behind such.
2	2.1 Interviewing Students During Class	4:49	Mrs. Miller Grade 4	In this clip, the teacher, Mrs. Miller, interviews a few students during her fourth-grade class as a quick way to check in about their learning.
2	2.2 Partners Working on an Open-Ended Task	2:43	Ms. Anderson Grade 4	In this clip, partners are working on an open-ended task in Ms. Anderson's fourth-grade class. The task is part of a multiplication Think Tac Toe, a format for organizing student choices (see Chapter 7 for more on Think Tac Toe).
2	2.3 Using Student Work to Differentiate Instruction	3:21	Mr. Geiger and Mrs. Miller Grade 4	In this clip, we observe a planning session between Mr. Geiger, the math coach, and Mrs. Miller, a fourth-grade teacher. They are looking at student work from a quiz to make decisions about what activities to put on a menu and what the role of the teacher will be during the work time.
3	3.1 Thinking About Differentiation and the Common Core State Standards	1:54	Mixed Grades	In this clip, authors Linda Dacey and Rebeka Salemi Eston reflect on the Common Core State Standards for Mathematics in the context of differentiating instruction.
3	3.2 Fostering the Common Core State Standards for Mathematical Practice	1:43	Mrs. Thompson Grade 3	In this clip, Mrs. Thompson checks in with two of her third-grade students. They are working on a problem that is part of a tiered activity (see Lesson Idea 4.3: *Mystery Puzzles* in Chapter 4).

CHAPTER	VIDEO CLIP	LENGTH	TEACHER AND GRADE	DESCRIPTION
4	4.1 Giving Students a Choice of Their Challenge	1:02	Ms. Corpas Kindergarten	In this clip, Ms. Corpas discusses choice time with her kindergarten class. Ms. Corpas uses a math menu to differentiate her instruction (for more about math menus see Chapter 7).
4	4.2 "There's Many Solutions!"	3:00	Mrs. Leon and Mrs. Thompson Grade 3	In this clip, Mrs. Thompson summarizes the tiered lesson that her third-grade students experienced (for the entire lesson plan and open-ended problems, see Lesson Idea 4.3: *Mystery Puzzles* in Chapter 4). We then observe the planning session that Mrs. Thompson and the math coach, Mrs. Leon, held following the lesson. They collaborate to make decisions to support next steps for students working on the open-ended problem.
4	4.3 *Mystery Puzzles* (A Tiered Activity)	10:12	Mrs. Thompson Grade 3	In this clip, we see excerpts from Mrs. Thompson's use of the tiered activity *Mystery Puzzles* with her third-grade class.
5	5.1 Tapping Into Multiple Intelligences: Choose Your Center	12:28	Ms. Cocuzzo Grade 2	In this clip, Ms. Cocuzzo carries out her lesson plan designed to tap into the multiple intelligences of her second graders. Read Ms. Cocuzzo's reflection in this chapter before watching the video.
6	6.1 Asking Questions	1:04	Mixed Grades	In this clip, consider the medley of questions that teachers ask on a day-to-day basis in their classrooms.
6	6.2 If It Works in Reading . . .	1:37	Ms. Cocuzzo Grade 2	In this clip, Ms. Cocuzzo supports her students in sharing what they learned during their work at centers (for a more thorough look at the entire lesson see Video Clip 5.1). The student, Mary, has just finished writing another poem; Ms. Cocuzzo is especially interested in the strategies Mary used to complete this task.

(continued)

Video Clips by Chapter *(continued)*

CHAPTER	VIDEO CLIP	LENGTH	TEACHER AND GRADE	DESCRIPTION
6	6.3 Fostering Collaborative Student Partnerships	4:38	Mixed Grades	In this clip, teachers reflect on student partnerships and students collaborate on various tasks.
6	6.4 Using Word Banks	4:35	Mr. Geiger Grade 5	In this video clip the math coach Mr. Geiger is working with a small group of fifth-grade students.
7	7.1 Focusing on the Goal in a Math Workshop	6:42	Ms. Loguidice Grade 5	In this clip, the teacher, Ms. Loguidice, facilitates a math workshop with her fifth graders.
7	7.2 Working within a Math Menu: *Scoop and Count*	8:19	Ms. Corpas Kindergarten	In this clip, the teacher, Ms. Corpas, sets her kindergarteners up for work within a math menu. She interacts with the children at the *Scoop and Count* center (one of the activity choices on the menu).
7	7.3 Think Tac Toe	5:04	Ms. Anderson Grade 4	In this clip, Ms. Anderson works with her fourth graders on a Think Tac Toe (see Chapter 7 for the Think Tac Toe activity choices).
8	8.1 A Do-Now Routine	2:06	Ms. Loguidice Grade 5	In this clip, Ms. Loguidice's fifth-grade class engages in a "do-now routine"—a daily routine Ms. Loguidice plans for the first five minutes of each class.
8	8.2 A Math Clinic	7:49	Mrs. Miller Grade 4	In this clip, Mrs. Miller facilitates a division math clinic with a group of her fourth graders. These fourth graders have chosen to do this clinic.
9	9.1 Student and Parent Interviews	2:19	Ms. Corpas Kindergarten	In this clip, Ms. Corpas meets with one of her kindergarten students, Aurora. After the school day, Ms. Corpas then meets with Aurora's mom.
9	9.2 Sustaining Your Differentiation Efforts	1:07	Mixed Grades	In this clip, authors Linda Dacey and Jayne Bamford Lynch share some advice to support you in continuing to sustain your differentiation efforts.

Video Clips by Grade, Including Demographics

GRADE	TEACHER	SCHOOL AND DEMOGRAPHICS	VIDEO CLIPS
K	**Ms. Corpas** teaches junior kindergarten and kindergarten. She has been teaching for seven years and loves using creative methods to teach math, such as having her students act out math problems with puppets or incorporating movement and dance into her lessons. Ms. Corpas also credits using the practice of math talk—specifically having her students repeat their peers' solutions to math problems during class discussions—for helping her students develop a deeper understanding of mathematical ideas.	**Dr. Martin Luther King, Jr. School** There are twenty students in Ms. Corpas' kindergarten class (eight boys and twelve girls). The student body at this school in Cambridge, Massachusetts, is composed of 21 percent Caucasian, 45 percent African American, 17 percent Asian, 13 percent Hispanic, and 4 percent Multi-Race, Non-Hispanic. Fifty-six percent of the students qualify for free or reduced lunch. Thirty-eight percent of the students do not have English as their first language.	4.1 Giving Students a Choice of Their Challenge 7.2 Working within a Math Menu: *Scoop and Count* 9.1 Student and Parent Interviews
2	**Ms. Cocuzzo** teaches second grade. She is in her second year of teaching and continuously refers to Howard Gardner's theory of multiple intelligences when planning differentiated math lessons and centers. By providing students with centers that focus on a range of specific intelligences, Ms. Cocuzzo is able to offer students choice and a variety of approaches they can use to support and explain their mathematical thinking.	**Kennedy–Longfellow School** There are eighteen students in Ms. Cocuzzo's second-grade class (eight boys and ten girls). The student body at this school in Cambridge, Massachusetts, is composed of 37 percent Caucasian, 31 percent African American, 10 percent Asian, 18 percent Hispanic, and 4 percent Multi-Race, Non-Hispanic. Sixty-two percent of the students qualify for free or reduced lunch. Thirty percent of the students do not have English as their first language.	5.1 Tapping Into Multiple Intelligences: Choose Your Center 6.2 If It Works in Reading . . .

(continued)

Video Clips by Grade, Including Demographics *(continued)*

GRADE	TEACHER	SCHOOL AND DEMOGRAPHICS	VIDEO CLIPS
3	**Mrs. Thompson** has taught second grade and is currently teaching third grade. She has been teaching for six years. She believes every student should have a voice and be able to explain their strategies for solving math problems to others. She employs many 'math talk' moves, including the turn-and-talk method and having students repeat what other students have said. Mrs. Thompson believes that these teaching moves help *all* of her students, including those with special needs and English language learners.	**Dr. Martin Luther King, Jr. School** There are seventeen students in Mrs. Thompson's third grade class (five boys and twelve girls). The student body at this school in Cambridge, Massachusetts, is composed of 21 percent Caucasian, 45 percent African American, 17 percent Asian, 13 percent Hispanic, and 4 percent Multi-Race, Non-Hispanic. Fifty-six percent of the students qualify for free or reduced lunch. Thirty-eight percent of the students do not have English as their first language.	3.2 Fostering the Common Core Standards for Mathematical Practice 4.2 "There's Many Solutions!" 4.3 *Mystery Puzzles* (A Tiered Activity)
4	**Mrs. Miller** teaches fourth grade. She has been teaching for six years and feels that providing structured choice in her classroom has finally given her the time to engage in meaningful differentiation. With her students more invested in the work, Mrs. Miller is able to meet all students' needs in a more thoughtful and deliberate manner.	**The Maria L. Baldwin School** There are sixteen students in Mrs. Miller's fourth-grade class (eight boys and eight girls). The student body at this school in Cambridge, Massachusetts, is composed of 50 percent Caucasian, 25 percent African American, 10 percent Asian, 8 percent Hispanic, and 7 percent Multi-Race, Non-Hispanic. Thirty-six percent of the students qualify for free or reduced lunch. Nineteen percent of the students do not have English as their first language.	2.1 Interviewing Students During Class 2.3 Using Student Work to Differentiate Instruction 8.2 A Math Clinic

GRADE	TEACHER	SCHOOL AND DEMOGRAPHICS	VIDEO CLIPS
4	**Ms. Anderson** teaches fourth grade. She has been teaching for fifteen years. To promote comprehension of math concepts and the awareness of misconceptions, she encourages strong communication skills through speaking, listening, and writing. Ms. Anderson is optimistic about the Common Core State Standards raising the level of student performance within her own classroom as well as the nation at large.	**Kennedy–Longfellow School** There are twenty students in Ms. Anderson's fourth-grade class (nine boys and eleven girls). The student body at this school in Cambridge, Massachusetts, is composed of 37 percent Caucasian, 31 percent African American, 10 percent Asian, 18 percent Hispanic, and 4 percent Multi-Race, Non-Hispanic. Sixty-two percent of the students qualify for free or reduced lunch. Thirty percent of the students do not have English as their first language.	2.2 Partners Working on an Open-Ended Task 7.3 Think Tac Toe
5	**Ms. Logiudice** teaches fifth grade. She has taught third, fourth, and fifth grades over the past fifteen years. She credits differentiated math instruction and class discussion techniques for increasing the engagement level of her students, especially the bored, disconnected, or unmotivated. She feels that with these approaches, the energy in the classroom changes from relative productivity to alive and vibrant. Ms. Logiudice's advice to teachers on differentiating instruction is to start small—one talk move, a differentiated menu, a small group—and elicit help when possible. Then just let it grow; soon it will be the only way you can imagine teaching math!	**The Maria L. Baldwin School** There are twenty-two students in Ms. Logiudice's fifth-grade class (eleven boys and eleven girls). The student body at this school in Cambridge, Massachusetts, is composed of 50 percent Caucasian, 25 percent African American, 10 percent Asian, 8 percent Hispanic, and 7 percent Multi-Race, Non-Hispanic. Thirty-six percent of the students qualify for free or reduced lunch. Nineteen percent of the students do not have English as their first language.	7.1 Focusing on the Goal in a Math Workshop 8.1 A Do-Now Routine

(continued)

Video Clips by Grade, Including Demographics *(continued)*

GRADE	TEACHER	SCHOOL AND DEMOGRAPHICS	VIDEO CLIPS
Instructional Math Coach	**Mrs. Leon** has been a JK–5 instructional math coach for eight years. In weekly collaboration meetings she supports teachers in using formative and summative data to make instructional decisions. She finds differentiation strategies from *How to Differentiate Your Math Instruction* highly effective in challenging and engaging every student—a goal not easily achieved but exceptionally rewarding!	**Dr. Martin Luther King, Jr. School** The student body at this school in Cambridge, Massachusetts, is composed of 21 percent Caucasian, 45 percent African American, 17 percent Asian, 13 percent Hispanic, and 4 percent Multi-Race, Non-Hispanic. Fifty-six percent of the students qualify for free or reduced lunch. Thirty-eight percent of the students do not have English as their first language.	4.2 "There's Many Solutions!"
Instructional Math Coach	**Mr. Geiger** is currently a math coach and has been teaching elementary school for 20 years. He sees a real opportunity to motivate both reluctant and enthusiastic math students when they are given a chance to choose "just right" problems and activities. Mr. Geiger enjoys seeing children experience that "aha" moment when there is a perfect intersection between the challenge of the task at hand and the student's level of mathematical experience.	**The Maria L. Baldwin School** The student body at this school in Cambridge, Massachusetts, is composed of 50 percent Caucasian, 25 percent African American, 10 percent Asian, 8 percent Hispanic, and 7 percent Multi-Race, Non-Hispanic. Thirty-six percent of the students qualify for free or reduced lunch. Nineteen percent of the students do not have English as their first language.	2.3 Using Student Work to Differentiate Instruction 6.4 Using Word Banks

Teaching with the Common Core: Lesson Connections

CHAPTER	LESSON IDEA AND GRADE	LESSON CONNECTION					
		Counting and Cardinality (CC)	Operations and Algebraic Thinking (OA)	Number and Operations in Base Ten (NBT)	Number and Operations— Fractions (NF)	Measurement and Data (MD)	Geometry (G)
1	*Even Steven and Odd Todd* (Grade 4)					X	
2	Solving Story Problems Involving Addition and Subtraction (Grade 2)			X			
3	Decompose and Compose Groups (Grade 1)		X				
3	Represent and Compare Fractions (Grade 4)				X		
4	Sum Investigations (A Tiered Activity) (Grade 2)			X			
4	Shape Puzzler (A Tiered Activity) (Kindergarten)						X
4	Addition Facts (Grade 1)	X					
4	Finish the Story (A Tiered Activity) (Grade 3)					X	
4	Hopping Robots (A Tiered Activity) (Grade 4)		X				
4	Real-World Connections (A Tiered Activity) (Grade 5)					X	

(continued)

Teaching with the Common Core: Lesson Connections *(continued)*

CHAPTER	LESSON IDEA AND GRADE	LESSON CONNECTION					
		Counting and Cardinality (CC)	Operations and Algebraic Thinking (OA)	Number and Operations in Base Ten (NBT)	Number and Operations—Fractions (NF)	Measurement and Data (MD)	Geometry (G)
4	*Mystery Puzzles* (A Tiered Activity) (Grade 3)			X			
5	*Facts I Know!, Making Progress,* and *Too Hard Right Now.* (Grades 1 and 2)		X				
6	What We Know About Fractions (Grade 4)				X		
7	Polygons Poster (Grade 4)						X
7	Measurement Menu (Grade 4)			X		X	
7	Counting Think Tac Toe (Grade 1)			X			
7	Telling Time RAFT (Grade 2)					X	
7	Measurement Station (Grades 1 and 2)					X	

PART I

Getting Started with Differentiation

· ·

Overview

The chapters in this section provide a vision for getting started with differentiated instruction. They address multiple strategies for assessing your students' readiness, learning styles, and interests, and important features of the Common Core State Standards for Mathematics. Knowing your students and the standards are essential first steps to differentiated instruction, but making decisions about what content and teaching strategies are appropriate is where you begin the challenging work of providing all your students with access to mathematical learning. It is in the conscious act of matching your students' needs with what the curriculum and pedagogy have to offer that differentiation helps you meet your instructional goals most effectively.

1

Chapter 1 What Is Differentiation?

Introduction

What Does Differentiation Look Like?

This introductory video clip gives glimpses of classrooms in which differentiated instruction is happening, as well as thoughts behind such.

As you watch the clip, consider:

1. What do you see happening in the clip that indicates differentiating instruction is part of these classrooms?
2. What surprises you?
3. What is familiar to you?
4. What do you have questions about?

Erin's Case: The Child Who Needs More Challenge

This year Erin, a kindergarten teacher, has a student whose mathematical ability far exceeds any student she has ever taught before. Erin feels as if she is constantly working to challenge this student without using activities that the child will explore in future grades. She wants to provide the child with work that relates to what the other students are doing, but at a more sophisticated level. Erin finds this situation particularly difficult. Although she has a strong background in early childhood education, she has never been taught how to teach more complex mathematical skills. She worries that she is not serving this child well.

Christa's Case: The Child Who Is Just Learning English

Christa, a first-grade teacher, worries about a child who joined the classroom in November. The student is just learning English and Christa has noticed that the child often isn't able to concentrate for more than five minutes at a time. The child is able to focus longer when students are using interlocking cubes to represent numbers or when students are building patterns, but much of the current content work is related to story problems. Christa isn't sure whether the problem is rooted in learning a new language, a result of the child's level of attention, or caused by difficulty with understanding mathematics. She wonders whether she should do a unit on geometry and not focus so much on word problems for a while.

David's Case: The Child Who Only Wants the Answer

David, a third-grade teacher, is worried about a student who seems to care only about getting the right answer. The student seems uninterested when other students share how they solved a problem and she resists representing her ideas on paper. David knows from his contact with her family that they, too, focus on whether their daughter is getting the correct answers. When given an open-ended problem, she seems to lack the confidence or initiative to just give it a try. Instead, she persistently asks, "What am I supposed to do? Can't you just show me?" When David asks a series of questions beginning with, "What's one thing you can tell me about this problem?" he can often get her to relate one idea about how to begin the task. David is particularly troubled about how she will perform on state-mandated tests. He is concerned that she will not have the confidence to try the open-ended response questions and so the results won't really reflect what she knows.

Jesse's Case: The Child Who Struggles with Visual Input

Jesse teaches fifth grade and worries most about a student in her class who has difficulty processing visual information. The student reverses numbers, confuses mathematical symbols, and miscopies information. Jesse tries to make sure that a verbal description accompanies everything that she or other students write on the board so that this student will receive auditory as well as visual input. Because this student is known to jump from one problem to another without completing his work, Jesse has also started to give him only one problem at a time. She is hopeful that this technique will help him to focus. Although Jesse is clear that this student struggles with visual input, she sometimes thinks that the level of mathematical challenge is also a factor. The student does do better when he works with another student who can read the problem aloud and record their work.

These four teachers are like most teachers of elementary school children. They want to provide for the needs of all of their students. They want to recognize the unique gifts and developmental readiness each child brings to the classroom community. These teachers also realize that addressing the variety of abilities, interests, cultures, and learning styles in their classrooms is a challenging task.

Philosophy of Differentiated Instruction

Differentiated instruction is a philosophy of teaching based on the belief that all learners are different and that all students are capable

> Differentiated instruction is a philosophy of teaching based on the belief that all learners are different and that all students are capable of learning.

of learning. Taken together, these beliefs mandate that teachers differentiate instruction. This resource takes the approach that differentiated mathematics instruction is most successful when teachers do the following.

Differentiated Mathematics Instruction Is Most Successful When Teachers:

- believe that all students have the capacity to succeed at learning mathematics and should be held to high standards;
- recognize that multiple perspectives are necessary to build important mathematical ideas and that diverse thinking is an essential and valued resource in their classrooms;
- know and understand mathematics and are confident in their abilities to teach mathematical ideas;
- focus assessment on gathering evidence that can inform instruction and provide a variety of ways for students to demonstrate what they know;
- are intentional about curricular choices; that is, they think carefully about what students need to learn and how that learning is best supported;
- develop strong mathematical learning communities in their classrooms; and
- support each other in their efforts to create and sustain this type of instruction.

It is important to think about differentiation as a lens through which you can examine your teaching and your students' learning more closely, a way to become even more aware of the best ways to ensure that your students will be successful learners. Looking at differentiation through such a lens requires us to develop new skills and to become more adept at a number of skills. Consider the following.

Differentiating Instruction Requires That Teachers Be Adept At:

- identifying important mathematical skills and concepts;
- assessing what students know, what interests them, and how they learn best;
- creating diverse tasks through which students can build understanding and demonstrate what they know;

- identifying ways to accommodate students' learning preferences;
- providing students with choices to make; and
- managing different activities that take place simultaneously.

It is also important that you be realistic about your goals for differentiated instruction. Just like your students, if you take on work for which you are not prepared, you will fail. Like your students, you need to set clear goals for yourself and adjust them as your skills increase. Moreover, you must remember that the goal is not to create twenty-five to thirty different plans for every mathematics lesson and task. Such a goal is not only impossible, it is ill-advised. It is important that your students share their thinking with others and participate in supportive, flexible learning environments.

Creating a Differentiation Planning Chart

When we work with teachers, we suggest they use a chart to identify ways to differentiate. We encourage teachers to use the chart as a brainstorming tool. They might think about individual students, identify resources, or pose questions, but not necessarily commit themseves to following up on all the ideas they generate. There are two main parts of a Differentiation Planning Chart:

1. Readiness, interests, and learning profiles
2. Content, process, and product

Readiness, Interests, and Learning Profiles

Carol Tomlinson, a leader in the field of differentiated instruction, urges teachers to differentiate based on students' *readiness*, *interests*, and *learning profiles* (Tomlinson 2003, Tomlinson and Eidson 2003, Tomlinson et al. 2008, Tomlinson and Imbeau 2010). The key is to make adaptations in ways that give all students access to the curricular content.

Readiness

To differentiate according to *readiness*, teachers:

- identify the content students are to learn at their grade level. The first step in this task is to be familiar with the local, state, or national standards for mathematics.

  See also CHAPTER 3, Know Your Standards

- assess what students already know. A decision to adapt content should be based on what you know about your students' readi-

  See also CHAPTER 2, Know Your Students

ness. Embedding assessment in your instructional practices is essential to differentiated instruction.

- evaluate the assessment data to determine the level of content that students can investigate and the pace at which they can do so. This might involve materials at varied readability levels, preteaching or frontloading vocabulary, and creating various levels of scaffolding, tiered assignments, flexible grouping strategies, and extended or collapsed time for learning.

Interests

To differentiate according to *interests*, teachers:

- identify their students' favorite books, activities, and pastimes;
- identify ways to link mathematical content to a variety of real-world contexts; and

See also CHAPTER 7, Support Choice

- support student choice through interest centers, technology, and assignments with built-in choices.

Learning Profiles

To differentiate according to *learning profiles*, teachers:

- determine the circumstances in which students learn best and provide opportunities to work alone or with others, in quiet and less quiet environments, and in a variety of locations;

See also CHAPTER 5, Tap Into Multiple Intelligences

- include visual, auditory, and kinesthetic modes of learning; and
- consider different intelligences when preparing lessons.

Content, Process, and Product

Teachers can differentiate three aspects of the curriculum: (1) what the students will learn (content), (2) how the students will learn it (process), and (3) how the students will demonstrate their knowledge (product). These components form the second part of a Differentiation Planning Chart.

Consider a second-grade teacher getting ready for a two-week mini-unit on measuring and estimating lengths. He has already collected data related to students' readiness, interests, and learning profiles and is now thinking about ways to differentiate the content, process, and product components

Take Action!
Make a differentiation planning chart.

of this unit. As part of his planning, he completes a Differentiation Planning Chart as shown in Figure 1–1A (a template of this chart is available as
Reproducible 1).

REPRODUCIBLE 1

Differentiation Planning Chart: Second Grade

	CONTENT	PROCESS	PRODUCT
Readiness	• Preteach comparitive-length terms to Mei and Sasha. • Kyle, Natalie, and Regan: extend to crooked paths. • Is anyone ready for yards yet?	• Make inch and foot strips so that some can use multiple units to measure lengths. • Could Massie and I work together to make leveled logic problems for other students? • Does pbs.org have measurement activities that model using different tools to measure?	• What sentence stems would support Mei and Sasha?
Interests	• Let the students choose items to measure in the classroom.	• Create interest centers that require students to measure: insect fact cards? art projects? • Create a reading corner with books about measurement: *Inch by Inch* by Leo Lionni.	• Write about ways measurement is used in a favorite activity. • Make a poster (for example, Measurement and My Pet). • Dictate a story about the adventure of the inchworm using real measurements.
Learning Profile	• What tasks need audio directions? • Have Jon and Carla make rulers by pasting inch strips.	• Have Mei and Carlos take lead partner roles with centimeters. • Velcro models of inch and foot strips for Jake to feel. • Competition: team estimation Olympics.	• Use gestures, oral language, or written descriptions to show how to estimate lengths. • Measure independently.

Figure 1–1A. Differentiation Planning Chart completed by a second-grade teacher planning a mini-unit on length measures.

Differentiation Planning Chart: Fifth Grade

	CONTENT	PROCESS	PRODUCT
Readiness	• Vary factors (one whole number, two fractions) and include mixed numbers. • Zak and Micki need to review area model of multiplication with whole numbers.	• Create mini-workshops: Use pattern blocks to model word problems; Use area model to find products. • Could I tier some homework assignments?	• Could students create a video on how to multiply fractions? • Does mathplayground.com offer models for students to represent their thinking?
Interests	• Give choices of leveled word problems to solve.	• Adapt favorite food recipe for larger group.	• Write word problems for others to solve with real-life applications.
Learning Profile	• Have completed examples available for models.	• Could Ned, Casey, and Nardia work in the hall to avoid distractions? • Connect to reading music?	• Complete a graphic organizer for multiplying fractions. • Have Sami, Arturo, and Kiki suggest extensions.

Figure 1–1B. Differentiation Planning Chart completed by a fifth-grade teacher planning a unit on division.

> Thinking about differentiating content, process, and products according to readiness, interests, and learning profiles prompts teachers to provide a variety of ways in which students can gain access to and demonstrate their understanding of mathematical concepts and skills.

Figure 1–1B is another example from a fifth-grade teacher thinking about a unit on multiplication of fractions.

It is not necessary, or even possible, to differentiate in all of these ways all the time; many teachers find that the categories overlap. However, thinking about differentiating content, process, and products according to readiness, interests, and learning profiles prompts teachers to provide a variety of ways in which students can gain access to and demonstrate their understanding of mathematical concepts and skills. It is also not likely that all attempts to differentiate will be successful, but keeping differentiation in mind as you plan and reflect on your mathematics instruction is important and can transform teaching in important ways. It reminds you of the constant need to fine-tune, adjust, redirect, and evaluate learning in your classrooms. You can also learn from watching experts.

The Research: Common Characteristics of Differentiated Instruction

Carolan and Guinn (2007) observed teachers identified as experts at differentiated instruction. Although they focused on middle school teachers, the findings are generalizable to the elementary level. They identified the following four common characteristics of instruction among these expert teachers. The teachers:

1. provided personalized scaffolding. To accomplish this personalization, these teachers needed to be aware of students' readiness, interests, and learning profiles.

2. used flexible means to reach the same ends. This means that differentiated ways to meet clearly defined goals were identified.

3. had expert knowledge of their content and content pedagogy. This knowledge allowed them to identify and address common misconceptions and to view their students along a learning trajectory for various skills and concepts.

4. created welcoming classrooms where differences were considered assets.

The importance of the last characteristic cannot be overstated. It reminds us of a drawing a first-grade student made in a language immersion school. (See Figure 1–2.) It captures what we would wish for all students.

Take Action!

Reflect on your practice with these characteristics in mind.

Figure 1–2. A first grader's depiction of the classroom as "Everyone School."

So what might differentiated math instruction look like in a lesson? Consider the following vignette from a fourth-grade classroom.

Fourth-Grade Class: *Even Steven and Odd Todd*

Having just taken a workshop on differentiated instruction, the teacher wants to try something different in her classroom. She is thinking about a lesson she sometimes leads this time of year and decides to make some changes. She wants to provide more choice, be more open to variations in student thinking based on readiness, and have a variety of materials available for the students to use. She feels that she is a novice in this way of teaching and is unsure of where these changes will lead her.

Part I: Introducing

The teacher begins the class by introducing the students to the book *Even Steven and Odd Todd*, written by Kathryn Cristaldi (1996). She holds up the book and asks, "What do you think this book might be about?" Several children raise their hands.

John answers, "I think it is about two boys, one named Steven and the other named Todd."

Madelyn continues, "I think Steven will like even numbers and things, and Todd will like odd numbers and stuff like that."

The teacher begins reading the book and, sure enough, John and Madelyn are correct. Steven loves everything to be even and Todd loves everything to be odd. They are cousins and, early in the story, Steven learns that Todd is spending the summer with him. It is clear that this proximity will lead to some disagreements.

At this point, the teacher stops reading and asks, "Does anyone have a cousin?" All hands are raised as the students smile and look at one another. She follows up with, "Have you ever had to compromise to get along with your cousin?" Most heads nod and the students begin to tell stories.

"My cousin always likes to play sports when I visit and I don't like to play sports all the time," says John.

Sam adds, "My cousin always likes to watch TV and get up early."

Meghan rolls her eyes and remarks, "My cousin always gets to sleep in my bed when she sleeps over. I have to sleep on the floor."

"Well," says the teacher, "let's find out what happens to these cousins." As she reads, the students learn that when the boys order pizza, Steven orders four slices and Todd orders three. When they go to an ice cream shop,

Steven orders two scoops of double-dip chocolate ice cream and Todd orders a triple nutty fudge sundae. Throughout their summer together, Todd manages to disrupt Steven's desire to have everything be even. Toward the end of the visit, Steven plants a perfectly even garden and enters it in the garden contest. Without Steven's knowledge, Todd disrupts this plan by planting an odd number of cacti, each of which has five long needles. Fortunately, just as Steven proclaims that he can no longer stand his cousin, who is just "too odd," they win the contest.

The students appear relaxed as they listen to the story, and they giggle during the boys' conflicts. When the teacher finishes the book, she closes it and asks, "If Even Steven and Odd Todd made a rectangular garden together, could they compromise by having an even perimeter and an odd area or an odd perimeter and an even area?"

Initially, the students seem perplexed by the question. Usually, the teacher would now offer a review of area and perimeter, but this time she decides to probe the students' ideas first. She asks, "What are *area* and *perimeter*?"

Kim Su raises her hand quickly and states, "Area is the middle of a box."

The teacher responds, "Tell me about the box."

Kim Su continues, "The box has cubes in it. Can I show you?" When the teacher nods, Kim Su walks to the board and draws a 5-by-3 rectangle with grid lines on the board:

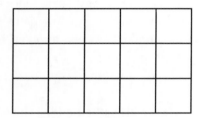

The teacher asks, "How do you know the area, Kim Su?"

"Well," she says, "you just count the boxes!"

It appears from the looks on the students' faces that this technique makes sense to them and helps some who may have forgotten the meaning of *area*.

Lisa comments, "I don't like to count them all. I multiply them."

After the students restate these ideas, the teacher redirects their thinking to perimeter. She asks, "Why might we want to know the perimeter of a garden?"

"Oh, I know!" responds Pedro. "It's for making a fence around the garden."

John then jumps up and gets permission to go to the board. He writes a 5 and a 3 on the two unlabeled sides of Kim Su's drawing and tells the class, "All you have to do is add up all of the numbers."

Jill looks excited when she offers, "I remember now. The perimeter is the distance around the figure."

The teacher asks, "What is *distance*?" and Jill walks to the board and begins to count her way around the figure. She points to each intersection on the outline of the grid and arrives at the answer of sixteen.

Jill turns to the class and says, "See? It's sixteen." The teacher asks if the students agree with Jill and most nod their heads. She then asks, "Sixteen what?" Jill and several other students in the class shrug their shoulders.

The teacher explains that perimeter is measured in units. She then asks the students to identify the units they counted, the distance from one intersection to another. As they count sixteen of them, they realize the perimeter is 16 units.

The students seem more confident about this idea, so she asks what they count to find the area. She points to one of the squares in Kim Su's figure and "Squares!" is said in a chorus. The teacher responds, "Yes, squares. We measure area in square units." She then asks them to restate the area of the figure as 15 square units.

"So back to the cousins," says the teacher. "Can they have a garden that will make both Even Steven and Odd Todd happy?" She draws a rectangle on the board, writes *Garden* above it, and asks, "Does anyone have an idea of what measurements the boys might want for their garden?"

Marcia replies, "I would make one side an even number and the other side an odd number, like four and seven."

The teacher asks Marcia to come up to the board and label the rectangle accordingly.

"What would be the area of this rectangle?" the teacher queries.

Rex responds, "Twenty-eight."

The teacher repeats "Twenty-eight," but says it in such a way that lets Rex know that she is waiting for him to identify the unit of measure as square units. After he responds to her prompting, the teacher asks the class, "Do any of you think you know how Rex got this answer?"

Dana notes, "He could have just multiplied four by seven."

Christa adds, "Or he can make rows and count the squares."

The teacher goes back to the board and draws a grid to highlight and connect these students' ideas. Many students nod their head with apparent understanding.

"Now what about the perimeter?" asks the teacher. "How can we find the perimeter of Marcia's garden?"

Josh eagerly calls out, "You just need to add another seven and four and then add them all up." He walks to the board, records *4* and *7* along the corresponding sides, and then writes *4 + 4 + 7 + 7 = 22 units* to the side of the figure. The teacher organizes the information by writing it in a list:

length = 7 units

width = 4 units

area = 28 square units

perimeter = 22 units

As she writes, she waits for the students to identify the name of the units before she records them. She then pauses and asks, "Do you think both cousins would be happy? Talk it over with your neighbor."

The consensus of the group is that both cousins would not be happy because three of the four numbers are even, and that isn't fair to Todd. The teacher then wonders aloud, "Hmm, will both the area and perimeter always be an even number or an odd number of units if the cousins make rectangular gardens?" She waits a moment and then declares, "This is what we will be investigating today during math class. I would like for you to explore the relationship between area and perimeter, and lengths of odd and even numbers of units."

Part II: Exploring

At this point in the lesson, the teacher makes another change. Normally, she would assign rectangular figures for all of the students to investigate. This time, she offers the students a bit of a choice. She posts a chart on the board with four regions, labeled *area = 24 square units*, *area = 21 square units*, *perimeter = 24 units*, and *perimeter = 21 units*. (See Figure 1–3 on page 16.)

Knowing that her students enjoy working together, she invites them to sign up, in pairs, for one of the four investigations. She explains, "When you sign up for *area equals twenty-four square units*, for example, you try to find out all the different perimeters you could have with that area. What do you think you should do if you sign up for the perimeter that equals twenty-four units?" she asks. When the students respond and the teacher is assured that they understand the tasks, she invites students to sign up on the chart, one table at a time.

Now the teacher is ready to provide another change; she gives students more choice among materials. This time, she places string, color tiles, and centimeter graph paper at each workstation, along with traditional dot paper to complete the exercise. The students sign up for their chosen tasks and head for a place to work.

Take Action!

Provide students with choices about tasks and materials.

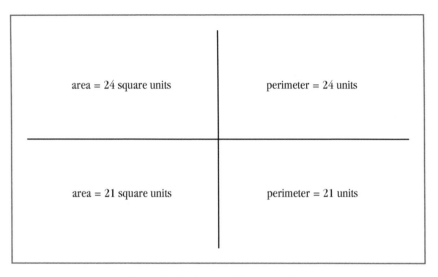

area = 24 square units	perimeter = 24 units
area = 21 square units	perimeter = 21 units

Figure 1–3. A chart with task choices.

Josh: That Just Can't Happen! As students choose their tasks, the teacher overhears Josh talking to Pete as they stand in front of the chart.

"I'm not going to sign up for the perimeter problem of twenty-one because that just can't happen," Josh declares with authority.

"How do you know?" asks Pete.

"You see," begins Josh, "any two numbers doubled is even, so if you have seven and seven and three and three, then you would have to have an even number."

The teacher decides to ask a question: "Would this be true for all perimeters or just twenty-one units?"

Josh looks off to the right for a minute while he ponders this question, then he says, "For rectangles, the area has to be even, but I don't know about other shapes. Can I do that?" he pleads.

"Sure, who are you going to work with?" the teacher asks. She smiles as Josh heads off looking for a partner. She enjoys Josh, but isn't always quite sure how to manage him in a classroom setting, particularly during math time. He is quite enthusiastic about his ideas and works at a fast pace. He frequently yells out answers and can get frustrated when others do not understand his thinking or appear not to appreciate his passion for the topic. He finds it hard to sit in his seat when he gets excited and often stands alone when he works. The teacher is pleased to see Josh find a partner and begin to work eagerly.

Kim Su: Square Units or Boxes?　The teacher checks in with Kim Su to make sure she is now referring to square units of area and not boxes. After this conversation, she looks up and notices that all pairs of students are engaged in their investigation. She wonders whether this is because they were able to choose their own problem to solve and which materials to use.

Samantha and Ellen: Making a T–Chart　Samantha and Ellen are investigating a rectangular garden with an area of 24 square units. Rather than using manipulatives, they make a T-chart to organize the factors of twenty-four. They decide that if they start with a factor pair, they can divide one side in half and double the other side to find the next factor pair. (See Figure 1–4.)

　　Samantha and Ellen draw rectangles systematically on a piece of dot paper using the factor pairs. (See Figure 1–5 on page 18.) When all the rectangles are drawn, they count around each one to find the perimeter and conclude that all of the perimeters are even. Encouraged by the teacher, they explore other areas in the same systematic way, exhausting all pairs by relating to what they know about multiplication and then making corresponding figures. Samantha and Ellen find it interesting that all the rectangles they make have a perimeter with an even number of units, but they do not yet trust that this happens all the time.

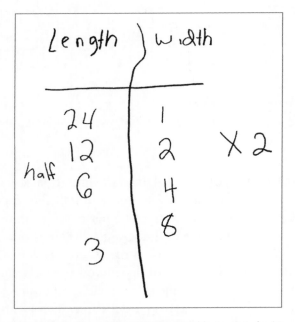

Figure 1–4. Samantha and Ellen's list of factor pairs for 24.

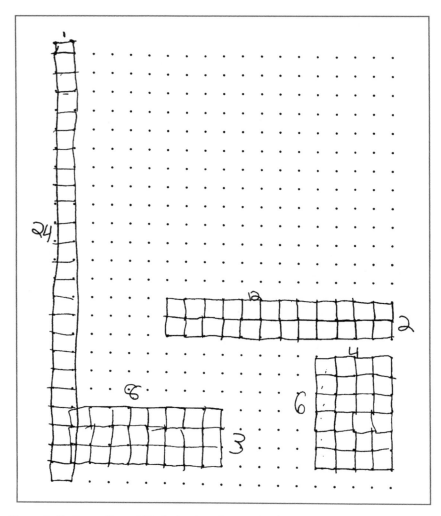

Figure 1–5. Samantha and Ellen's drawing of rectangles that correspond to their factor pairs.

Len and Marietta: Using Dot Paper Len and Marietta also use dot paper to draw rectangular arrangements of 24 square units. The teacher notes that they add the lengths of the sides to find the perimeter of these figures. They then count the dots on each side and notice that there is one more dot than the number of units they have recorded for length. This distracts them for a bit, but they decide to ignore it and depend on their knowledge of multiplication to determine the length measures. The teacher notes this behavior, marveling at their ability to ignore apparent contradictory information. She realizes that they have counted both end points on the line and that is why their count has increased by one. She decides to bring this up in the whole-group discussion that will follow because she is sure other students might run across this as well.

Corey and Tim: Using String   Several student pairs are using manipulatives. Corey and Tim decide to experiment with the string. They cut a string 21 inches long to represent the perimeter. As the teacher watches them work, she can see that they are forming rectangles with the string and then measuring the sides with a ruler. At first, they are not sure what to do when their side lengths do not measure a whole number of inches. Then, they simply stretch the string a little to make the length "so it works." But in doing so, they change the length of the string. The corners or angles of the rectangle are slightly rounded, again making it difficult to measure accurately. The teacher recognizes the difficulty of using string and offers the pair a 10-by-10 geoboard, thinking they can use the string with the board, which might help to avoid these difficulties. Corey and Tim are not interested in the board, however, and so their data are inaccurate.

Maggie and Katie: Using Color Tiles   Maggie and Katie use the color tiles to build their figures with areas of 21 square units. They appear to need to sort all the tiles by color before using them, and this takes them a great deal of time. They form two rectangles for this area, but do not have time to explore other figures.

Matt and Jacinta: Using Color Tiles   Matt and Jacinta also use the color tiles. They are investigating rectangles with an area of 24 square units. They discover that all of the perimeters are an even number of units. They explore a couple of other examples on paper, discuss the properties of even and odd numbers, and conclude that the perimeter of a rectangle will always be an even number of units. Although they discuss their ideas together, their explanations show different perspectives. (See Figures 1–6 and 1–7 on page 20.)

Part III: Summarizing

A whole-class discussion provides an opportunity for students to share their ideas. Most students are confident about their individual data, but only a few have come to any generalizations. When Matt and Jacinta share their ideas, some students look confused and other students challenge them. Their thinking remains firm and, as they continue to explain their ideas with additional examples, more heads begin to nod in agreement. The teacher is pleased with their progress. It feels good to see students beginning to form generalizations and to have the work led by the students themselves.

Take Action!
Encourage students to share their thinking and grapple with the ideas of others.

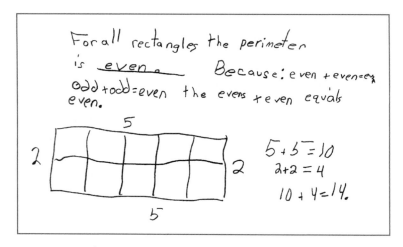

Figure 1–6. Matt's explanation of perimeter.

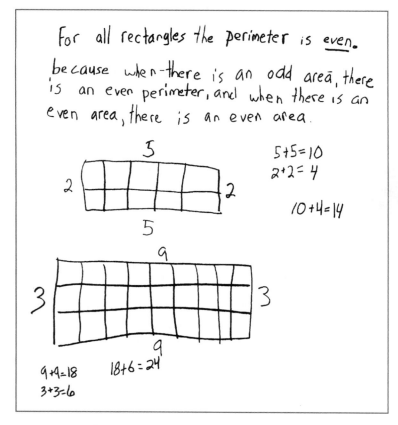

Figure 1–7. Jacinta's explanation of perimeter.

How to Differentiate Your Math Instruction

Although the book about Steven and Todd is written for younger students, it only takes a few minutes to read and it really motivates this lesson. Also, I know most of my students like to listen to stories. This is a good problem for the class to work on. Many students know *area* and *perimeter* in isolation, although they sometimes get confused between the two. In addition, they haven't explored relationships between these measures. At first, when Kim Su started talking about a box with cubes in it, I thought she was confusing area and volume. Her drawing helped me to realize that it was just an issue with vocabulary.

Many of these students tend to think just about the problem at hand, and not about how that problem might relate to a bigger mathematical idea. But, they have made progress this year. The range of abilities in this class speaks to the need to differentiate.

I don't think I would use the string again. I imagined them placing it around the centimeter paper and then counting the units. The string was too flexible and I think it just confused the students who used it.

I wish Maggie and Katie hadn't spent so much time sorting the tiles. Perhaps I should have refocused them, but Katie can become quite upset when she isn't allowed to finish something she has started. Perhaps I should have limited her choice of materials, but I don't like to single her out. Maybe I'll presort the tiles by color so that this doesn't become an issue next time.

I was pleased with how students remained on task, but because of all the different levels of learning, I know all of the students didn't understand the suggested generalization.

Our next unit is fractions and decimals, and I'll revisit this idea then. I want my students to realize that it is possible to have a perimeter with an odd number of units, such as a rectangle that is $4\frac{1}{2}$ units by 6 units. Making conjectures and then finding when they do and do not apply is an important aspect of mathematical thinking. Overall, though, I think the students did well.

> "At first, when Kim Su started talking about a box with cubes in it, I thought she was confusing area and volume."

This *Even Steven and Odd Todd* activity provided several types of differentiation. Even though the children were allowed to choose which of the four conditions they wanted to investigate, there was room for different readiness levels, including a challenge for a particularly adept student. A variety of materials from which to choose was offered to the students to complete their task, and they used different methods of recording to demonstrate their understanding. After the activity, the teacher reflects on what she learned.

This teacher is not as much of a differentiation novice as she might think, and this is true of most teachers. Every day teachers try to meet their students' needs without necessarily thinking about their teaching as differentiated instruction. Seeing teaching and learning through the lens of differentiation helps teachers meet students' needs more completely and more consciously. Over time, you can develop the habits of mind associated with differentiated instruction.

Questions to Plan By: Differentiated Instruction

1. What mathematical skills do I want my students to acquire?

2. What do my students already know? What is my evidence of this? How can I build on their thinking?

3. How can I expand access to this task or idea? Have I thought about interests, learning styles, use of language, cultures, and readiness?

4. How can I ensure that each student is challenged?

5. How can I scaffold learning to increase the likelihood of success?

6. In what different ways can my students demonstrate their new understandings?

7. Are there choices students can make?

8. How prepared am I to take on these challenges?

Connecting the Chapter to Your Practice

1. What concerns do you have about meeting your students' mathematical needs?

2. What ways have you found to integrate students' interests with mathematics instruction?

3. Which is easiest for you to differentiate in your instruction: content, process, or product? Why do you think so?

4. How do you decide when to interject yourself into student conversations?

Even Steven and Odd Todd

To see insights on how this lesson is carried out in a classroom, see page 12.

Recommended Grade: 4

Common Core State Standards for Mathematics

- Apply the area and perimeter formulas for rectangles in real-world and mathematical problems.
- Look for and make use of structure.
- Reason abstractly and quantitatively.

Time

60 minutes

Materials

- the book *Even Steven and Odd Todd*, written by Kathryn Cristaldi (1996)
- chart (see the figure presented later in Part II: Exploring)
- manipulatives at various workstations (color tiles, centimeter graph paper, and traditional dot paper)

Directions

Part I: Getting Started

1. Introduce students to the book *Even Steven and Odd Todd*. Hold up the book and ask, "What do you think this book might be about?"
2. Start reading the book. When Steven learns that Todd is spending the summer with him, stop reading and ask your students, "Does anyone have a cousin?" Then ask, "Have you ever had to compromise to get along with your cousin?" Allow some students to share their experiences.
3. Continue reading the story until the end, then ask, "If Even Steven and Odd Todd made a rectangular garden together, could they compromise by having an even perimeter and an odd area or an odd perimeter and an even area?"
4. Probe students' ideas. Ask key questions such as the following:
   - What are *area* and *perimeter*?
   - Why might we want to know the perimeter of a garden?
   - What is *distance*?

5. Revisit the question, "Can they have a garden that will make both Even Steven and Odd Todd happy?" Draw a rectangle where everyone can see it, write *Garden* above it, and ask, "Does anyone have an idea of what measurements the boys might want for their garden?" Solicit ideas. Have one student label the garden with measurements.

6. Now ask, "What would be the area of this rectangle?" As students provide answers, ask key questions, and highlight and connect their ideas.

7. Then ask, "What would be the perimeter?" Once again, as students provide answers, ask key questions, and highlight and connect their ideas.

8. When the area and perimeter of the garden have been determined, ask, "Do you think both cousins would be happy?" Have students turn to a partner and discuss.

9. Return to a whole-group discussion and solicit students' opinions. Ponder out loud, "Hmm, will both the area and perimeter always be an even number or an odd number of units if the cousins make rectangular gardens? This is what we will be investigating today during math class. I would like for you to explore the relationship between area and perimeter, and lengths of odd and even numbers of units."

Part II: Exploring

10. Post the following chart where everyone can see it.

area = 24 square units	perimeter = 24 units
area = 21 square units	perimeter = 21 units

(continued)

11. Invite students to sign up, in pairs, for one of the investigations. Explain, "When you sign up for *area equals twenty-four square units*, for example, you try to find out all the different perimeters you could have with that area."

12. Check for understanding. Ask, "What do you think you should do if you sign up for the perimeter that equals twenty-four units?"

13. Each pair of students should head to a workstation to being the investigation. Make sure the workstations offer string, color tiles, and centimeter graph paper, along with the traditional dot paper.

14. Circulate, observe students at work, and make note of their thinking. Encourage exploration. Think about what you'd like to bring up in a whole-group discussion after the investigations.

Part III: Summarizing

15. After students finish their investigations, have a whole-class discussion. Ask key questions such as the following:

    - What did you learn about area? Perimeter? The relationship between area and perimeter?
    - How did you organize your data?
    - Would you choose a different task or different materials next time? Why?

Chapter 2 Know Your Students

(continued)

Introduction

Just before the school year begins is a time filled with varying degrees of anticipation, enthusiasm, and apprehension. As the start date draws near, many students wonder: What will my teacher be like? What will I be learning this year? Who will be my friends? Teachers have their own questions: What will the students be like this year? Will they get along well as a group? What challenges will I face in meeting their needs? For students and teachers, the first few weeks of school can set the tone for the year. As you establish rituals and routines, you help students learn what is expected of them. As you get to know your students, you begin to identify how to differentiate their learning.

We believe that getting to know each student is at the heart of differentiation. By using specially designed data-gathering techniques and a wider variety of assessment practices, teachers can have a better understanding of each student as a unique learner and, as a result, have a deeper and broader view of the learning trajectory for each student. Making decisions about for whom, why, and when to differentiate becomes clearer when it is based on what you know about your students and your curriculum. Information about students' readiness, learning preferences, and interests enables you to offer different ways for students to develop and to demonstrate their mathematical knowledge. This chapter focuses on three main avenues to collecting information on your students: questionnaires, formative assessment strategies, and collaborations with other teachers.

Questionnaires and Interviews

Too often, teachers differentiate instruction only according to students' readiness. Although essential, you also need to differentiate instructional activities according to students' interests, preferred learning styles, and mathematical dispositions. Responses to questionnaires and interviews, from parents or guardians and children, can provide you with vital information to allow you to facilitate learning in different ways. In addition to gathering relevant data quickly, questionnaires and interviews let children and their families know that you expect your students to be different from one another and that you want to get to know them as individual learners. In the following pages, we offer several examples of questionnaires and interviews that we recommend using for getting to know your students.

> Too often, teachers differentiate instruction only according to students' readiness. Although essential, you also need to differentiate instructional activities according to students' interests, preferred learning styles, and mathematical dispositions.

Examples of Questionnaires and Interviews for Getting to Know Your Students

- Parent or Guardian Questionnaire
- What Interests You? Questionnaire
- Who Are You as a Learner? Questionnaire
- What Do You Think About Mathematics? Questionnaire
- A Mathematical Autobiography
- Interviewing Students During Class

Parent or Guardian Questionnaire

Some teachers ask parents or guardians to complete questionnaires. These questionnaires not only give teachers important insights into their students, they also help build school and family connections, and provide a heads-up if families need to receive communications in a language other than English. Although questionnaires are not always returned, when they are, the information gleaned can be important. An example of a narrative-style questionnaire is provided in Figure 2–1 (on p. 30, also available as Reproducible 2).

In deference to parents' busy lives, some teachers prefer to use forms that do not require narrative responses. These forms can be created and distributed electronically via online survey services such as www.surveymonkey .com. An example of a survey-style questionnaire is provided in Figure 2–2 (on p. 30, also available as Reproducible 3).

REPRODUCIBLE 2

Take Action!

Gather information about your students through parent or guardian questionnaires.

REPRODUCIBLE 3

Narrative–Style Parent or Guardian Questionnaire

Distribute to parents at the beginning of the school year.

Student name: _____

Dear Parent or Guardian:

I am always so excited about the start of the school year and a roomful of eager students. I am looking forward to getting to know each and every one of them, as well as their families. Because no one knows your child as well as you do, I am hoping that you will have the time to answer these few questions. There are no right or wrong answers, just responses that will help me to meet your child's needs more completely when he or she is learning math. I am very interested in helping children realize that math is an important part of the world, and is exciting to learn. I believe that by connecting the learning of math to other important aspects of your child's life, I can make it more relevant and exciting. Please feel free to call me if you have any questions. Thank you.

1. What are your child's favorite hobbies, interests, pastimes, books?

2. In what ways is mathematics part of your child's life at home?

3. What, if any, concerns do you have about your child's knowledge of mathematics?

4. What is a mathematical strength that you see in your child?

5. Describe your child's experience with math homework.

Figure 2–1. Narrative-style parent or guardian questionnaire.

Survey–Style Parent or Guardian Questionnaire

Distribute to parents at the beginning of the school year.

Dear Parent or Guardian:

This first day has been a wonderful start to the school year. I am excited about getting to know each of my new students. I hope that you will help me by completing this questionnaire about mathematics. There are no right or wrong answers! Please feel free to call me if you have any questions. Thank you.

Student name: _____

Please circle the number next to the statement that corresponds to the number key listed here:

1 = agree
2 = somewhat agree
3 = somewhat disagree
4 = disagree

My child will stick with a math problem, even when it is difficult.	1 2 3 4
My child lacks confidence in mathematics.	1 2 3 4
My child has strong computational skills.	1 2 3 4
My child's favorite subject is mathematics.	1 2 3 4
My child becomes frustrated solving math problems.	1 2 3 4
My child does math homework independently.	1 2 3 4
As a caregiver, it is my job to help my child with math homework.	1 2 3 4
Math is talked about at home and is part of our everyday life.	1 2 3 4
I do not always understand the way my child thinks about math problems.	1 2 3 4
Math is taught better today than when I was in school.	1 2 3 4

Comments:

Figure 2–2. Survey-style parent or guardian questionnaire.

The following reflection shows how one fifth-grade teacher gained respect for the information parents and guardians can provide.

TEACHER REFLECTION

When I first started teaching fifth grade, I thought my job was to teach children, that only primary teachers had to focus on families. I didn't give much thought to the parents or guardians of my students and what my relationship would be with them. How quickly I learned! Now in my fifth year of teaching, I have made progress in finding ways to connect with my students' caregivers.

At the beginning of the year I send home a parents and guardians survey, which asks questions about how their child learns and about their attitudes toward learning mathematics. I ask for the surveys to be returned prior to the first open house at the end of September. I gather this information to use as a guide when I am addressing the parents or guardians. I am as surprised by the variety among the parents and guardians as I am by the differences in my students! I have parents who feel strongly that their role is to help their child with homework as well as parents who feel it is solely the child's responsibility to complete his or her homework. Likewise, I have many parents who support the recent changes in math education and those who think: The way we were taught is fine. Why are we changing the rules?

In addition to the survey, I share with each parent or guardian their own child's survey done in class. Often, how a child answers the questions surprises the adult. One child, Wanda, wrote *Excellent!* in response to the question: How do you feel about multiplication? Her mother was shocked, but happy, and told me, "Last year my daughter always cried while doing her homework. I tried to help her, but I think she got more confused. She was not comfortable with me helping her because she said I don't do multiplication the right way. I am glad to see that she is liking multiplication now." It's so easy for all of us to hang on to a perception that may no longer be true. It was important for Wanda's mother to realize that her daughter was now comfortable with multiplication. I think this knowledge will help Wanda's mother treat her daughter as someone who is successful in math, which will in turn reinforce that idea in Wanda.

When it comes to talking about math, parents or guardians frequently tell me that they were not successful in or didn't like math. Sometimes I worry that these parents don't hold high enough expectations for their children. Other parents tell me how much they excelled at math and how they want the same for their children. They tell stories of how their child has impressed them at an early age, and they identify family traits and interests they share: "We love to look at the football stats in the newspaper." "We play cards all the time and race to see who can add up the points first." These comments give me a perspective on how the families view mathematics and how mathematics is embedded in their daily lives. I can't believe how much more I learn about my students now that I have built family connections.

> " I have parents who feel strongly that their role is to help their child with homework as well as parents who feel it is solely the child's responsibility to complete his or her homework. Likewise, I have many parents who support the recent changes in math education and those who think: The way we were taught is fine. Why are we changing the rules? "

What Interests You? Questionnaire

Questions about students' hobbies, collections, and activity choices in and out of school provide insight into interests students have that may connect to mathematics. Knowing these interests allows you to position tasks in contexts that can help capture students' curiosity and illustrate the usefulness of what they are learning. Collecting coins, playing cards or logic games, doing puzzles, having an interest in sports-generated statistics, and constructing intricate block designs often relate to skills that support and use mathematical thinking. The following is an example of a What Interests You? Questionnaire given to fourth-grade students early in the fall (Figure 2–3; also available as Reproducible 4). A similar questionnaire can be used at the primary level if it is completed at home with an adult reading and recording the information.

Reproducible 4

What Interests You? Questionnaire

Distribute to students early during the school year. For younger children, ask the parent or guardian to complete this questionnaire at home, with the adult reading and recording the information given by the child.

Student name: _____

What Interests You?

1. What activities do you like to do after school?

2. What are your favorite sports or games?

3. What do you like to do during indoor recess?

4. If you could plan a field trip, where would you want to go?

5. Who is your favorite character from a book or a video?

6. In the following list, place a 1 next to the things you like the most. Place a 2 next to the things you like second best.

   ____ music   ____ reading

   ____ sports   ____ nature walks

   ____ acting   ____ drawing or art projects

   ____ being with friends   ____ building things

   ____ science experiments   ____ field trips to historical places

---

Figure 2–3. What Interests You? Questionnaire for fourth graders to complete at the beginning of the school year.

Who Are You as a Learner? Questionnaire

Students can also tell us about how they learn best—for example, whether they like to work in groups or alone, the levels of challenge they prefer, the noise level they find comfortable, and where they like to work in the classroom. Asking children about these preferences helps them realize that we care about how they learn best. It also allows them to reflect on their learning preferences. Depending on your preferences and the ages of your students, the Who Are You as a Learner? Questionnaire (Figure 2–4; also available as Reproducible 5) can be completed independently in class or as homework, can be talked about in small groups (with you reading the questions and jotting notes from oral responses), or can be completed by you as individual student interviews.

Take Action!
Have students describe their learning preferences.

REPRODUCIBLE 5

Reproducible 5

Who Are You as a Learner? Questionnaire

Distribute to students early during the school year. For younger children, ask the parent or guardian to complete this questionnaire at home, with the adult reading and recording the information given by the child.

Student name: _____

Who Are You as a Learner?

1. If you could learn about anything at school, what would you choose?

2. What do you know a lot about?

3. How do you work best in school (check all that describe you)?
   ___ alone   ___ partner   ___ small group   ___ large group

4. Where do you like to work at school (check all that describe you)?
   ___ desk   ___ table   ___ hallway   ___ floor   ___ library area   ___ other

5. You learn best when your classroom is (check all that describe you)
   ___ quiet   ___ somewhat quiet   ___ somewhat noisy   ___ noisy

6. Do you like schoolwork to be (check all that describe you)
   ___ easy   ___ somewhat easy   ___ somewhat hard   ___ hard

7. What else helps you to learn?

8. What makes it hard for you to learn?

Figure 2–4. Who Are You as a Learner? Questionnaire for students to complete at the beginning of the school year.

What Do You Think About Mathematics? Questionnaire

It is also worthwhile to gain insight into students' mathematical dispositions, or their attitudes toward mathematics. As all teachers know, positive attitudes contribute greatly to successful learning. Ideally, all students enjoy mathematics, have positive mathematical learning experiences, think of themselves as successful learners and users of mathematics, and view mathematics as a useful tool in their lives. Simple observations, such as noting how a child sits or looks during mathematical activities, can often provide quite a bit of information. Does her body language suggest that she is tense? Do his eyes indicate that he is disinterested? Is the position of her shoulders a sign that she is confident? Is the angle of his upper body an implication of eager anticipation? These behaviors can often be observed during the first week of school and can alert teachers to those students who might need closer attention.

Student responses to the What Do You Think about Mathematics? Questionnaire suggest a variety of beliefs about mathematics. For example, when asked, "Why is math important to learn?" some students may indicate its relevance to their daily life with comments such as "It is everywhere" or "In life, you need to be smart in math or you will lose money." Other responses may be school based, containing expressions of concern about a student's future education, with comments such as "You need it for middle school" or "to go to college." The questionnaire offered in this resource (Figure 2–5; also available as Reproducible 6) has been used to collect data from first-through fifth-grade students about their mathematical dispositions.

Responses to the questionnaire also reveal how students feel about math. Many students may give short positive answers such as "really happy," "smart," "great!", "cool," or "excited." Unfortunately, even in elementary school, difficulties and ill feelings are also indicated with responses such as "nervous"; "like I'm thinking so much that my head will pop off"; "confused"; "sad, because I don't do math well"; or "like I want to hide."

Interestingly, when completing the questionnaires, students most often named an arithmetic operation as what they were good at, not good at, or wanted to learn more about. All the students are usually able to identify something they are good at, with "adding" or "pluses" being the most common response among younger children who identify negative feelings when learning mathematics. As students advance, fractions are more frequently identified as something they are not yet good at. Teachers who collect the data are always pleased that some of the students identify "doing problems" or "learning different ways to do problems" as either their strength or as something they want to learn. Teachers may be disappointed at how few students comment on the usefulness of math outside of school. Teachers also recognize that their students' responses alert them to feelings that could potentially impact learning, both positively and negatively.

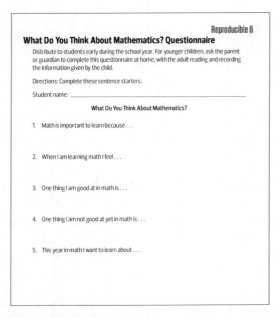

Figure 2–5. The What Do You Think about Mathematics? Questionnaire.

VIDEO CLIP 2.1 ·

Interviewing Students During Class

In this video clip the teacher, Mrs. Miller, interviews a few students in her fourth-grade class as a quick way to check in about their learning.

As you watch the clip, consider:

1. What structures are in place to make it possible for Mrs. Miller to conduct these interviews?
2. Having viewed Mrs. Miller collecting information about the students' strengths and weaknesses, what would you recommend for an action plan going forward? How could you include the student in designing their own action plan?
3. In your own classroom, how could interviewing your students inform your instruction to make the math accessible to each student?

To see an example of an in-class interview happening in a Kindergarten classroom, see Video Clip 9.1.

A Mathematical Autobiography

REPRODUCIBLE 7

In grades 3 to 5, you may want to go beyond the format of a questionnaire. Some teachers ask their students to write their mathematical autobiography (Figure 2–6 on page 37; also available as Reproducible 7), integrating the assignment with an English and language arts unit on personal narratives. A fourth-grade teacher, for example, offers a variety of questions in her assignment to help students brainstorm ideas and make connections, but she does not require them to respond to each question because she thinks it might feel oppressive or repetitive to them.

Dino begins his response by declaring that he likes math, although his later comments suggest otherwise. (See Figure 2–7 on page 37.)

Formative Assessment Strategies

One way of categorizing assessment is by when it occurs. Such a categorization leads to terms such as *preassessment*, *interim assessment*, and *postassessment*. As teachers, it is important to assess students at each of these stages of learning. However, in terms of differentiation, it is the *purpose* of the assessment that is most important. Traditionally, assessment has been tied to the purpose of evaluation—for example, to assign a grade or ranking. Such assessments are most closely related to postassessments because, theoretically at least, they occur after students have had the opportunity to learn the content. Called *summative assessments*, these are now thought of as assessments *of* learning. Although not always recognized, it should be remembered that such data can also inform instructional decision making (Dunn and Mulvenon 2009).

In contrast, formative assessment is associated more closely with pre- or interim assessment practices and is thought of as assessments *for* learning. Such assessments can occur before, during, or after an instructional sequence. The purpose of a formative assessment is to gather data that allow you to monitor student progress, provide feedback to students, reflect on instructional techniques used, and make or adjust future instructional plans. As teachers, you can use all evidence of learning to inform your teaching, regardless of whether it is collected before, during, or after learning. What is important is your intentionality to use the data to help ensure student success.

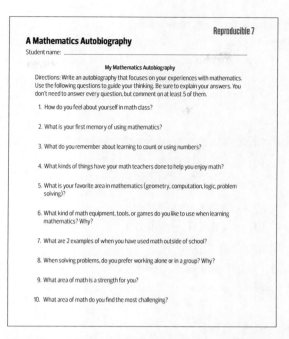

Figure 2–6. My Mathematics Autobiography assignment.

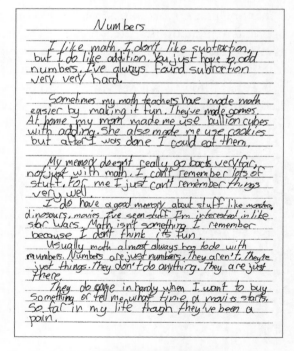

Figure 2–7. Dino's autobiography.

So, how can we make the practice of what Dana Islas (2011) calls "assess while you teach" an integral part of our practice and how can we use such data to support the goal of differentiated instruction? In the following pages, we suggest several formative assessment strategies that will help you acquire data on your students with the goal of differentiating your instruction.

Formative Assessment Strategies for Getting to Know Your Students

- Preassessment
- Anecdotal records
- Interviews
- Open-ended problems
- Student work
- Quick assessments

Preassessment

Take Action!

Assess for readiness.

To differentiate according to readiness, you need to determine what your students already know. Many activities can provide us with preassessment data if they include opportunities for discussion, group work, or recorded responses and explanations. Often, it can be the inclusion of simple prompts such as "Who can tell me what they remember about squares?" or "Draw a line that you think is close to three inches long." It is the teacher's clarity of purpose that allows such activities to become sources of preassessment data. Let's consider another teacher's words as she reflects on preassessment.

TEACHER REFLECTION

When I am thinking about preassessment, I know I am trying to identify children's zones of comfort and proficiency. I am looking for data that will help me answer questions such as the following: How familiar are my students with this concept? What working knowledge, skills, and strategies do they have in place to support further learning in this area? What misconceptions might they have? How comfortable are they with the mathematical language associated with this topic?

I try hard not to make assumptions about my students anymore. Some of them come to school with a wealth of mathematical knowledge and experience. Many students do not, and the range among them seems to be increasing each year. I want to meet each child where he or she is. It's hard to find that edge for each student, that place between where things are too hard and out of reach, and too easy and potentially uninteresting or not challenging. Although I know in reading that it can be fun and good practice to read a book that is too easy, I also know that if that is all you are asked to read, you have considerably less opportunity to improve and become a more proficient, analytical reader. When a book is too hard, the reading experience can also be frustrating and can lead to reluctance to read and lack of productivity. The same is true in math. I want to identify the tasks and investigations that will be just right for my students, that will challenge their thinking without overwhelming them. And, I want to do this frequently, so that we all feel good about what we are doing.

> **I want to meet each child where he or she is. It's hard to find that edge for each student, that place between where things are too hard and out of reach, and too easy and potentially uninteresting or not challenging.**

Many aspects of the importance of all types of assessment have been identified by this teacher. Keep her words in mind as you read about other formative assessment strategies.

Anecdotal Records

During the first week of kindergarten, teachers might begin to collect anecdotal data about their students' mathematical understandings by observing them explore mathematics-related manipulatives and become familiar with the possible uses of these materials. As children dive in, so do their teachers, who listen, watch, and often record what they see and hear. The following notes were recorded by a kindergarten teacher:

Anecdotal Notes by a Kindergarten Teacher

- Marcus counted to seven as he stacked blocks to make a tower.
- Mikeala didn't seem to want to explore the materials. She kept gravitating back to the baskets of books.

(continued)

Take Action!
Keep track of your observations.

- Ana and Roman were using Cuisenaire rods. They made "stairs." "This is the tallest," Ana said.
- Hue and Kayla stopped at each bin but moved on quickly. "Now what?" Hue kept asking.
- Counting buttons—Evan got to nineteen but said, "Thirteen, thirteen, sixteen, seventeen, eighteen, nineteen."

Anecdotal notes such as those just listed help teachers get a feel for students' comfort level, engagement, and working knowledge. Over time, patterns of thinking or behavior might emerge for an individual as well as for the whole class that can help teachers make more informed decisions for instruction. Recording such observations can help teachers focus and remember what they have witnessed.

One fourth-grade teacher uses a list of questions to help manage her data collection. She has purposely chosen to include items that align with aspects of the Common Core State Standards for Mathematics. She has also established the habit of underlining one or two phrases in her notes that will help her to differentiate instruction.

A Fourth-Grade Teacher's List of Questions Aligned to Aspects of the Common Core State Standards

- What strategies does the student use to make sense of the task?
- Does the student use equations, arrays and/or area models to represent the situation or calculations?
- Does the student use place value strategies, properties of the operation, and relationships to other operations to compute?
- Does the student use precise language when describing his or her solution strategies?
- What misconceptions are suggested?
- Does the student understand the thinking of others? Interested in such thinking?
- Does the student demonstrate both strong procedural skills and conceptual thinking?

Sometimes teachers want to dig deeper. They often listen to their students read to gather data about their literacy fluency and decoding skills. Such close individual attention makes sense in mathematics as well.

Interviews

Early assessment interviews are usually designed to help teachers learn relatively quickly about students' abilities in relation to numbers and operations, including counting, place value, computation, and fractions. Often, teachers construct their own interviews and use their state standards as a way to decide what kinds of questions to ask, focusing on standards expected to have been mastered the previous year. Questions to consider across the grade levels are presented in Figure 2–8. These suggestions are not comprehensive, but are intended to serve as examples. It is assumed that teachers would include phrases such as *explain your thinking* or *tell me more*, as appropriate.

GRADE LEVEL	INTERVIEW QUESTION EXAMPLES
K	How high can you count? What numbers can you write? How many counters are there? Can you show me a set of five (then ten, and then twenty) objects?
1	Can you show me a set of thirty counters? If you were counting, what number would you say after seventeen? Before forty? What is four more than five?
2	Can you show me a set of one hundred counters? How high can you count by tens, starting at twenty-five? What is an equation you can write? What is six plus eight?
3	If you were counting, what number would you say before five hundred sixty? What is forty-six plus thirty-nine? What number goes in the blank when I write $13 + 7 = 14 +$ ___ ? How would you estimate seventy-three plus twenty-nine?
4	Is three-fourths closer to zero or to one? What is six hundred thirty-four minus ninety-nine? What is five times nine? When might you use multiplication?
5	Which is greater: three-eighths or four-sevenths? How do we write twenty-four tenths? What is six times twenty-four? When might you need to find one hundred divided by five?

Figure 2–8. Interview question examples.

Take Action!

Talk with a special educator about comprehensive assessment interviews available in your school.

General and special educators often work together to collect more data about particular students identified as being at risk. Many math educators, researchers, and research groups have designed more comprehensive assessment interviews. The following are insights on a few of them.

Comprehensive Assessment Interviews

Assessing Math Concepts

Leading mathematics educator and consultant Kathy Richardson has developed a series of assessment tasks designed for use as individual interviews. *Assessing Math Concepts* (Richardson 2003) includes a continuum of assessment for students in grades K–3. Each of these short assessments is tailor-made to help a teacher find the place at which a student transitions from a comfortable, grounded under-standing of mathematics to a place where more practice, application, or instruction is required—that is, to determine a student's edge of understanding. Richardson (2003) also suggests how the teacher can make strategic decisions for future instruction based on data gained through interviews and provides ways to continue to assess students' work.

First Steps in Mathematics

First Steps in Mathematics (Willis et al. 2007) is designed for use in pre-K–9 classrooms. Originally developed in Australia and Canada, this diagnostic resource has since been field-tested in the United States. Although its implementation requires special training, it provides diagnostic tasks that are integrated easily into interactions. It also links assessments to instructional activities and is designed for use with all students.

Key Math 3 Diagnostic Assessment

Key Math 3 Diagnostic Assessment (Connolly 2008a) is for educa-tors looking for a norm-referenced assessment. This diagnostic can be used to assess counting through algebraic expressions. Because the assessment takes 30 to 90 minutes to administer, it should be used to assess those students who require a more extensive diagnosis. Instructional materials that correlate to the tool are also available (Connolly 2008b).

Similar to Vygotsky's (1978) zone of proximal development, your job is to challenge students' comfort level and then to help them find their next boundaries. Through assessment, we try to identify evidence for what the child knows or has mastered, areas where initial ideas are formed but additional experience with them is needed, and those concepts and skills that require further scaffolding or additional readiness development.

Teachers need to determine their own best way to use data gathered from an assessment, be it formal or informal. There was a time when such initial data were used to determine ability groups in mathematics. These groups were thought to be homogeneous in nature, and students tended to be assigned to these groups for the long term. That is not the goal assumed here. Although we do recommend that students' instruction be differentiated based on readiness, we do not assume—nor do we recommend—that groups always be formed or that, when groups are appropriate, they be homogeneous or that the group members remain the same. Remember to continue to collect data about students' preferred mathematical models, learning styles, and personal connections to mathematics.

Open-Ended Problems

Some open-ended tasks or problems can provide us with several types of insights into student thinking. The following are several examples of these types of tasks.

Task: *What Do You Know About 12?*

One second-grade teacher offers her students the following task early in the year:

What do you know about 12?

Show 12 in as many different ways as you can.

Haley's response contains a variety of ideas. (See Figure 2–9 on page 44.) Her inclusion of standard notation, along with the creation of a word problem, shows that she is aware of the kinds of problems we explore during math time, and some of the symbols we use to communicate mathematical ideas. She tells her teacher that her first drawing shows, "ten ones together to make one large one with two small ones left." This lets Haley's teacher know that she has some understanding of working with tens and ones, and some familiarity with a model of the base ten system. Haley then draws twelve "ones" as an additional representation; she indicates her awareness of another mathematics manipulative when she says, "These are twelve tiles." Haley seems

> **Take Action!**
> Establish expectations for flexible groups.

> "We do recommend that students' instruction be differentiated based on readiness, we do not assume—nor do we recommend—that groups always be formed or that, when groups are appropriate, they be homogeneous or that the group members remain the same."

> **Task Idea!**
> **Focus:** Number sense
> **Domain:** Numbers and operations in base ten
> **The Task:** *What do you know about 12? Show 12 in as many different ways as you can.*

Figure 2–9. Haley's response to the open-ended task *What do you know about 12?* shows connections to equations, physical models, and a story problem.

to have some ideas about the commutative property for addition because she writes *12 + 0 = 0 + 12* as well as *11 + 1* next to *1 + 11*.

Haley's teacher was particularly pleased to see the equation with two addends on each side because it shows an initial understanding of the equals sign as indicating equality or balance, rather than the traditional misconception many children have that it is the sign to tell you where you write the answer. In the following reflection, you see how the teacher thinks about this task as a way to gather data about her students.

The range of responses to this task is pretty amazing. I have found that twelve is a number that most, if not all, of my students feel comfortable with and yet it still provides mathematical interest. Some children try to dazzle me by writing a long list of equations, others try adding "clever" responses, such as "I know twelve is a dozen," or "Twelve on the clock is for noon and midnight." My second-grade students know we use problems like this one to get a feel for what they know and can do.

Although the range of responses is great, I don't want to read too much into them. After all, it's only one task, but it is a place to begin and the responses do help me develop some ideas about what my students know. I don't have a specific number of responses that I am looking for, although I do look for accuracy, flexible thinking, and engagement. I also check to see whether there is any evidence of a child looking uncomfortable during this work.

> "Although the range of responses is great, I don't want to read too much into them. After all, it's only one task, but it is a place to begin and the responses do help me develop some ideas about what my students know."

This teacher's thoughts should remind you of the balanced way you need to think about assessment tasks. No one task can be given too much attention, and yet each appropriate task does provide some relevant data.

The Importance of Gathering Student Data from Multiple Sources

It is particularly important to take a balanced perspective on information that is passed from grade to grade. In many schools, data are shared from one grade to another by way of lists of test scores and portfolios that contain end-of-year assessment interviews or packets. Some teachers who receive this information find it to be very helpful, whereas others prefer to begin to make their own judgments before reviewing any of the previous data. In either case, it is important to remember the significance of gathering evidence from multiple sources.

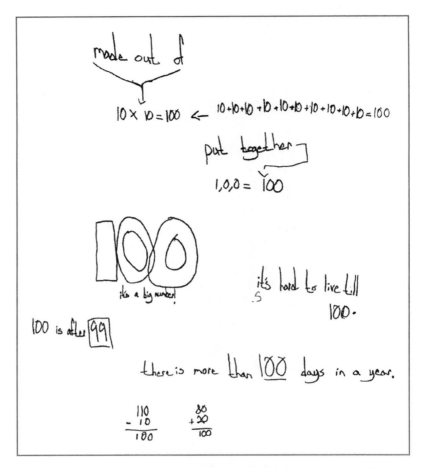

Figure 2–10. Sam's response to the task *What do you know about 100?*

Task: *What Do You Know About 100?*

The type of open-ended question explored earlier can be adapted easily across the grades. One third-grade teacher asks her students to respond to a similar question: What do you know about one hundred? Sam's response identifies one hundred as ten times ten. (See Figure 2–10.) He indicates this relationship through repeated addition of tens as well, suggesting that he understands the relationship between addition and multiplication. He indicates flexibility in his thinking as he connects one hundred to several different ideas. He writes that it *is after* 99 and that it is *a big number*. He writes a subtraction example with one hundred as the difference and an addition example with one hundred as the sum. He demonstrates his number sense when he relates

Task Idea!

Focus: Number sense

Domain: Numbers and operations in base ten

The Task: *What do you know about 100?*

one hundred meaningfully to the real world. He writes that it would be hard to live to be one hundred and that *there is [are] more than 100 days in a year*. The teacher notes that Sam often refers to one hundred as a landmark number in terms of computation, but from responses to this task, Sam realizes that one hundred is important for number sense as well.

Task: *What Do You Know About $\frac{3}{4}$?*

A fifth-grade class is working on equivalent fractions in preparation for applying these ideas to addition and subtraction with unlike denominators. The teacher notices the variation among the students in response to what he thought of as a lesson to connect to previous knowledge. He decides to step back and collect some data. He presents the task *What do you know about $\frac{3}{4}$?* He chooses this question because he is confident that all of his students can respond in some way. The teacher is struck by Michaela's response, in which there is a list of related mathematical ideas (Figure 2–11). Michaela

. . . .

Task Idea!

Focus: Number sense

Domain: Numbers and operations, fractions

The Task: *What do you know about $\frac{3}{4}$?*
. . . .

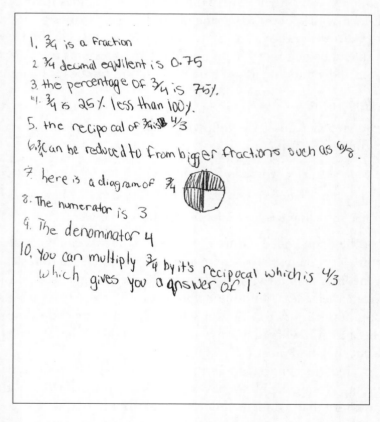

1. ¾ is a fraction
2. ¾ decimal equivilent is 0.75
3. the percentage of ¾ is 75%.
4. ¾ is 25% less than 100%.
5. the recipocal of ¾ is 4/3
6. ¾ can be reduced to from bigger fractions such as 6/8.
7. here is a diagram of ¾
8. The numerator is 3
9. The denominator 4
10. You can multiply ¾ by it's recipocal which is 4/3 which gives you a answer of 1.

Figure 2–11. Michaela's response to the task *What do you know about $\frac{3}{4}$?*

makes connections to decimals and percents, and uses the terms *reciprocal*, *numerator*, and *denominator*. She includes references to ideas of equivalency by connecting three-fourths to six-eighths, seventy-five percent, and seventy-five one-hundredths. She also demonstrates knowledge of multiplication of fractions when she refers to multiplying three-fourths by its reciprocal to give an answer of one. The teacher also notes that Michaela's is one of the few responses that does not include a real-world connection, and he wonders whether she needs more work in this area, perhaps while other students are focused on concepts that Michaela already knows.

Student Work

We cannot overemphasize the importance of looking carefully at student work. A variety of resources are available that provide examples of assessment tasks along with rubrics that can make it easier to assess work, including *INFORMative Assessment: Formative Assessment to Improve Math Achievement, Grades K–6* by Joyner and Muri (2011). Sometimes it is best just to look at student work, perhaps sorting it into three categories or noting similarities and differences for further instructional purposes. While reviewing the work, it can be helpful to focus on follow-up questions to ask so that an ever-greater understanding about student thinking can be gleaned.

INFORMative Assessment: Formative Assessment to Improve Math Achievement, Grades K–6 by Joyner and Muri (Math Solutions, 2011)

Task: *Telling Time*

A first-grade teacher poses the following task to her students at the end of a unit on time:

> Your younger sister wants to learn how to tell time. Make a list of the most important things she needs to know. Or, describe how you would teach her to tell time using pictures, numbers, and words.

Because of the open-ended nature of the task, students can control some of the difficulty level themselves—for example, by limiting their illustrations to times on the hour. Similarly, students may choose to emphasize drawings to communicate their ideas, without including much prose. This task also gives teachers an opportunity to discover what their students choose to include, perhaps because it is what they know best or what they believe is most important or what they find most interesting.

As expected, the children are intrigued by the task. At this age, even children without a younger sibling are aware of and proud of the fact that they now know more than younger children. They are often solicitous to kindergarteners who get upset on the playground, and they are proud to use their

Task Idea!

Focus: Telling time

Domain: Measurement

The Task: *Your younger sister wants to learn how to tell time. Make a list of the most important things she needs to know. Or, describe how you would teach her to tell time using pictures, numbers, and words.*

Partners Working on an Open-Ended Task

This video clip shows one example of partners working on an open-ended task in Ms. Anderson's fourth-grade class. The task is part of a multiplication Think Tac Toe, a format for organizing student choices (see Chapter 7 for more on Think Tac Toe).

Place the numbers: 3, 4, 6, 15, 20, and 30, so that the product of each side is 360.

○

○ ○

○ ○ ○

Write one more problem like this one and trade it with a classmate.

Figure 2–12. Multiplication Think Tac Toe example for fourth-grade students.

Before you view the clip, solve the problem. (See Figure 2–12.) What is the mathematics in this task? What makes this an open-ended task?

As you watch the clip, consider:

1. What skills does each learner demonstrate?
2. What misconceptions did you notice?
3. What question(s) would you want to ask to check each student's understanding of the mathematics?
4. When students work with a partner, what strategies do you use to support students sharing the ownership of the mathematics?

newly acquired literacy skills to read to younger children. The teacher views this task as a way to celebrate her students' mathematical knowledge modestly. The teacher chuckles as she hears Jason announce, "There's a lot I can teach my sister about time. She hardly knows anything and I know bunches of stuff."

The range of responses can be represented by the following three examples. Madison relies mostly on a clock face to explain her thinking. She draws a recognizable clock and writes the corresponding time correctly. She also notes the different sizes of the hands. (See Figure 2–13.)

Jessica is the only child whose response shows people and, most notably, connects analog and digital representations of the same time. (See Figure 2–14.) The teacher is not surprised by Jessica's drawing because she knows that relationships are important to Jessica. She is surprised by Jessica's inclusion of the fact that there are sixty minutes in an hour, a detail that many students do not recognize at this level. Jessica does not, however, focus on how to tell time, so the teacher plans to have a follow-up conversation with her and a couple of other students to gain more insight into their thinking.

Derek uses a list format to communicate what he would teach his sister. (See Figure 2–15.) The teacher notes his preference for using words in this response. She also notes his reference to counting by fives, because she knows that this goes beyond the standards for this grade level.

The teacher writes the following comments for follow-up questions about these student responses. Note that she references the student work directly. She will show the work to the student as she asks the question. Teachers of older students can write the questions directly on the paper as part of their feedback.

Take Action!

As you read student work, note follow-up questions that you want to address to deepen or clarify student thinking.

Teacher's Follow-up Questions for Each Student

1. For Madison: Why do you think one of the hands on the clock is little and the other is big?
2. For Jessica: What do you know about the minute hand?
3. For Derek: What picture could you make that might help your sister?

little big
hand hand
5:00

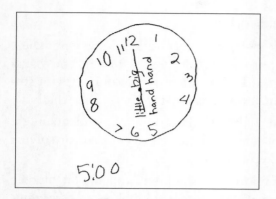

Figure 2–13. Madison's response shows the numbers on a clock and the different-size hands.

the little hand tells the hour. Sixtee minets are in a hour.
the big hand tells the minits.
okay

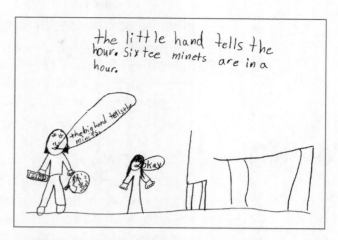

Figure 2–14. In response to this task, Jessica shows herself teaching her little sister how to tell time.

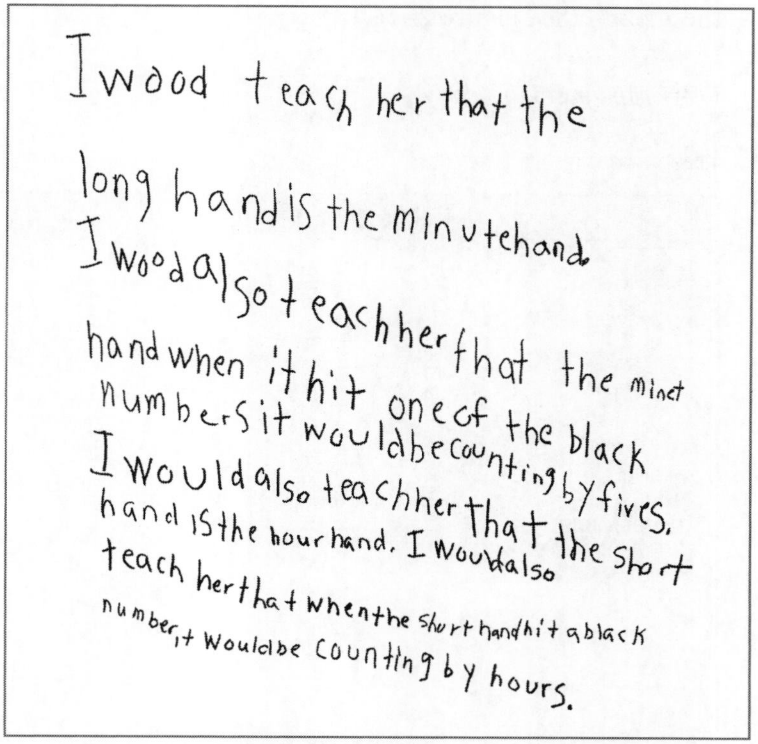

I wood teach her that the
long hand is the minutehand.
I wood also teach her that the minet
hand when it hit one of the black
numbers it would be counting by fives.
I would also teach her that the short
hand is the hour hand. I would also
teach her that when the short hand hit a black
number, it would be counting by hours.

Figure 2–15. Derek provides a narrative response to this task.

Identifying Purposes in Student Work

Another way to think about student work is to consider its purpose. Diezmann and McCosker (2011) suggest we consider text, symbols, and visual models when we consider student work. They identify two purposes for student representations: to represent their thinking and to support their thinking.

Take Action!

Keep track of how students represent their thinking.

1. *Represent their thinking*: To represent their thinking, students might depict the context of the problem, the key strategy used for solving the problem, or the entire step-by-step process.

2. *Support for thinking*: To support their thinking, students might keep a record of their computational steps or make drawings and diagrams that can identify and organize information and relationships.

When you keep track of how students use a combination of drawings, symbols, and text to support and express their thinking, you collect data that can inform your teaching. Such data allow you to recognize the ways in which students do and do not use their representations, and thus indicate how and with which students you should work to increase their ability to develop and communicate their thinking. We created a rubric for organizing these data. (See Figure 2–16.)

Check all purposes that apply.

Task: Date:

Student Name	TOOL FOR THINKING			TOOL FOR COMMUNICATION		
	Keeps track of computation steps	Draws or makes notes to highlight and interpret data	Uses diagrams, drawings, or notes to organize data	Labels key strategies and answer	Shows or relates to problem context	Provides step-by-step solution process

Figure 2–16. Rubric for organizing data.

Giving Feedback on Student Work

Along with examining student work and making instructional plans based on that work, teachers must decide what feedback to give to their students. Whether given orally or in writing, feedback is an important part of the assessment process. Most teachers understand that feedback is more effective when it is given promptly, that it should be specific, and that it should describe the work, not their attitude toward it. The feedback should motivate students to improve their learning. Yet, nearly all teachers sometimes struggle with what comments to make to students. It can be hard to find the right balance between too little and too much commentary.

Differentiation requires another layer of reflection as we decide what kind of feedback is best for which work and which students. Konald and coauthors (2004) suggest different responses, depending on how a student states a verbal response. For example, if a quick, but hesitant, response is given by the student, the teacher should take the time to reinforce the student's thinking, perhaps by reiterating the statement or giving another example to affirm the student's thinking. Teachers make such decisions, often subconsciously, throughout the day.

Feedback to written work is more intentional. Here are some questions that are designed to help you better differentiate such feedback.

> **Take Action!**
> Give feedback that is prompt, specific, and individualized to student needs.

Questions to Help You Better Differentiate Your Feedback

- Would this student best understand feedback given in writing, in a mini-conference, or in a casual conversation?

- What is the key concept or skill on which feedback should focus for this student right now?

- What aspects of this student's work should I reference specifically?

- What growth has this student shown over time that I could point out based on this work?

- What feedback could I give that would motivate this student to improve?

- How could I involve this student in the feedback process? For example, could I ask him or her to identify what the focus should be?

Providing meaningful feedback is not an easy task, and it is still not guaranteed that students will look at the feedback and make changes. One third-grade teacher realized this as she watched her students stuff their backpacks with their papers that contain feedback, without looking at them, as they got ready to go home. She wondered what she could change in her classroom to support students valuing feedback. She decided to add a new routine at the end of each day. Now, before getting their backpacks, students are given five to ten minutes to organize and read over returned papers. During this time, her role is to circulate around the room and to focus on five or so students a day. Throughout the week, she finds she can talk individually to every student. After a few weeks of implementation, she notices that students have begun to ask her questions about the comments she made on their papers, and she starts to follow up these questions with comments about the student's own performance goals. Over time, students make clear connections between the work they are doing and the goals they set. Students took ownership of their own learning, and the feedback provided validation of what they had mastered as well as support for what they were still working on learning.

Looking at Student Work Across Grade Levels

Looking at your students' work closely is always a valuable experience. Unfortunately, as teachers, you are often alone when you examine such products. There is great value to sharing such work with others who teach at the same or at other grade levels. Here we focus on looking at work across grade levels.

Task: *What Do You Know About Shapes?*
Three colleagues—a third-grade teacher, a fourth-grade teacher, and a fifth-grade teacher—want to get a better idea of how their students compare across grade levels in terms of their geometric thinking. The range in ability levels in their classrooms seems vast to these teachers, and they hope that by working with teachers at other levels, they will understand more completely what might be normative at their level and how they might better support and challenge students at different points along the learning spectrum. The teachers decide to assign the same task across the grades. They design a question so that a broad range of responses can be captured:

> *What do you know about shapes?*
> *Write and draw to communicate your ideas.*

The teachers pose the task and, before sending their students off to work, talk with them about task expectations. In the fourth-grade classroom, the students create the following list to guide their work:

- Focus on shapes.
- Use words and drawings to explain what you know.
- Use geometric vocabulary.
- Organize your ideas.
- Give several examples.
- Think about real-world connections.

After this brief conversation, the students are eager to begin the task. Some students use shape templates whereas others prefer drawing freehand. Most students begin by drawing a shape on their paper and then writing some words above or below it. A few students begin by writing an idea or the name of a shape, which they then illustrate.

Lisa focuses on two-dimensional shapes. Lisa is a third-grade student. Her response focuses on two-dimensional shapes. (See Figure 2–17.) She classifies shapes by their number of sides, and provides the correct name for three-,

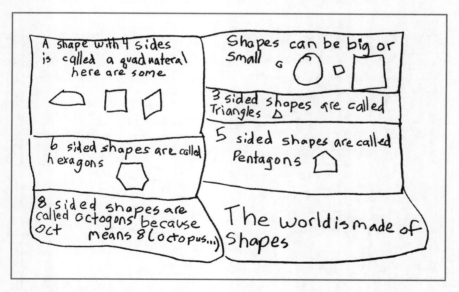

Figure 2–17. Lisa, a third-grader, focuses on classifying two-dimensional shapes.

four-, five-, six-, and eight-sided shapes. Although she does not name the shapes that she draws in her quadrilateral category, she does include a trapezoid, a square, and a parallelogram. She provides one example of a triangle, a pentagon, and a hexagon. Note that the sides within these figures have approximately the same length and that the figures are drawn with a base parallel to the bottom of the page. Such orientations are common; in fact, many students do not identify some of these figures when their sides are not congruent or when they are not placed in traditional positions.

Nick identifies several figures. Nick, a third-grader, identifies several figures, although he makes no attempt to classify them or to associate their names with the number of sides in the figures. (See Figure 2–18.) His notation, *They all are different and simalar [similar] in lots of ways*, suggests that he may know more than he is indicating in this task, and his teacher decides to follow up with him orally. She laughs as she reads, *Shapes rock!* Nick is an enthusiastic student who genuinely enjoys learning.

Tai includes several geometric terms. Responses by fourth- and fifth-grade students are much more complex and illustrate how many geometric terms and ideas upper-elementary school students are exposed to today. Tai, a fourth-grade student, includes references to concave shapes and polygons, and makes connections between two-dimensional and three-dimensional

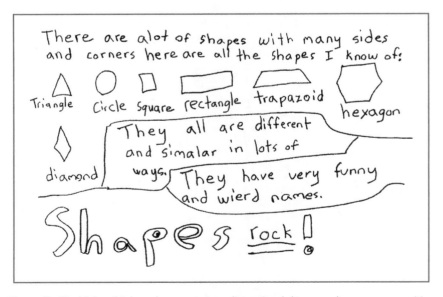

Figure 2–18. Nick, a third-grader, names two-dimensional shapes and expresses a positive attitude toward geometry.

figures. (See Figure 2–19.) Because these ideas are not necessarily related, he often records a thought and then draws a ring around it to separate it from his other recordings. He also introduces pyramids, right angles, and the terms *concave* and *parallel*. The teacher is not surprised to see references to angles and lines in the work; they are part of the fourth-grade curriculum, although connections between two-dimensional and three-dimensional figures are not. Tai is excited as he works. He records one idea and then his eyes light up as he thinks of another.

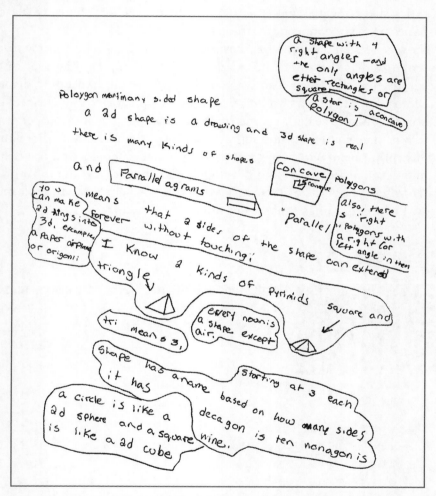

Figure 2–19. Tai, a fourth grader, includes several geometric terms to describe lines, angles, and shapes.

Emily writes descriptions of each drawn figure. Emily, a fifth-grade student, uses templates to draw her shapes. (See Figure 2–20 on page 59.) Classification of two-dimensional shapes was a significant focus of the geometry unit, involving the identification and comparison of properties of shapes. Her teacher wonders if Emily's attention to individual two-dimensional shapes, rather than broader categories, results from using templates or if it reflects a lack of clear categorization on Emily's part. Emily draws several shapes; illustrates right, acute, and obtuse angles; and then gives detailed lists of the properties she associates with each figure she draws. She does not classify the shapes or make connections among them.

The teachers talk about what they see. The fourth- and fifth-grade teachers recognize that their students' work was more complex than that of the third grade, but there was also some overlap. After all, had Emily demonstrated any further understanding of geometric categories than Lisa? They also note that Nick's zeal for geometric shapes was missing at the upper grade levels. Was there something about the formality of the curriculum that dampened his enthusiasm? Working together helps the teachers focus more clearly on grade-level expectations and developmental changes. As the third-grade teacher notes, "Looking at this work with you has helped me to look more closely. I'm seeing things I might not notice by myself."

Take Action!
Review student work with colleagues.

▶ VIDEO CLIP 2.3

Using Student Work to Differentiate Instruction:
In this video clip, we observe a planning session between Mr. Geiger, the math coach, and Mrs. Miller, a fourth-grade teacher. They are looking at student work from a quiz to make decisions about what activities to put on a menu and what the role of the teacher will be during the work time.

As you watch the clip, consider:

1. What do you notice about the decisions Mrs. Miller is making?
2. What does the student work tell Mrs. Miller about their mathematical understanding in order for her to make decisions about her instruction?
3. What types of questions does Mr. Geiger ask to help Mrs. Miller clarify her decisions?
4. How can you better use student work to differentiate your own instruction?

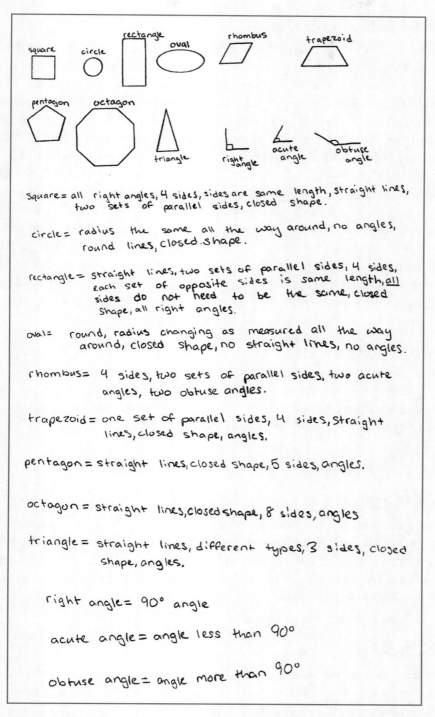

square = all right angles, 4 sides, sides are same length, straight lines, two sets of parallel sides, closed shape.

circle = radius the same all the way around, no angles, round lines, closed shape.

rectangle = straight lines, two sets of parallel sides, 4 sides, each set of opposite sides is same length, <u>all</u> sides do not need to be the same, closed shape, all right angles.

oval = round, radius changing as measured all the way around, closed shape, no straight lines, no angles.

rhombus = 4 sides, two sets of parallel sides, two acute angles, two obtuse angles.

trapezoid = one set of parallel sides, 4 sides, straight lines, closed shape, angles.

pentagon = straight lines, closed shape, 5 sides, angles.

octagon = straight lines, closed shape, 8 sides, angles

triangle = straight lines, different types, 3 sides, closed shape, angles.

right angle = 90° angle

acute angle = angle less than 90°

obtuse angle = angle more than 90°

Figure 2–20. Emily, a fifth-grade student, writes descriptions of each figure she draws.

Quick Assessments

Take Action!

Give quick assessments to collect assessment data during a short period of time.

Getting to know your students does not happen overnight, nor is it only accomplished during the first few weeks of school. Most important, the information you acquire about them is not static; attitudes, interests, and readiness change throughout the year. Thus, the daily routines and lessons provide teachers with the greatest source of assessment data for the greatest number of students. Teachers are always gathering data during their normal classroom activities and adjusting lessons accordingly. Probing questions (How do you know? Can you tell me more? Can you restate what she just said?) allow teachers to gain a better understanding of what their students know and how they think about mathematical ideas. Asking students to record their thinking with words, numbers, or drawings also provides mathematical artifacts that teachers can compare over time. Conversations at recess or lunch can update teachers on their students' current interests or concerns. It is important to realize that assessment data do not need to be collected in a time-consuming manner. In the following paragraphs, consider the different ways to collect assessment data in a quick and efficient manner.

Range Questions

Range questions can be asked at the beginning of an activity or lesson to identify quickly who might require more support or challenge. These questions are open-ended by design so that they can capture a variety of responses. Examples of range questions include the following:

- What are some numbers greater than ten?
- How many numbers are between four and five?

Hinge Questions

Hinge questions are used during an activity or lesson and can inform what to do next. They often address key misconceptions or incomplete ideas. The notion is that whether the teacher can proceed as planned hinges on students' responses. For example, in the following question, the numbers with more digits would be distractions:

- Which number is greater: 0.4, 0.81, 0.39, or 0.100?

Exit Cards

To see an example of exit cards in use in a classroom, see Video Clip 7.1, Focusing on the Goal in a Math Workshop.

Exit cards can be used at the end of a lesson or activity. For younger children, they can merely be a picture of three faces, one that is smiling, one that is neutral looking, and one that is frowning. For older students, exit cards are sometimes given in a 1-2-3 format. For example, students might be asked to reflect on a lesson just completed and state one question they have, two connections they can make to other things they know, and three new ideas they learned. These students can also be asked to create the equivalent of a tweet, such as: Using no more than 140 letters and spaces, write an interesting statement about what you learned today.

Correct the Error

Correct the error involves giving students a completed computation example and asking students to correct the error. Students can deepen their own conceptual development when they reflect on common misunderstandings (Shaughnessy 2011). Common errors can be highlighted, such as in the following example, where a student merely subtracted the ones in the reverse order:

$$\begin{array}{r} 34 \\ -\ 17 \\ \hline 23 \end{array}$$

One–Minute Definitions

One-minute definitions can be used before, during, or after an activity or lesson. Simply provide the term and give students one minute to respond. Names of geometric shapes work well for this task.

Just a Few Minutes a Day . . .

Questionnaires, observations, anecdotal records, and student work— what do we do with all these data? Many teachers comment that they get overwhelmed by the amount of information they collect. In a professional development course, one teacher moaned, "Sometimes I feel like I am drowning in paperwork. Every piece is important; I don't want to give it back to the student in case I need to refer to it in some way. It's all so interesting, but I'm beginning to want to find a way to figure out what I need to know versus what is nice to know."

One recommended practice is to take a few minutes a day to write two to three items about what you know about five students. The idea is to have focused on each student by the end of the week. Over time, teachers begin to see patterns among their students that can be useful to understanding developmental sequences. Furthermore, these notes can serve as summative statements of what teachers feel confident that their students understand. Or, the notes can provoke the next questions to guide instruction, such as "Can you tell me more about three-dimensional shapes?" or "Tell me why we use protractors." Throughout this process, teachers are frequently asking: What more do I need to know about my students to offer them an effective and engaging math program? Creating thoughtful rubrics and checklists can also help teachers to assess student work in a more expedient manner.

Teacher Collaborations

Sometimes teachers experience uncertainty or confusion with regard to particular students. No matter how much data they collect, they feel that they still have not gathered information that allows them to figure out how best to reach these students. Some teachers who face this situation have learned the benefit of turning to each other for assistance. In an example earlier in this chapter (see "Looking at Student Work Across Grade Levels," page 54), we saw teachers collaborate to gain insights into their students. Margie and Ellen are another example of such a partnership. Both experienced second-grade teachers, they have been teaching for more than twenty years and have been introduced to many math curricula during that time. They are now in the third year of implementing another new series. Although they both embrace the curriculum, they also feel that the professional development provided by the school system is not enough for them to feel completely confident while teaching the units. They both want additional support in their classrooms, but their system has no more funding for mathematics education this year, and has plans to focus next year's professional development on science.

After many conversations in the teachers' room, Margie and Ellen decide to provide for their own professional development. With the support of their principal, they develop a plan that they hope will work for them. They agree to meet once at the beginning of each unit to consider it together. Also, they plan to visit each other's classroom during each unit and look for *evidence of learning*, a term their professional development presenter used when they were looking at student work. They also agree to meet before the classroom visits to review the mathematics in the lesson and any particular concerns they might have. Last, they plan to debrief the lesson. Let's take a look at an example of this plan in action in the following lesson, Solving Story Problems Involving Addition and Subtraction.

Take Action!

Be proactive about your own professional development.

Second-Grade Class: Solving Story Problems Involving Addition and Subtraction

Today's lesson is in Ellen's classroom. Ellen has twenty-three second-grade students with many different levels of mathematical understanding. The focus of the lesson is solving story problems involving addition and subtraction. Ellen has introduced her students to a hundreds chart and encourages them to use this tool to help solve problems.

During their preconference, Ellen indicates that she wants Margie to listen to how her students are solving the problems and to determine whether their representations on paper match their mathematical thinking. Ellen is also concerned that some of the students are not using the hundreds chart effectively. During the fall, the students had many opportunities to use the chart; Ellen is hoping to see more growth. She wants all of her students to count forward or backward by tens and ones, not always just by ones. Her students have shown confidence in decomposing numbers into tens and ones in class, but Ellen is concerned that some of her students do not apply this skill when using the hundreds chart and are not developing fluency with addition to one hundred. She expresses particular concern about Josh, who rarely explains his thinking.

When the lesson begins, the students are asked—based on their interests—to solve one of three problems. As the students work, Margie and Ellen interact with them and make notes about their conversations and observations. After the lesson, they meet to share what they saw and heard.

After Ellen is assured that Margie thinks the lesson was successful, they begin to review their notes. Margie is anxious to tell Ellen of her interactions with Josh when he was working on the following problem:

Lucinda had 28 pennies in her pocket.

She spent 17 of them.

How many pennies does Lucinda have now?

Margie describes how Josh took the hundreds chart, started on 28, and counted back seventeen ones. Because Margie knows Ellen's concern about Josh using this strategy too often, Margie asks Josh if there is another way to solve the problem. Josh says, "I could go up ten and then back seven. Is that what you mean?"

Lesson Idea!

Focus: Adding by tens and ones, not just ones

Domain: Numbers and operations in base ten

Context: Solving story problems

For this Lesson at a Glance, see Lesson Idea 2.1, page 66.

Take Action!

Encourage the use of mathematical tools and models.

Take Action!

Give different tasks to different students.

Margie tells Ellen that she was confused by Josh's use of *up* and *back*, so she asked him to show her on the hundreds chart. Josh put his finger on 28 and said, "See, I am going to go up ten," then moved his finger up one row to land on 18. "Then," he continued, "I count back one to seventeen." To Margie, *up* meant *forward* and she would have expected a greater number to result. She was glad she asked Josh to show her what he was doing.

Margie then goes on to tell Ellen what happened next: Margie explains to Josh that it is time for him to record his thinking on paper. Josh groans and clearly doesn't want to write what he just verbalized. When Margie looks at his folder, she finds that Josh explains his work on the first problem by simply writing *I went backwards*. Margie then tells Ellen that she wonders whether Josh counts by ones because it is an easy strategy to record.

After working with Josh for a bit, Margie thinks that a different visual model might be helpful to him, so she shows him an open number line. She demonstrates how he can use this model to indicate his moves on the hundreds chart. Josh decides to try out this method of recording. (See Figure 2–21.)

This example should help you to remember to take the time to understand your students' thinking and not to assume that different is incorrect. This awareness speaks to the importance of differentiating mathematical models within assessment tasks and instruction. It also reminds us to adjust our lenses constantly as we look for evidence of student understanding.

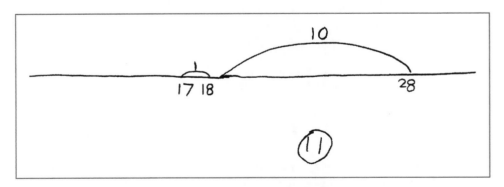

Figure 2–21. Josh used an open number line to communicate his thinking.

Connecting the Chapter to Your Practice

1. How have you communicated with your students' parents to learn more about their child's learning preferences?

2. Sometimes students' self-assessments given in response to questionnaires do not match what teachers have observed in the classroom. What do you think teachers should do when this happens?

3. What techniques help you to organize assessment data?

4. Who are the colleagues who help you the most? What do they do that you find most helpful?

Solving Story Problems Involving Addition and Subtraction

To see insights on how this lesson is carried out in a classroom, see page 63.

Recommended Grade: 2

Common Core State Standards for Mathematics Correlations

- Add and subtract within one hundred fluently using strategies based on place value, properties of operations, and/or the relationship between addition and subtraction.
- Represent and solve problems involving addition and subtraction.
- Use appropriate tools strategically.

Time

30 to 45 minutes

Materials

- 10 strips of paper that are printed with Problem 1
- 10 strips of paper that are printed with Problem 2
- 10 strips of paper that are printed with Problem 3
- 30 envelopes, 1 for each problem
- hundreds charts
- number lines

The Problems

Create a variety of problems based on the following three, changing the settings to match your students' interests and/or the numbers to provide more or less of a challenge. These problems were written for a small group of students who liked to count money.

1. *Lucinda had 28 pennies in her pocket.*

   She spent 17 of them.

   How many pennies does Lucinda have now?

2. *Carlos needs 57 pennies.*

   He has 39 pennies.

   How many more pennies does Carlos need?

3. *Jaswanda has 46 pennies.*

   Nicki has 34 pennies.

   How many pennies do they have in all?

Directions

1. Make hundreds charts and number lines available for students to use.

2. Make sure that each envelope contains one problem. Tell the students to select one envelope; let them know that the envelope contains one problem that they are to solve. Indicate that they may work with a partner who has the same envelope or they may work alone. Circulate among the students as they work, noting their strategies and representations. Pay particular attention to those students who are still counting by ones, rather than tens and ones.

3. Call the students together and have a few volunteers share their thinking.

4. Ask questions to help students make connections among the different strategies used:

   • Why might we add or subtract one ten rather than ten ones?

   • How is a hundreds chart different from a number line? How do these tools help you to add or subtract?

Chapter 3

Know Your Standards:
The Common Core State Standards for Mathematics

(continued)

Introduction

Thinking About Differentiation and the Common Core State Standards

In this video clip authors Linda Dacey and Rebeka Eston Salemi reflect on the Common Core Standards for Mathematics in the context of differentiating instruction.

As you listen to the authors, consider:

1. What strikes you as most interesting about their observations?
2. What changes do you anticipate or have you made in your instructional practice as a result of the Common Core State Standards?

More than ever before, *common* expectations for learning are clear. Described as focused and coherent (Dacey and Perry 2012), the Common Core State Standards are key for supporting the development of conceptual understanding and procedural skills. In this chapter, we take a close look at the Common Core State Standards for Mathematics (CCSSM) and how you can best navigate through these standards with differentiating instruction in mind.

To start, the CCSSM does not provide teachers with insights into how to differentiate mathematics. In fact, in terms of readiness, the document clearly states, "The Standards set grade-specific standards but do not define the intervention methods or materials necessary to support students who are well below or well above grade-level expectations" (National Governors Association Center for Best Practices and Council of Chief State School Officers 2010, 5). However, the lack of specification regarding curricular materials puts such decisions where they belong, in the hands of teachers. As you realign your curriculum based on these standards, you have the opportunity to rethink *how* you teach, not just *what* you teach.

Working Together: Factual, Procedural, Conceptual, and Metacognitive Knowledge

Some people describe mathematics as a subject that requires you to learn how to follow a series of prescribed steps to find the one correct answer. Such a description reflects the way mathematics is sometimes taught, but not the subject itself. Instruction that emphasizes a rule-based approach to mathematics focuses on factual and procedural knowledge such as basic facts and standard algorithms for addition, subtraction, multiplication, and division. It's not that facts and procedures aren't important—they are—but we do *not* want to teach them in ways that keep students from developing the conceptual understanding that underpins their procedures and connects the facts that they know. We also want students to develop the metacognitive skills necessary to integrate and manage their learning. Ideally, all four types of knowledge—*factual*, *procedural*, *conceptual*, and *metacognitive*—work together to build mathematical understanding. As we differentiate instruction, we must make sure that all students are expected to develop a conceptual understanding of the procedures on which they rely, to use the correct vocabulary, and to reflect on their thinking.

Think About the Content Standards

When navigating through the CCSSM, you might first start by looking at the content standards and gaining an understanding of the learning progressions.

Questions to Ask When Thinking About the Content Standards

- How do the concepts and skills I'm teaching develop across grade levels?
- Am I using language that might cause misunderstandings later?
- Am I oversimplifying mathematical ideas?

How Do the Concepts and Skills I'm Teaching Develop Across Grade Levels?

For the purposes of differentiating instruction, teachers need to be aware of how concepts and skills develop across grade levels in the CCSSM. This perspective makes the learning progression clear and is helpful when thinking about readiness. For example, consider addition with whole numbers, which begins in kindergarten and is completed in grade 4. (See Figure 3–1.) Students find sums using a variety of representations, which we label *exploration*. Over time, students are expected to gain fluency, although not necessarily tied to a standard algorithm. Note there is time to develop conceptual underpinnings before use of the standard algorithm becomes an expectation.

Am I Using Language That Might Cause Misunderstandings Later?

Another reason for you to think about learning progressions is to make sure that, when trying to make mathematical ideas accessible, you are not using language that will cause misunderstandings later. For example, when students are working with the traditional algorithm for subtraction, you might hear a teacher say, "You can't take a bigger number from a smaller one." Such a statement is often made with the intention of reminding a student to regroup. Yet, when negative numbers are involved, the generalization no longer holds true. You *can* subtract three from five; the difference is negative two. This new idea may confuse some students. Consider the examples in Figure 3–2 (page 74) of ways a

The CCSSM and Changes in Grade Level

It's important to note that the CCSSM has changed the grade levels at which several mathematical concepts and skills are introduced. Sometimes, ideas are introduced earlier, such as when children start thinking about the teen numbers as tens and ones (now in kindergarten), and sometimes ideas are delayed, such as when students find the fraction of a collection of objects (now in grade 5). Teachers need to be clear about content expectations at the grade level they teach. Such a perspective makes it clear what must be accomplished at one grade level for students to be successful the following year.

GRADE LEVEL	EXPLORATION	FLUENCY	STANDARD ALGORITHM
K	Use objects, drawings, and actions to find sums to 10.	Sums to 5.	
1	Use models, drawings, and strategies to find sums to 100.	Sums to 10. Adds 10 to two-digit numbers.	
2	Use models, drawings, and strategies to find sums to 1,000.	Sums to 20. Adds with sums to 100.	
3		Adds with sums to 1,000. Adds hundreds to hundreds, tens to tens, and ones to ones.	
4			Adds multidigit whole numbers using the standard algorithm.

Figure 3–1. Progression of CCSSM standards for addition with whole numbers.

Progression documents for CCSSM can be found at http://ime.math.arizona.edu/progressions/; this site offers detailed descriptions of how topics develop across grade levels.

WHAT MIGHT BE SAID	CONTRADICTION
You can't take nine from six.	Differences can be negative numbers.
Line up the numbers on the right that you are going to add.	This does not apply to addition with decimals.
Eight doesn't go into four.	Quotients can be less than one.
Always line up the decimal points.	This does not apply to multiplication with decimals.
There is no number multiplied by itself that gives you eight.	This does not hold true when irrational numbers, such as the square root of eight, are introduced.

Figure 3–2. Misleading language that is contradicted later.

simple rule conflicts with later learning, when students are no longer limited to working with whole numbers or when considering different operations.

Am I Oversimplifying Mathematical Ideas?

Last but not least, as a teacher thinking about learning progressions, you need to make sure that you are not oversimplifying mathematical ideas for less ready students. You should get into the habit of asking yourself the following questions:

- Is there a mathematical concept that will help students understand what to do, regardless of the type of numbers?
- Am I depriving some students the opportunity to develop mathematical concepts by giving them simple procedural rules?

Think About the Standards for Mathematical Practice

Along with content standards, the CCSSM identifies eight Standards for Mathematical Practice that describe what mathematically proficient students do. These standards raise new questions for teachers regarding how best to support all students meeting these goals. A list of the practices follows, along with examples of questions related to differentiated instruction. The questions could be adapted to match each of the practices, and related ideas are interwoven throughout this resource.

The verbs used in the Standards for Mathematical Practice emphasize that learning mathematics is an active process, one that involves students in exploring ideas, making and investigating conjectures, discovering relationships, representing ideas, and justifying thinking. Such activity often results when students pursue real-world mathematical problems or explore open-ended tasks—that is, problems for which they don't already recognize a procedure or a representation that will lead them to a solution, or tasks that may be completed in a variety of ways. When exploring these types of problems, students wrestle with ideas and are less likely to follow the same solution paths. Allowing for different approaches to mathematical tasks can lead to rich discussions that help students establish and agree on facts, construct and use procedures, and develop and solidify concepts. This way of teaching has two advantages: It encourages deeper mathematical thinking and it supports alternative learning preferences.

Teaching with this mind-set is part of our changing expectations of mathematics instruction. Teachers facilitate mathematical discourse, rather than delineate specific steps and demonstrate how to follow prescribed procedures. Teachers focus on questions such as: Why do you think so? What are you thinking? How do you know? As teachers, when you engage in this approach, you often will be surprised at the range of what your students are thinking. You come to recognize differences in readiness levels, in approaches to tasks, in the connections students make among ideas, and in the ways students model, represent, and describe their thinking.

Integrate Content and Practices

It takes time to develop the habits of mind associated with the eight Standards for Mathematical Practice. Although explicit attention needs to be given to the development of these individual practices, for the most part they need to be integrated within the daily investigations of content (Russell 2012). Following are three classroom scenarios that focus on differentiating instruction and illustrate concomitantly the integration of the content standards with the Standards for Mathematical Practice.

First-Grade Class: Decomposing and Composing Groups

Part 1: Introducing

Let's consider a vignette from a first-grade classroom. It is late November, the children are gathered in a circle, and the teacher has prepared visual image cards to help students connect the composition and decomposition of numbers to symbolic notation. (See Figure 3–3.) She knows that the development of visual models of numbers is vital. Studies have indicated the importance of the visual cortex in mathematical thinking (Sousa 2011). Activities that explicitly help students develop their visual perceptions of numbers further provide learners with models that students can reference, manipulate, and think about when solving problems.

Lesson Idea!

Focus: Decomposing and composing groups

Domain: Operations and algebraic thinking

Context: Quick visual images

See Lesson Idea 3.1, page 101.

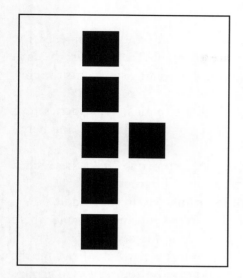

Figure 3–3. Example of a visual image card.

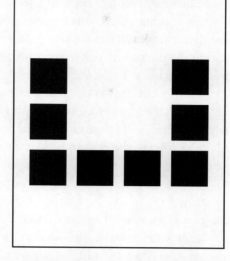

Figure 3–4. A visual image card of eight.

Initially, the teacher holds up a card briefly and then asks the children to identify the number of squares that they see. Over time, she believes this repeated activity will support them in learning to break the whole into recognizable and manageable parts, and then combine those parts to be able to relate how many parts make up the whole. This activity also offers her students an opportunity to use numbers and number sentences to describe what they see, and it helps some students in their transition from counting all to counting on.

The teacher begins with simple examples to make sure all of the children are successful. After a few examples of sets of six or less, she holds up a card of eight squares. (See Figure 3–4.) There are a variety of responses to this more difficult example. A couple of the children raise their hands immediately. Nicolita looks like she will burst if she can't share her answer soon. Nat taps his finger on his forehead as if he is trying to recapture the image as he counts. Macy immediately drops her head, avoiding her teacher's eyes. The teacher looks around and says, "Before you tell me how many you saw, I want you to tell me what you think about this card."

"This one is harder," replies Jim.

"What makes it harder?" the teacher asks.

"There are so many," offers Macy.

"I couldn't count each one," explains Paul.

"I did! There are eight," claims Nicolita.

"I got eight, too," confirms Joey.

The teacher asks if anyone else got eight and some hands rise in response. She then queries, "How did you know there are eight?" and shows the card again. She purposely does not confirm the answer because she wants the children to decide for themselves.

While pointing to the bottom row Nicolita explains, "See there's four here," and then pointing to the top two groups of two explains, "and here's four up here. So four and four, that's eight."

"Do you see the groups of four that Nicolita is showing?" asks the teacher. Heads nod and she asks, "Did anyone see eight a different way?"

Joey responds, "I saw two groups of three and two in the middle."

"Oh!" responds the teacher. "Can someone come up and show me where you think Joey sees two groups of three and two in the middle?"

After Carla shows the groups and Joey confirms her identification, the teacher says, "So Nicolita saw two groups of four and Joey saw two groups of three and two in the middle. How did this help them know there were eight squares in such a short amount of time?"

"I didn't have to count each one," responds Nicolita.

"What does Nicolita mean by that?" asks the teacher.

"Oh, I know!" Mimi says. "She just saw four. She didn't count them."

Then Leo's eyes light up and he remarks, "So if you can see a lot at once, you can get it faster."

The teacher then suggests that they try some more cards. This time, she returns to some easier examples, but in a purposeful way. First she shows a card with a row of two squares, followed by a card with a row of four squares. In both cases, the children recognize the number of squares immediately.

After a few more examples, the teacher decides that they have done enough of this activity for today. The idea that decomposing numbers can help you find the total number has been introduced, and the children have recognized that numbers can be decomposed in different ways. It's time to let these ideas incubate.

Part II: Exploring

The next day, the teacher shows a new card with an arrangement the children have not seen before and asks, "Who can tell me what we did yesterday with cards like this?" After the students have connected with their previous learning, a few more of the visual image cards are considered. Today, more of the children are able to decompose the numbers to find the number in all. After the final example, the teacher notes, "Cam sees four and six squares and Mike sees two and eight squares, and they both saw ten in all. How could

Take Action!
Expect students to justify their thinking.

Take Action!
Make connections to previous learning.

78   How to Differentiate Your Math Instruction

we write this?" After students respond, the teacher writes the corresponding number sentences on chart paper and introduces the next activity.

"I want each of you to make your own arrangement of squares. When you go to your tables you will see some glue sticks, white paper, and some cut-out squares. Pick a number four through ten. Take that number of squares and make a design. Then, I want you to write what you see." After the students repeat the directions and the teacher is confident of their understanding, students move to the tables where the materials are ready for use.

Paul makes a design with the squares and then writes the number of squares in each of the three components of his configuration. (See Figure 3–5.) Note that he doesn't record the total number. Mimi and Gina record

Take Action!
Support auditory, visual, and kinesthetic learners.

Take Action!
Provide students with choices.

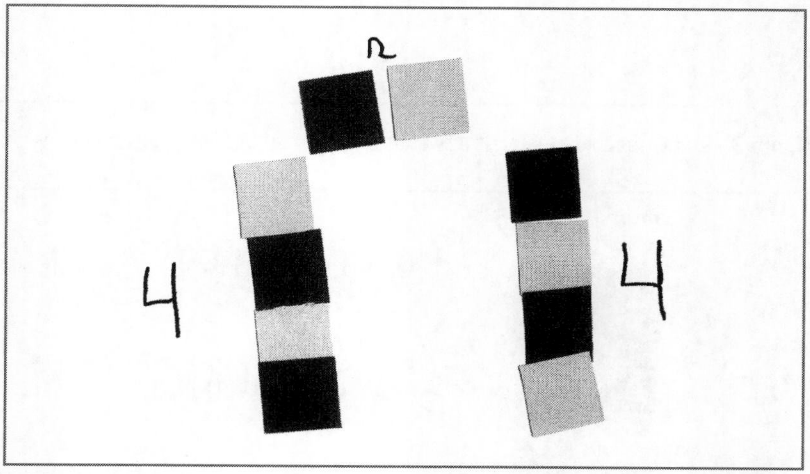

Figure 3–5. Paul writes numbers for each part of his design, but does not record the total.

numbers for parts of the whole and the total numbers. Mimi doesn't use the standard notation of addition, but circles the 3 and 7 to indicate that, together, they make 10. (See Figure 3–6, page 80.) Gina records numbers for three parts and marks 7 to indicate the total. (See Figure 3–7, page 80.) As is often the case with first graders, she has recently lost a tooth and is excited when she decides that her design looks like a toothbrush. It is important to her to communicate this as well.

Leo makes a design using eight squares and writes *4 + 4 = 8*. The teacher asks him where he sees the two groups of four and he replies, "I just know that." When asked what he can see, he adds the second number sentence *5 + 3 = 8*. (See Figure 3–8, page 81.) The teacher is pleased that Leo is able to connect with the visual image and asks if there is another way he can see his design. He turns his paper around and says, "I can also see three plus five."

Take Action!
Support a variety of representations.

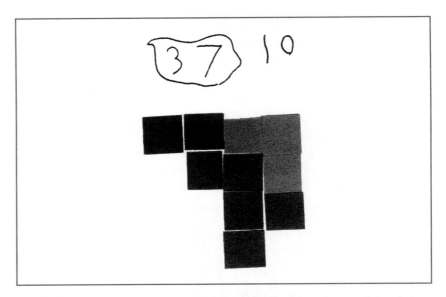

Figure 3–6. Mimi records subtotals as well as the total number of squares in her design.

Figure 3–7. Gina records three subsets and the total and identifies her design as a toothbrush.

Paul, who is sitting next to Leo, watches this response and remarks, "You can turn the paper and the numbers."

Nicolita's work is the most complex. She sees and writes six different number sentences without teacher assistance. (See Figure 3–9.) When she shows her work to the teacher, she is able to recreate the connections between the equations she has recorded and her design. She uses her hand to show each way she decomposed the figure. When she gets to her last sentence,

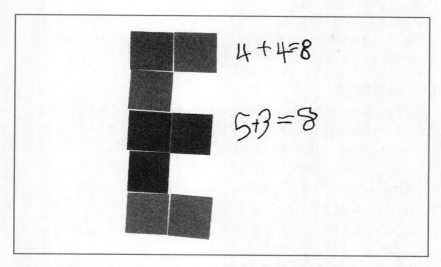

Figure 3–8. Leo identifies two different equations for the same design.

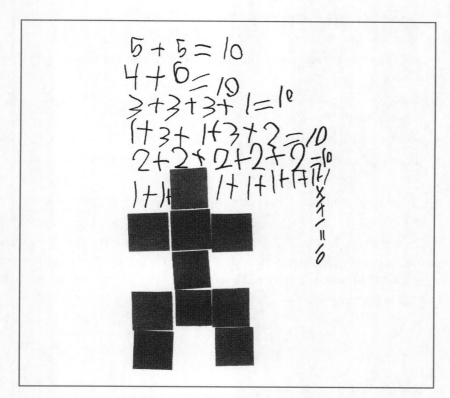

Figure 3–9. Nicolita describes her design with numerous equations.

1 + 1 + 1 + 1 + 1 + 1 + 1 + 1 + 1 + 1 = 10, she just chuckles and says, "Well, I just put that because I knew it and wanted to write a long sentence. You can always do that, right?"

Part III: Summarizing

The lesson ends with the teacher inviting the students to the rug area to share their thinking. As the students show their representations, she asks them to talk about the similarities and differences in their work.

The teacher used several techniques for differentiating instruction. She:

- provided auditory, visual, and kinesthetic inputs;
- gave students choices;
- encouraged students to represent ideas in multiple ways; and
- expected all students to justify their representations.

With such support, students can be more successful learners of mathematics.

Simultaneously, these students demonstrated several behaviors associated with the Standards for Mathematical Practice. Among them, the students:

- made sense of a visual model by decomposing it;
- reasoned quantitatively about visual models;
- discussed their reasoning and attended to the reasoning of others;
- wrote one or more addition sentences to model a visual representation;
- counted with precision;
- identified an example of the commutative property of addition; and
- noted that you could always write a sum using as many ones as needed.

Although not every lesson will result in so many (all but the use of tools) of the practices being demonstrated, you do need to keep these standards prominent in your thinking and find ways to ensure that all of your students are held to these expectations.

Take Action!

Develop the habits of mind associated with the eight Standards for Mathematical Practice.

Fourth-Grade Class: Represent and Compare Fractions

Part 1: Introducing

Let us now consider a vignette from a fourth-grade classroom. It is October and the students are working on fractions. With denominators of ten or less, the students can identify or represent fractions shown as congruent parts of a region, although they are not always sure about where to place fractions on a number line. With common fractions such as halves, fourths, and eighths, many of the students can identify and represent equivalent relationships, but the teacher feels they do so in a rote manner and would like them to have more experience applying the ideas. The students integrate fractions easily into their real-world activities, demonstrated with comments such as "I only ate half of my lunch" or "It's quarter after one. Is it time to go to music?"

The teacher wants to help his students develop better number sense with fractions and to become more comfortable with length or linear models of fractions. He wants them to be able to use their conceptual understanding of fractions to compare them and to place them on a number line between zero and one. He knows that the Common Core sets the expectation that his students understand that one-fourth can be defined as what is *iterated* (copied) four times to make a whole, or it is the part you get when you *partition* (subdivide) a whole into four equal parts (Suh et al. 2008).

The teacher is particularly interested in the ways in which students use representations of fractions. He knows that, too often, his school's adopted textbook provides models for students. For example, it shows a number line with an arrow and asks the students to write the fraction. Earlier in the week, the school held a schoolwide metric Olympics day, so he gathers his students around the rug to pose a question about a race.

A student reads aloud the problem posted on chart paper: "At Olympics Day, two friends are running in a race. One friend is five-eighths of the way to the finish line and the other friend

Lesson Idea!

Focus: Represent and compare fractions

Domain: Numbers and operations, fractions

Context: Who is winning the race?

See Lesson Idea 3.2, page 103.

Aha! Moments with the Standards for Mathematical Practice

Many teachers who begin to teach in ways that align with the Standards for Mathematical Practice are truly amazed at what they see and hear. Teachers recognize that they have uncovered information about their students that they never knew before. Focusing on the development of mathematical ideas and on making links among factual, procedural, and conceptual knowledge is a significant transformation in the teaching of mathematics, and it raises two essential questions:

1. How do you best reveal the different ways your students think?

2. When revealed, how do you support differentiated thinking about mathematics while still focusing on unified mathematical ideas?

is three-quarters of the way. Who is winning?" After the problem is read aloud, the teacher asks a couple of students to restate the problem.

Part II: Exploring

When the teacher is confident that students understand the task, he sends them to their tables and asks that they use pictures, numbers, and words to represent their thinking.

Take Action!
Use flexible grouping strategies.

This is a routine with which they are familiar, and the students are eager to get started. They know that, because they haven't been told otherwise, they are free to work alone or with partners. The teacher realizes that some of his students prefer to work alone. When they have ideas, they want to work on their solutions before they share their thinking. Other students find it easier to talk to a partner and come up with a plan together. When a new idea is being investigated, such as this problem, the teacher likes to let them choose their preference. This way, they are working in their preferred manner as they wrestle with the challenges of new ideas.

There is a buzz in the room as some students quickly draw solutions on their papers and others look off to the side, tapping their pencils as they create a plan. After a bit more time, most students are writing, but as the teacher looks about the room, he notices that Isabelle and Kara have not yet recorded anything. He sits down next to them and listens to their conversation.

"I think the three-fourths kid is winning," says Kara.

"I think five-eighths is winning," Isabelle argues.

The teacher encourages them to explain their thinking to each other.

Kara starts with, "Three-fourths is closer to the finish line because three and four are littler numbers, but in fraction math the little number is the highest number and five-eighths is the lowest."

Isabelle looks confused and states, "I don't agree. I think that five-eighths is closer because three-fourths is still near the beginning. We want big numbers." Both girls look toward the teacher for direction or approval. He asks them to write and draw their ideas on paper so he can understand their thinking. He also believes that drawing images of fractions may initiate a change in their thinking.

The teacher continues to walk around the classroom, looking for evidence of understanding or the need for help. He checks in with a few more sets of partners to get a better sense of the levels of thinking about the fraction problem. Many students agree with Kara; they identify the runner that is three-fourths of the way to the finish line as winning. (See Figure 3–10.) They note the importance of three and four being less than five and eight.

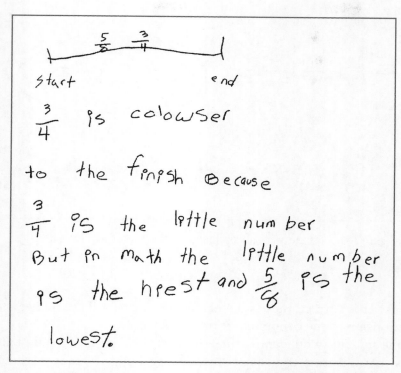

Figure 3–10. Kara's work focuses on the size of the numbers.

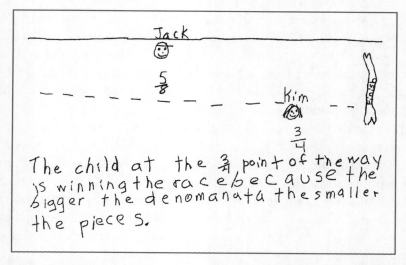

Figure 3–11. This explanation focuses on the size of the numbers and a generalization.

Some students explain this choice further by reasoning that the greater the denominator, the smaller the pieces will be. (See Figure 3–11.) Although

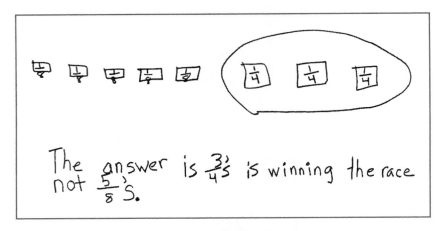

Figure 3–12. Manny's work includes proportional drawings of eighths and fourths.

their answer is correct, these students seem to disregard the numerator and its relationship to the denominator or to the whole.

Some students who identify three-fourths as the greater fraction provide models that illustrate equivalent fractions. Although Manny does not use words to explain his thinking, his drawing shows proportional models of fourths and eighths. (See Figure 3–12.) Janice and Quinn use length models. In fact, Quinn uses a ruler to make his drawing. (See Figure 3–13.) Janice identifies equivalent fractions correctly, but has some difficulty placing them on her model of the race. (See Figure 3–14.) Note that she records the quarters in the spaces rather than at the end of that distance. This common misconception is recognized as an end point problem. Many students have a similar misconception when using a ruler.

Xavier makes a region and a length model to represent his thinking. Note that although his pie drawing depicts the relationships between fourths and eighths correctly, the linear model does not. (See Figure 3–15.) His written explanation, however, clarifies his understanding and he gives the teacher a verbal explanation as the teacher stops by his desk. Xavier summarizes his ideas by saying, "Three-fourths is bigger because two-eighths is equal to one-fourth and there are five-eighths, and if two-eighths equals one-fourth, then five-eighths would only be two-fourths and one-eighth."

Some students believe that the friend who is five-eighths of the way is the winner. They make a drawing of the race that coincides with their thinking,

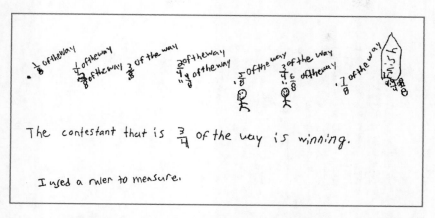

Figure 3–13. Quinn uses a ruler to make his model of the race.

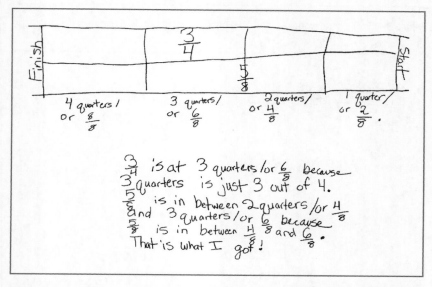

Figure 3–14. Although not placed correctly, Janice's work includes equivalent fractions.

but they do not model the fractions, and their explanations contain only a restatement of the relationship between the two fractions. (See Figure 3–16.)

Other students make a model of the fractions, but then only attend to the numerators or don't use the same unit to create the fractional parts. By disregarding the denominators or by changing the unit, they are actually only comparing three and five, and so identify five-eighths as their answer. (See Figure 3–17 and Figure 3–18 on page 88.)

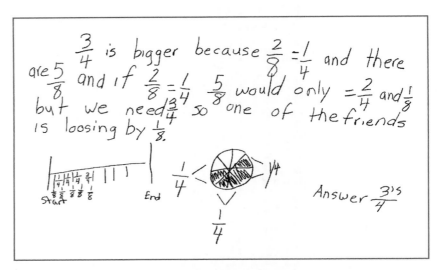

$\frac{3}{4}$ is bigger because $\frac{2}{8} = \frac{1}{4}$ and there are $\frac{5}{8}$ and if $\frac{2}{8} = \frac{1}{4}$ $\frac{5}{8}$ would only $= \frac{2}{4}$ and $\frac{1}{8}$ but we need $\frac{3}{4}$ so one of the friends is loosing by $\frac{1}{8}$.

Start   End $\frac{1}{4} <$ $\frac{1}{4}$ Answer $\frac{3's}{4}$

Figure 3–15. Xavier's work includes a region and a length model to compare the fractions.

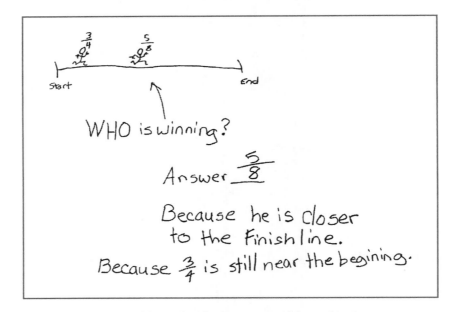

$\frac{3}{4}$ $\frac{5}{8}$

Start   End

WHO is winning?

Answer $\frac{5}{8}$

Because he is closer to the Finish line.
Because $\frac{3}{4}$ is still near the begining.

Figure 3–16. Work without a correct model or explanation.

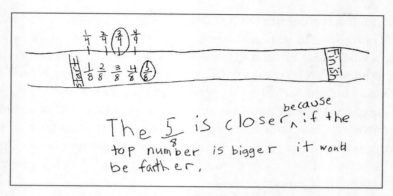

The $\frac{5}{8}$ is closer because if the top number is bigger it would be farther.

Figure 3–17. This student focuses only on the numerators while making this linear model.

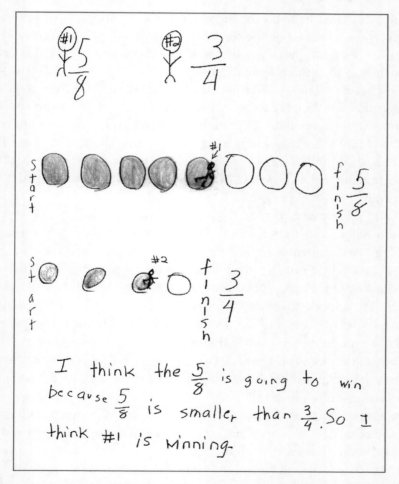

I think the $\frac{5}{8}$ is going to win because $\frac{5}{8}$ is smaller than $\frac{3}{4}$. So I think #1 is winning.

Figure 3–18. This student uses a set model, but focuses only on the numerator even though he identifies that five-eighths is less than three-fourths.

As a teacher, it is essential that you think carefully about the mathematical concepts embedded in students' representations. Such a focus allows you to meet individual needs better and to address misunderstandings more quickly.

The students are getting louder as they reach some agreement among themselves. The teacher claps his hands and they pause and look up as he announces, "In a few minutes we will share solutions. Think about what you want to say about your work and talk with a partner about your ideas." For many students, this opportunity to share with a partner before a whole-group discussion allows them to practice the language they are going to use and to solidify their thinking.

Part III: Summarizing

Take Action!

Make time for students to share their thinking after an investigation.

Take Action!

Ask questions that encourage students to be responsible for their own learning and support metacognitive awareness.

The students gather back on the rug to share their solutions. Most of the initial conversation focuses on the size of the numbers three and four versus five and eight. Then a couple of the students who thought in terms of equivalent fractions begin to explain their thinking.

Janice begins, "The second friend is winning because, for them to be equal, the first friend would have to be six-eighths of the way to the finish line."

Liam nods in agreement. The teacher asks the students if they understand Janice and Liam's thinking and hears a common initial response from Trevor, who states, "I don't get it."

The teacher asks Trevor, "What would make it easier for you to understand?"

"Could you draw a picture?" questions Trevor.

The teacher holds out chalk to Janice and Liam and they walk to the board. The two students confer briefly and gesture toward their individual drawings, then Liam draws four short vertical lines on the board. Next, Janice draws eight similar lines on top of Liam's, but hers are clustered closer together. They work together to draw arrows from the four lines on the bottom to pairs of the eight lines above. When the drawing is complete, they take turns explaining their work. Liam tells his classmates that the bottom four lines show three-fourths and then he draws a ring around three of the four lines. Janice continues explaining that for each one-fourth, you have to draw two lines for eighths. She then draws a ring around six of her lines to show that six-eighths is the same as three-fourths. Without pausing, Janice then concludes, "So five-eighths is only five-eighths not six-eighths, so he is losing and three-fourths is winning." (See Figure 3–19.)

The teacher looks at the group of students, who seem quite impressed with their friends' thinking, even if they were not necessarily clear about all of the ideas. He decides that enough has been done for today. The teacher

$$\frac{3}{4} = \frac{5}{8}$$

$$\frac{2}{8} = \frac{1}{4}$$

$$\frac{4}{8} = \frac{2}{4}$$

$$\frac{5}{8} = \frac{2\frac{1}{2}}{4}$$

The second friend is winning because for them to be equal the first friend would have to be $\frac{6}{8}$ of the way to the finish line.

Figure 3–19. Liam and Janice's explanation of five-eighths versus three-fourths.

Take Action!
Sort student work.

thanks Janice and Liam for sharing their work and tells the class that they will continue to think about these ideas over the next few days.

At the end of the day, the teacher looks at the students' work more closely. He finds that he can separate their papers into three piles. There is a group of students who did not demonstrate an understanding of three-fourths and five-eighths as fractions or who used incomplete ideas to compare these fractions. There is a group of students who knew the correct answer but could not explain their thinking fully or whose single representation needed revision. Last, there is a group of students who identified the correct answer and demonstrated a clear understanding of the situation using at least one model.

The teacher takes some notes to help him think about tomorrow's lesson. In doing so, he focuses on what he learned from sorting the student representations. As you can see from his notes, he plans to start with the whole class and then have the students follow up with somewhat different versions of the game. (See Figure 3–20 on page 92.)

The teacher starts the next lesson by asking, "If two children are running a race and one friend is one-half of the way to the finish line and the other friend is three-quarters of the way there, who is winning?" This time he draws a line on the board, labeling *Start* and *Finish,* and asks, "Who can answer this question?"

Many hands are raised. After asking the students to whisper their answer to each other, the teacher asks Brandy to share her answer with the class. Brandy identifies the friend that is three-quarters of the way as winning, and the teacher asks her to come up to the board and use the line to explain her thinking. He asks the class, "How did Brandy know that three-fourths was closer to the finish line than one-half?"

Teacher Notes

1. Model the use of benchmarks on a number line.

2. Introduce *Closer to 0 or 1?* game.

3. Have students work in three groups:

NEED MORE WORK WITH MODELS	CAN PRACTICE USING BENCHMARKS	READY FOR A CHALLENGE
Start with warm-ups.	Have students play game as done in class.	Have students play game and place several fractions.
Connect region to linear models.	Use fractions on a number line.	
Use strip models to play game.		

Figure 3–20. The teacher's planning notes.

Take Action!

Ask questions that require students to build on the ideas of others.

Lesson Idea!

Focus: Use strategies to compare fractions

Domain: Numbers and operations, fractions

Context: Playing a game

For game directions, see Lesson Idea 3.2, page 103.

Kevin raises his hand and states, "One-half is in the middle and three-fourths is more than that."

When the teacher asks him how he knows that, Kevin just shrugs his shoulders, but Xavier suggests, "Two-fourths is the same as one-half and three is more than four."

Kevin responds, "Oh! I get it."

The teacher records $\frac{1}{2} = \frac{2}{4}$ on the board and asks, "What if the one-half is being compared with a fraction with a denominator of six, eight, or ten? What would we do?"

Quinn explains, "We'd find half by making the number on top half the number on the bottom."

The teacher pauses for his students to process what Quinn has said and then asks if anyone can restate Quinn's idea.

Janice responds, "To be half, the number on the top has to be half the number on the bottom."

"Is this always true?" asks the teacher. The students respond with a loud "Yes!" and he is delighted with their confidence. Then the teacher introduces a game. He asks for two students to come to the front of the room. He then divides a deck of cards (forty cards made up of four sets of the numbers 1, 2, 3, 4, 5, 6, 8, and 10) into two equal stacks and hands a stack to both children. He draws a number line on the board and labels one end *0* and the other end *1*, then he tells the student to the left that he will stand for zero, and tells the

After today's work, I realized my students were at many different levels of thinking about fractions. I was surprised by how many students had incomplete understandings and used nonlinear models. How much do students think about the context of a problem when they think about models to use? Janice and Liam's thinking was much more sophisticated than I ever expected.

It is clear that I need to support these students in different ways. When I can, I like to differentiate by having students involved in a very similar activity, but in a slightly different manner. This way, I can maintain my focus better while providing for individual differences. I'd like to model the use of the benchmark numbers zero, one-half, and one to compare numbers—a standard for fourth-grade students—but I know they need to explore this idea with different levels of support.

Over time, I have become more respectful of the different ways my students think about mathematical ideas. A couple of years ago I would have just told them to use a linear model for this problem. Now I realize that they have strong preferences for which models they use, and try to spend more time connecting the various representations they make. I am eager to return to a similar problem tomorrow and see if the students can use benchmarks to compare fractions, as well as common equivalent fractions, in ways that also deepen their understanding of fractions.

> "Over time, I have become more respectful of the different ways my students think about mathematical ideas. A couple of years ago I would have just told them to use a linear model for this problem."

student on the right that she will stand for one. The teacher has each child turn over their top card and asks them to make a fraction with the numerator less than the denominator. The students announce that their fraction is five-sixths. The teacher continues to explain the game by saying, "Your job is to decide if five-sixths is closer to zero or to one. The person representing the whole number that is closer to the fraction gets the two cards. So, who is the winner of this round?"

The two students at the board confer and the teacher asks the other students to discuss the problem as well. With discussion, the students agree that five-sixths is closer to one, and so the student representing the number 1 gets the cards. As a whole class, they play a few more rounds. During the process, they decide that if the fraction is equal to one-half, then each person gets one card because it is not closer to zero or one; it is equidistant.

So far, students have been able to participate in the same activities by thinking about the mathematics in different ways, but the teacher thinks it is now time to differentiate their next steps. He turns over the top page of a pack of chart paper, revealing a list of three groups of students, with partners indicated. He gives decks of cards to the pairs of students who need more practice (which he identified the day before) and releases them to sit in pairs at available desks. The students begin to play the game.

The teacher then asks the group of students who need more work with models to deepen their understanding of fractions to go to the large table in the back of the room, talk in pairs about the materials he has left in front of each seat, and complete the warm-up questions. The teacher knows he can't leave this group on their own too long, but is comfortable that he has provided them work that they can do in pairs and that the task will get them ready for what he has in mind after he joins them.

As these students move to the table, the teacher organizes the group of students who remain: those who need more challenge. He gives each pair of students a bin that contains a deck of cards, some tape, several small pieces of paper, a strip of adding machine tape with a line drawn across the middle of its length, and a direction sheet. The directions modify the game a bit for these more advanced students. This time, after they decide who wins a round, they are supposed to write the fraction on one of the small pieces of paper and tape it along the long line to show where it is in relation to zero and one. As their play continues, they need to compare each number they form with both the benchmarks and with other numbers already on the line. The teacher realizes that these students would rather just write along the number line, but he wants them to use more flexible materials. By recording the numbers on paper and using the tape, the students can adjust the positions of the numbers as the play continues and their thinking changes.

The teacher stays with these students for a bit to make sure that they understand the task and to get some insight into their thinking. They spread out around the area and are quickly engaged in the activity. He notices that Kyle and Liam immediately fold their long strip in half and record $\frac{1}{2}$ at this point on the line.

The teacher then joins the first group. As requested, they are looking at the copies of fraction strips and fraction pies that have been left for them and are exploring the warm-up questions. The teacher reviews one of the questions with them by asking how the circular model of thirds could help them figure out whether two-thirds is closer to zero or to one. The students agree quickly that two of the thirds are more than half of the circle. When asked how they could prove that to him, they use their hands to cover up half of the circle and tell him, "There's more left over." He then asks the same question using the strip model, and the students appear to agree that it is more than "half the way."

The students review the rules of the game. The teacher has already split the decks of cards in half, and the first four cards in each deck have been arranged so that the initial fractions will be one-fourth, seven-eighths, one-sixth, and four-fifths. He hopes that these examples are easier for these six students and will help to build their confidence.

As the students begin to play the game, the teacher shows Nicole how she can use a view window to help her. Nicole has some difficulty with visual perception and so the teacher cuts out a circle at the top and a strip at the bottom of a piece of heavy paper. By using the "viewer," Nicole can look at just one fraction circle or one fraction strip at a time. The teacher sits with Nicole and her partner for two rounds to make sure she is comfortable with the device.

The teacher then scans the group to see how the others are doing. He notices pairs using both the fraction strips and pies, except for Isabelle and Elise, who seem to be playing without reference to the models and without much conversation. When a fraction is made, one of them claims it and the other agrees quickly to that decision. The teacher decides to intervene by asking, "Can you tell me why Elise gets three-fifths?" Both girls look at him blankly and so he tries another approach, "Is there something you could show me to convince me?"

Isabelle replies, "I think we are supposed to use those things [pointing to the strips], but I'm not sure how."

The teacher takes a copy of the fraction strip and places it so that both Isabelle and Elise can see it, then asks, "Do either of you see anything here that might help us to think about three-fifths?"

"Well, these are fifths," offers Elise.

"So, maybe, we should look at three of these," suggests Isabelle and counts three of the regions.

"But how do we know what's closer?" asks Elise as Isabelle looks up with questioning eyes.

The teacher is beginning to understand the conceptual difficulty and asks the girls to tell him where zero would be. Both Elise and Isabelle look perplexed at first and there is silence that he chooses not to fill.

Then Isabelle says, "Well, if it's nothing, I guess it's just before the first fifth."

The teacher asks Elise if that makes sense to her and, after she nods tentatively, he asks Isabelle to record 0 on the left edge of the first fifth. Then he asks the girls where the number 1 would be and Elise slowly places her hand at the end of the fifths. When Isabelle agrees, the teacher has Elise record *1* on the strip.

Isabelle's eyes then get wide and she exclaims, "So it's closer to one!"

The teacher is pleased with the connections these girls have made and asks them to share them with the rest of the group. He then asks the pairs to continue play as he checks in with the other students.

The teacher wants to be sure that his "middle" group also gets some of his attention, so he approaches a pair of these students and asks them how they are making their decisions about the fractions. They have just formed the fraction two-eighths.

Casey responds, "I would draw a circle and make eight parts. I'd color in two and not a lot would be colored, so that would be closer to zero."

"How do you see it Ben?" the teacher asks.

Ben replies, "I see it like we did on the board. Half of eight is between four and two is less than four, so it goes to the zero."

Satisfied that both students have developed techniques that work for them and provide for accuracy, he checks in with a few other partners. Then he feels a tapping on his arm and turns to Jim, who asks, "Is it better to be the zero or the one?"

The teacher turns around, wondering about the question and asks Jim what he means.

"Well, Jamie thinks it would be better to be the one because more fractions are closer to one."

The teacher and Jim make their way back to Jamie and he listens for a few minutes as they talk. Before too long, the math session needs to end for the day. Unfortunately, time does not allow for Jamie and Jim to reach a conclusion, but the teacher is interested in and surprised by this question.

Many times, students take you in directions you would not have thought about. Some of you would not think to put the zero and one along a fraction strip model. Most of you are not ready to answer questions related to the infinite number of fractions there are between any two numbers. But, having time for students to pose questions, listening for these opportunities, and finding ways to record these questions for further exploration is key. Differentiated "teacher moves"—such as allowing for flexible grouping, asking questions to probe thinking, sorting work according to learning expectations, and scaffolding learning—allow all students to engage in higher order thinking. There are so many rich ideas to consider when our students pursue worthwhile tasks.

Third-Grade Class, *Mystery Puzzles* (A Tiered Activity)

Let us now consider a lesson in a third-grade classroom. Instead of exploring this lesson through a vignette, we offer a video clip.

VIDEO CLIP 3.2

Fostering the Common Core State Standards for Mathematical Practice

This shows Mrs. Thompson checking in with two of her third-grade students. They are working on a problem that is part of a tiered activity (see Lesson Idea 4.3: *Mystery Puzzles* in Chapter 4).

As you watch the clip, consider:

1. Which of the eight Common Core State Standards for Mathematical Practice are the students engaged in?

2. There are symbols in this lesson used as variables. The teacher and the student use the descriptive term *diamond* rather than the geometric term *rhombus*. If you were teaching this lesson, how would you balance the need to support students making sense of the problem and their use of precise mathematical language, both called for in the Common Core State Standards for Mathematical Practice?

3. Think about how you integrate the Common Core State Standards for Mathematical Practice in your classroom. How does this offer opportunities for differentiation? Which practice standards do you find most prominent in your teaching? Most challenging to thread through your lessons?

Extend Your Learning: For additional insights, view Video Clip 6.4, Using Word Banks. Consider the questions above in the context of this clip. For more clips focused on this lesson, see Video Clips 4.2 and 4.3.

Identify Attributes of Tasks That Support the Mathematical Practices

The previous activities led to a lively exploration of mathematical concepts and practices. Relationships were discovered, affirmed, or reaffirmed; a variety of ideas emerged; misconceptions were uncovered; symbolic notation was connected to visual representations; and students were eager to explain their thinking and to listen to each other. What type of task yields such results? Although it is easier to recognize a specific task as being one that will support the mathematical practices when explored with a specific group of students, general attributes of such a task can be identified. The following is a close look at five such attributes.

Five Attributes of a Task That Support Common Core Mathematical Practices

1. The task focuses on significant mathematical ideas.
2. The task is developmentally appropriate.
3. The task is contextualized.
4. The task offers an appropriate level of challenge.
5. The task encourages multiple perspectives.

Attribute 1: The Task Focuses on Significant Mathematical Ideas

The task should be connected to big ideas in mathematics and be problematic—that is, the solution should not be apparent immediately to any learner in the class, or a variety of outcomes should be possible. This attribute requires students to make sense and persevere. In this case, number sense and connecting visual images to fractions are the big ideas. When instruction emphasizes significant ideas, students are more likely to make connections across mathematical strands or to pursue related ideas on their own. For example, a couple of weeks after Jim and Jamie thought about whether more fractions were closer to zero or one, they started talking about whether there were more whole numbers closer to zero or infinity. As they connect these ideas, they are making sense of mathematics.

> When instruction emphasizes significant ideas, students are more likely to make connections across mathematical strands or to pursue related ideas on their own.

Attribute 2: The Task Is Developmentally Appropriate

For elementary school students, Attribute 2 means that ideas are within reach both from a cognitive level and an experiential one. Students should be encouraged to construct their own strategies or ideas, and should be prodded to connect their intuition and natural language to their mathematical experiences. Concrete materials, visual models, and drawing materials should be available for use at all times to support their work as they explore representations

> Students should be encouraged to construct their own strategies or ideas, and should be prodded to connect their intuition and natural language to their mathematical experiences.

of mathematical ideas. As was demonstrated in the exchanges about fractions, asking students to explain their ideas or make comparisons among representations often extends students' thinking, requires them to justify their thinking, and compels them to critique the thinking of others.

Attribute 3: The Task Is Contextualized

Presenting mathematical ideas in connection to literature or shared events (such as field races) can help students enter mathematical activities. Situating mathematical tasks within everyday contexts also helps capture students' interests and gives them insights into how to begin open-ended tasks. These tasks also set the bar for mathematical precision. We need to know who won the race; we can't just estimate which fraction is greater.

Attribute 4: The Task Offers an Appropriate Level of Challenge

A task must offer a cognitive challenge that requires decisions to be made and new ideas to be explored, and yet not be so challenging that it feels overwhelming. When a task has multiple entry points, it is possible to engage students with a broad range of readiness, and thus help all of them believe that their efforts will lead to success. Without such a belief, it is unlikely students would bother to persevere.

Attribute 5: The Task Encourages Multiple Perspectives

An interesting task stimulates a variety of strategies, representations, and mathematical ideas, and thus encourages students to engage in mathematical discourse in which they explain and justify their thinking. In our earlier vignette, when students shared the different ways they *drew* a fraction, other students were able to extend their visual representations of fractions as well. As students make broader connections, they have the opporutunity to discover structure and make use of repeated reasoning.

Note that these characteristics of a task serve two purposes:

1. They provide attributes of a task that build broader and deeper mathematical ideas.

2. They support differentiated instruction.

That is, a task that is contextualized, is developmentally appropriate, offers an appropriate level of challenge, and encourages multiple perspectives makes room for a variety of learners and supports a variety of learning needs. Although a variety of tasks are available in published materials, teachers often find that they are more successful with tasks they adapt or create themselves. Whether using tasks as written, adapting them, or creating them from scratch, teachers first need to assess where their students are in comparison with the goals of the curriculum.

Connecting the Chapter to Your Practice

1. How does the clarity of the content standards in the Common Core change what you expect your students to be able to do?

2. Which of the Common Core mathematics practices are best reflected in your teaching? Which, if any, practices do you find more challenging to develop?

3. How do you support students' use of multiple representations of ideas? What do you do when a student relies, almost exclusively, on one type of representation?

4. What questions have your students asked that surprised you and perhaps changed your own mathematical thinking?

5. How do your favorite tasks relate to the attributes listed?

Decompose and Compose Groups

To learn insights into how this lesson is carried out in a classroom, see page 76.

Recommended Grade: 1

CCSSM Correlations

- Understand and apply properties of operations and the relationship between addition and subtraction.

- Add and subtract within twenty.

- Work with addition and subtraction equations.

Time

Day 1: 15 minutes

Day 2: 45 minutes

Materials

- visual image cards (Make images similar to the example shown in Figure 3–3, choosing the best complexity level for your students.)

- glue sticks

- cut-out paper squares

- sheets of white paper

Directions

Part I: Introducing

1. Hold up a card, for just a few seconds, with a set less than six and ask students to identify the number of squares they see.

2. Repeat Step 1 several times using different cards.

3. Now hold up a card with a set of six or more. This time, first ask students, "Before you tell me how many squares you see, I want you to tell me what you think about this card."

4. Then ask students, "How many squares did you see? How do you know?"

5. Return to various card examples in a purposeful way to ensure understanding.

Part II: Exploring

6. Show a new card with an arrangement students have not seen yet and ask, "Who can tell me what we did yesterday with cards like this?"

7. After students have connected with their previous learning, show a few more of the visual cards and solicit answers.

(continued)

Lesson Idea 3.1 *(continued)*

8. Now introduce the next activity. Say, "I want you each to make your own arrangement of squares. When you go to your tables you will see some glue sticks, white paper, and some cut-out squares. Pick a number four through ten. Use that number of squares and make a design. Then, I want you to write what you see."

9. Circulate and observe as students make their designs. Ask key questions such as the following:

    - What could you write to show me what you see?

    - Where do you see these numbers?

    - Is there another way to write an equation with these same numbers?

    - Is there another way to see numbers in this design?

Part III: Summarizing

Gather students to share their work.

10. Encourage students to think about and ask the following questions:

    - How are our designs the same? Different?

    - How are our equations the same? Different?

    - Do you have a new equation for someone else's design?

Represent and Compare Fractions

To learn insights into how this lesson is carried out in a classroom, see page 83.

Recommended Grade: 3

CCSSM Correlations

- Understand a fraction $\frac{1}{b}$ as the quantity formed by 1 part when a whole is partitioned into b equal parts; understand a fraction $\frac{a}{b}$ as the quantity formed by parts of size $\frac{1}{b}$.

- Understand a fraction as a number on the number line; represent fractions on a number line.

- Explain equivalence of fractions in special cases, and compare fractions by reasoning about their size.

Time

Day 1: 60 minutes

Day 2: 60 minutes

Materials

- problem written where everyone can see it

- paper and pencils

- 10 decks of cards (Each deck has forty cards made up of five sets of the numbers 1, 2, 3, 4, 5, 6, 8, and 10.)

- tape

- several small pieces of paper

- a strip of adding machine tape with a line drawn across the middle of its length

- pie models of fractions

- strip models of fractions

The Problem

At Olympics Day, two friends are running in a race. One friend is $\frac{5}{8}$ of the way to the finish line and the other friend is $\frac{3}{4}$ of the way. Who is winning?

(continued)

Lesson Idea 3.2 *(continued)*
Directions
Part I: Introducing

1. Read the problem (written where everyone can see it) and have students restate it on their own words.

2. Have students work alone or in pairs to solve the problem. Remind them to use pictures, numbers, and words to represent their thinking.

3. Circulate as students work, looking for evidence of understanding or the need for help.

4. When you think students have captured their thinking, note, "In a few minutes we will be sharing solutions. Think about what you want to say about your work. Talk with a partner about your ideas."

5. Call students together and have them discuss their solutions. Encourage students to ask questions of each other and to build on their classmates' thinking.

6. In preparation for the next day, review students' solutions, paying particular attention to their representations. Sort the work and plan appropriate follow-up activities.

Part II: Exploring

7. To introduce the strategy of making comparisons with one-half, ask, "If two children are running a race and one friend is one-half of the way to the finish line and the other friend is three-fourths of the way there, who is winning?" This time, draw a line on the board with the labels *Start* and *Finish*, and ask, "Who can answer this question?"

8. Record $\frac{1}{2} = \frac{2}{4}$ on the board and ask, "What if the one-half is being compared with a fraction with a denominator of six, eight, or ten? What would we do?"

9. Ask for two volunteers and give each one approximately half of a deck of cards. Describe the directions for participating in the game (listed later) and play a few rounds as a whole class.

10. Announce the three groups (from the sort you conducted the day before) and send your students to their assigned areas.

    - Group 1 plays the game with models of fractions available (pie and strip).

    - Group 2 plays the game as demonstrated.

- Group 3 plays the game as demonstrated, but after each fraction is formed, the students write it on a small piece of paper and place it on a number line.

11. Circulate as the students play. Ask key questions such as the following:

- What do you know about this fraction?
- Why do you think this fraction is closest to zero (or one)?
- How might thinking about one-half help you?

Part III: Summarizing

12. Bring students together to share their thinking. Ask key questions such as the following:

- What strategies did you learn to compare fractions?
- What strategies could you use to compare one-tenth and three-fourths? Explain.
- Which number is greater: three-tenths or five-eighths? How could you convince someone else you are correct?

Game Directions

1. Play with a partner. Divide a deck of cards in half and make sure each player has a stack of twenty cards.

2. Make a number line, labeling the left end *0* and the right end *1*. Decide which player will represent zero and which will represent one.

3. Draw two cards. Create a fraction using the number that is less as the numerator and the number that is more as the denominator.

4. Decide whether your fraction is closer to zero or to one.

5. The player who represents the closer number (zero or one) gets the cards.

6. Repeat Steps 3 through 5.

7. At the end of the game, the player with most cards is the winner. If both players have twenty cards, the game is tied.

Chapter 4

Transform Your Tasks

Introduction

Through assessment, you can uncover many of the similarities and differences among your students' thinking. Assessment offers you an opportunity to look for patterns in your students' learning, both as individuals and as a group. Inevitably, assessment data for any class reveal a range in students' experiences, interests, and readiness. In response to these differences, teachers work diligently to delineate standards for all learners, to build inclusive classroom environments, and to vary their teaching styles to address these differences. Yet, no matter how carefully learning outcomes are identified, habits are developed to encourage community, or diverse instructional strategies are used, teachers remain most concerned about the range, great or narrow, of student readiness. Consider the following words of this first-grade teacher.

TEACHER REFLECTION

I often struggle with finding what is "appropriate" for all my students. Even now, just days into the new school year, I am already feeling that I am not prepared to meet the different levels of math readiness in my students. Yesterday, Hazel spoke up at morning meeting and quickly, without knowing it, revealed to me some of the ways she thinks mathematically. It's only the second day of first grade and as we were talking about the number of children in our class, twenty-three, I hear her say, "I can make twenty-three with two tens and three more. I can also make it with eleven and twelve if I split up the tens and ones." I've been teaching for a few years and this is the first student who has demonstrated such thinking so early in the year. Just last night I was reviewing the first few lessons in our math curriculum and they are all about working with numbers less than ten. How is that going to challenge Hazel?

Later, I asked Hazel to talk with me about math. She beamed and exclaimed, "I love math! I love to count and figure out the numbers. My mom says I think in numbers." I took a moment to ask her a few informal questions. I know I will take the time in the coming weeks to assess her mathematical understanding more formally, but her eagerness and confidence called out to me. I don't want to wait too long to get a clearer picture of her abilities and to tap in to her obvious interest and potential in math. I just wish it were easier. I asked her to solve a few word problems that I remembered from the end of the school year. It was clear that she has fluency with adding and subtracting numbers to at least one hundred. She spoke in terms of values—ones, tens, hundreds, and thousands. She clearly is clever and accurate when calculating. Later, I also noticed her making complex patterns with Unifix cubes as the children explored materials during our first math lesson. When I spoke with her about her work she was very articulate and, again, accurate. Already I have the sense she meets or exceeds our first-grade curriculum goals.

Although this child seems particularly advanced in her understanding of numbers, I feel there are always children in my class who have already met some of the goals of the given curriculum. I'm just not sure how best to extend the lessons for them, especially when the curriculum seems right for the majority of students. I don't feel stuck like this when thinking about readiness in literacy. I know I have a host of books at varying levels to meet the challenges of my emerging, early, or independent readers. If I don't have enough titles for them at a given level, I feel comfortable asking the teachers at the grade level above mine if I can borrow some books. I wish it were that easy in math. Do I ask to borrow a copy of their math curriculum? If I do, will they feel like I'm stepping on their toes? I have a close friend who might be willing to share her curriculum, but then what will the children do next year?

> "I feel there are always children in my class who have already met some of the goals of the given curriculum. I'm just not sure how best to extend the lessons for them, especially when the curriculum seems right for the majority of students."

One of my students, Ryder, really concerns me. We're putting on a class play and I thought it provided an opportunity for some of my students to review their mathematical skills. The entire school is invited to the play and so the students are working in groups to solve problems related to planning for refreshments. Ryder is working in a group that has the responsibility of finding the number of students in the school. They decide to visit each class to find the number of students in that class. Ryder is assigned the classrooms in our wing of the building. He returns with his data: 17, 22, 21, 23, 23, 18. The numbers are written randomly on a small scrap of paper. Fortunately, his group leader knows that there are only five classes in this wing and she notices that Ryder has written six numbers. They decide that he wrote *23* twice. This may or may not have been the source of the mistake, but they all seem satisfied. Ryder's lack of organization often results in his making errors.

Ryder's next task is to find the sum of the five numbers to determine the total number of fourth graders. His sum is then checked by another member of his group. When we were working consistently with addition and subtraction, Ryder was fairly proficient. He would look for combinations of ten or split numbers into parts in ways that made sense to him. As Ryder begins to find his sum, he becomes agitated and erases several times. There are several tally marks written on his paper. Basically, he is trying to count on by ones. His final answer is eighty-nine.

> Ryder used to be able to do these basic math tasks. I review with him fairly often, but it never seems to be enough. I wish I knew how to help him hold on to his ideas.

What bothers me the most is that Ryder used to be able to do these basic math tasks. I review with him fairly often, but it never seems to be enough. I wish I knew how to help him hold on to his ideas.

If I had an assistant in the classroom during math time, I could work with him more often. I have a reading specialist in my room twice a week who works with the readers that struggle the most. That special time for them really makes a difference. My school system provides extra materials for reading and I have lots of books in my classroom that less advanced readers can enjoy, but I don't have these materials in math and can't just repeat the same problems he did last year.

Hazel may very well be the student who represents the more advanced students in her first-grade class this year. Perhaps she is not alone. More than likely, there are classmates whose profiles are dramatically different. A fourth-grade teacher provides us her thoughts on a student who is less ready for math challenges.

Considering ways to manage and meet the range of readiness in our mathematics classes is no easy task. Most early childhood and elementary teachers feel much as these teachers do. What you take on as a rudimentary challenge in literacy becomes seemingly impossible to many when it comes to mathematics. Teachers are often not sure how to challenge those students who are beyond grade level, and sometimes it feels as if the students who are less ready can slip easily through your grasp. At times, nothing feels just right or appropriate.

But how do you define *appropriate*? It is a word used frequently in the educational arena. Teachers usually aim for the middle or average group and adjust a little up or down, but is that enough? Reviewing Vygotsky's zone of proximal development (Vygotsky 1978) will help you think more clearly about what is appropriate for each student. It is that area that provides challenge, without going beyond the student's comfort zone or edges—that is, without being too easy or too hard. Teachers cannot possibly provide a separate curriculum for each of their students, nor would that be advisable. The social interaction and exchange of ideas among students is too important a component of learning. So how do teachers expand their curriculum so that it is appropriate for students whose grasp of mathematics differs greatly from that of the majority of students?

Choosing mathematical tasks is one of the most important decisions that teachers can make. Although it is difficult for one task to be appropriate for all learners, most tasks can be transformed to be more inclusive, to allow a greater number of students access, and to provide additional students with possibilities for more expansive thinking. When teachers do this, they are casting a wider net that can "catch" a broader range of students. Your goal, then, is to transform or adapt tasks to meet a wider range of readiness. (See Figure 4–1, page 112.) Note that the range of learners does not change, nor does the field that is deemed *appropriate*; rather, the tasks themselves are stretched to be better aligned with your students' needs. To do this, teachers begin with the tasks in their curriculum and consider how they can be modified.

We have discovered a variety of ways in which tasks can accommodate different levels of readiness. In this chapter, we explore some of these ways, offering ideas for implementing them immediately in your classroom.

> Choosing mathematical tasks is one of the most important decisions that teachers can make. Although it is difficult for one task to be appropriate for all learners, most tasks can be transformed to be more inclusive, to allow a greater number of students access, and to provide additional students with possibilities for more expansive thinking.

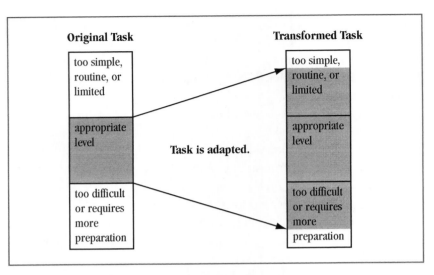

Figure 4–1. Tasks can be transformed to meet a wider range of readiness.

Ways in Which Tasks Can Accommodate Different Levels of Readiness

- Give students control over the difficulty level.
- Open up problems.
- Provide multiple models.
- Vary the challenge.
- Extend your resources.

Give Students Control Over the Difficulty Level

One adaptation to tasks that teachers can make is to allow students to have some control over the difficulty level. Two ways to do this are presented in the following paragraphs.

Take Action!

Identify ways for your students to have some control over the difficulty level of tasks.

▶ VIDEO CLIP 4.1 ·

Giving Students a Choice of Their Challenge

This video clip shows Ms. Corpas discussing choice time with her kindergarten class. Ms. Corpas uses a math menu to differentiate her instruction (for more about math menus see Chapter 7).

As you watch this clip consider:

1. How is Ms. Corpas setting expectations for the students during choice time?
2. How can giving students choice help make the mathematics more accessible to them?
3. Is student choice of problems a high priority in your classroom? Why or why not?

· ·

Students Provide the Numbers in the Problem

In story problems, instead of the standard format in which all the numbers are provided, the story may be written without numbers and the students asked to provide them. For example, students may be asked to write numbers in the following story so that it makes sense:

> Nora had _____ stamps in her stamp book. There were _____ stamps on each page. Then, Nora's uncle came to visit and gave her enough stamps to fill _____ more pages in her book and add _____ stamps to the next page. Now Nora has _____ stamps.

Students can choose numbers according to their comfort level, but *must* recognize the mathematical relationships among their chosen numbers. This is an important point. Whenever teachers expand tasks to allow more access, they never want to do so in ways that undermine the integrity of the mathematical challenge. All students must have access to tasks that require mathematical thinking, not just rote learning or less complicated thinking.

> **Whenever teachers expand tasks to allow more access, they never want to do so in ways that undermine the integrity of the mathematical challenge.**

Students Choose Exercises to Complete

Students can also make choices within simple practice assignments. Imagine a standard list of ten addition examples. By changing the directions *Complete exercises 1–10*, students can make choices according to their readiness. Consider the following alternatives.

Caution: Oversimplifying

Decisions to make task adaptations or to provide differentiated learning opportunities are grounded in knowledge of the CCSSM, your curriculum, and your students. As you choose among adaptations, you must remember that all students deserve challenging, thought-provoking problems and tasks. Too often, in the spirit of "helping," some students are provided with simplistic tasks or rules to follow that are not connected to conceptual understanding. For example, oversimplistic statements such as *take-away means subtract* do not allow students to understand the variety of language or uses associated with subtraction.

Open Up Problems

Tasks can be opened up to allow for one or more solutions and a wider range of responses and understandings. Examples are presented in the following paragraphs.

Problems with More Than One Answer

Open up a problem so that there is more than one answer. Problems with more than one answer allow room for expansion. Some students will be quite satisfied with finding one answer, and it may take them some time to do so. Other students may find one solution quickly, but may be able and interested to find more possibilities. By removing information or by creating a greater number of choices, many problems can be adapted to allow for multiple answers. Examples of such problems include the following.

Take Action!

Open up tasks to allow for one or more solutions and a wider range of responses.

Examples of Problems with More Than One Answer

Problem A

How might you color half of this figure?

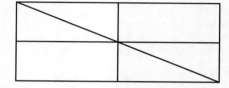

Problem B

Danny has some pennies and nickels.

He has 5 coins.

How much money could Danny have?

Problem C

Jocelyn has 15 pencils.

Some are sharpened and some are not.

How many of each type of pencil could Jocelyn have?

Problem D

Use graph paper. Draw 6 different quadrilaterals with an area of 6 square units.

What's the Question? Problems

Standard story problems can also be transformed by providing students with a number story and with answers. Students are asked to create questions within the given context that will yield the answers provided. Students can make choices about which questions they provide; they may also identify more than one question for some of the answers.

Open-Ended Problems

Some tasks have multiple solutions in that there are a variety of ways to respond to them. Examples of such problems were explored in Chapter 2. Teachers usually create these tasks by thinking about the topic and identifying a broad question that taps in to what children know, see, or recognize.

See CHAPTER 2

- *What are some patterns you see on the hundreds chart?*
- *How could you describe a parallelogram to someone who has never seen one?*
- *How is measurement used in your home?*
- *The answer is 5.25. What could the question be?*

VIDEO CLIP 4.2

"There's Many Solutions!"

This video clip first shows Mrs. Thompson summarizing the tiered lesson that her third-grade students experienced (for the entire lesson plan and open-ended problems, see Lesson Idea 4.3: *Mystery Puzzles* in this chapter).

We then observe the planning session that Mrs. Thompson and the math coach, Mrs. Leon held following the lesson. They collaborate to make decisions to support next steps for students working on the open-ended problem.

As you watch the clip, consider:

1. What are the challenges Mrs. Thompson faces?
2. How might Mrs. Thompson's use of the suggested questions impact student learning?
3. In your own practice what opportunities do you have to chat with a colleague about the mathematics in open-ended problems?

Provide Multiple Models

Teachers have long recognized that children operate on a variety of levels in terms of their needs for concrete models. Therefore, the types of materials available may make the difference with regard to whether a problem is accessible. Consider the problem that follows:

There are some strawberries on the table.

Maria and Tom each eat 2 of them.

Now there are 9 strawberries left.

How many strawberries were on the table in the beginning?

Teachers can make a variety of materials available to children when solving this problem, including real strawberries; strawberries made from felt;

individual pictures, stickers, or stamps of strawberries; red Unifix cubes, tiles, or counters; or arbitrary counters that aren't red. This is not to say that all students would choose to use these materials. Many students prefer to draw, whereas others feel they do not need any visual or concrete models to solve a problem. These students may have developed a deeper or more abstract sense of numbers or may visualize numerical situations more easily in their head. As you learn from the following teacher's reflection, having a range of materials available can provide students with access to this type of thinking.

TEACHER REFLECTION

> I came to realize that what children found helpful went beyond or differed from the continuum I had constructed in my mind. For example, orange Cuisenaire® rods are more abstract than pictures of real carrots for some children. For others, touching the rods is more important than the realistic images of carrots in pictures.

When I first began teaching kindergarten, I thought that as long as there were physical materials available, my students would be fine. *Hands-on* had been the buzzword in my teacher training and I knew that I would make sure my classroom was filled with math manipulatives. Throughout the years, I've come to recognize that using materials is more complex than I realized. I began to think about "concreteness" along a continuum that included real items, manipulatives related closely to the real object, random manipulatives or counters, and pictures. I always tried to have a variety of materials available that represented different levels of abstraction. I would assign my students to use different materials based on what I perceived their need to be for concrete representations. As I did so, I came to realize that what children found helpful went beyond or differed from the continuum I had constructed in my mind. For example, orange Cuisenaire® rods are more abstract than pictures of real carrots for some children. For others, touching the rods is more important than the realistic images of carrots in pictures. Now I think it's best to make many different kinds of materials available and let my students choose what works best for them. If I find a student struggling, I suggest a different model, and this strategy is often successful. But, I would rather intervene only when it is necessary than impose my thinking right from the beginning. I now realize that my students make fairly good choices, and this helps them to become more independent learners.

Teachers at the upper grades can sometimes forget that these students also benefit from using materials. The following teacher's reflection reminds us that all learners benefit from concrete materials.

When I first began teaching fifth grade three years ago, I thought my students would no longer need to use manipulative materials. I started my teaching career at grade 1 and so, of course, I expected my students to use concrete materials at that level. Throughout the years, I've come to recognize that mathematical models are important at any age.

This really hit home when I was taking a professional development course. We were solving a problem about twenty-seven small cubes arranged in one large 3-by-3-by-3 cube. The question was about how many cubes had one, two, or three faces showing. I saw some people making drawings and some others apparently able to figure this out in their head. There was no way I would be able to do that! I was so grateful for the small cubes that the professor had made available. At first I was embarrassed to need them, but then I saw other teachers starting to build with them, too. From that moment on, I vowed that I would always have different kinds of materials available for student use. I had learned that providing visual models for students to use may, in fact, extend their thinking and allow more students to stick with a task longer. I certainly would not have kept working on the cube problem without those small blocks to use!

> Throughout the years, I've come to recognize that mathematical models are important at any age.

Vary the Challenge

Sometimes even open-ended tasks need to be differentiated to be successful with a wide range of student readiness. Two examples of this are tiered tasks and curriculum compacting, which are presented in the following pages.

Tiered Tasks

Tiered activities allow students to focus on the same general concept or skill, but to do so according to their level of readiness. Consider the following example from a second-grade classroom.

Second-Grade Class: *Sum Investigations* (A Tiered Activity)

Part I: Introducing (Day 1)

The students are gathered in the meeting area where the teacher shows them four number cards: 4, 5, 11, and 17. He also has drawn a picture of these number cards on chart paper. He pulls out a black top hat from behind his chair. The students watch closely as he places the cards in the hat and then shakes it. He then looks quizzically at the hat and says, "If we pull out two of these numbers, I wonder what their *sum* would be? Can you help me find out?" Heads nod, and Jasmine and Andrew are invited to come to the front of the meeting area. The teacher holds the hat high enough so that the children have to reach to choose a card. Jasmine announces that her card is 5 and Andrew shows the class his card, 17. The teacher asks the children to talk briefly with their neighbors about the sum of these numbers. The students agree that the sum is twenty-two.

Part II: Exploring (Day 1)

After another example, the teacher shows the students' names listed in three groups on a piece of chart paper. Within each group, the students are recorded in pairs so that partnerships can be formed quickly. Each group is also color-coded to correspond to the folder in which students will find copies of tailor-made direction sheets for their group. Red is associated with the first level of the task, blue with the second, and green with the third. (See Figure 4–2; also available as Reproducibles 8, 9, and 10 for individual tasks identified by color.) Before releasing the students, the teacher explains, "Because we don't have enough top hats, we will be using paper bags. I can't wait to see what you discover. Let's get started!"

The teacher is thrilled by how seriously each group takes up its challenge. He is happy that the children are so engaged, and is delighted that they are getting a lot of practice with addition. The task also provides them an opportunity to recognize that there is only one possible sum for two given numbers. He wonders what his students will do when they come across the same two numbers to be added. Will they find these sums each time as though it was the first encounter or might some students notice the repetition? The teacher is also curious to see how students will determine the sums. As with

Lesson Idea!

Focus: Addition of single-digit and two-digit numbers

Domain: Numbers and operations in base ten

Context: Pulling numbers from a hat to find all the sums

See Lesson Idea 4.1, page 138.

Take Action!

Provide intriguing ways to introduce mathematical investigations.

Take Action!

Organize materials to support multiple tasks.

Reproducibles 8, 9, and 10

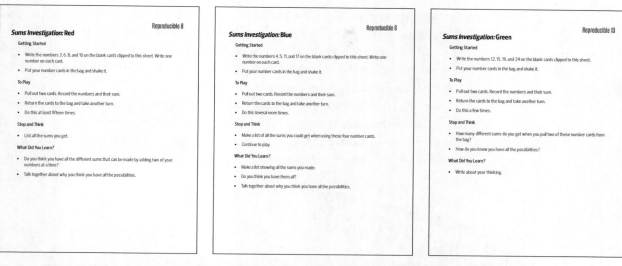

Figure 4–2. Task descriptions for tiered second-grade sums investigations (available as Reproducibles 8, 9, and 10).

any math lesson, counters are within reach for children who prefer to make the problems more concrete. Students know that hundreds charts are available to them as well. The teacher expects to observe a wide range of strategies from counting all, to counting on, to using some basic facts knowledge. He believes he will see some of these behaviors across the three groups red, blue, and green. That is, some students who are ready to work with greater numbers may sometimes rely on less complex strategies, whereas students not ready to work with greater numbers may occasionally feel enough comfort and familiarity with the particular numbers chosen to use more advanced strategies.

As the teacher checks in with the students working in pairs, he hears initial predictions.

"I think we'll have a ton [referring to the sums] because we have the highest numbers," Eliza says. Eliza and her partner are working with 12, 15, 19, and 24.

As the teacher moves on to Harry and Melissa, he hears Harry chime, "Same, same, same!" He thinks that Harry has recognized the fact that the number of sums is limited, but as he gets closer, he realizes that Harry is referring to having pulled the same two addends from the bag three times in a row. Over time, "Same!" becomes a common chant. One child even bemoans, "So boring. Same!" as he pulls out the 4 and the 11 for the fourth time. The teacher is hoping that this emotion will cause the students to look more closely at their growing list of combinations and sums, and begin to make a general statement about why the repetition might be happening. Because the

Take Action!
Consider learning trajectories and schemata as you observe students' thinking.

Take Action!
At the beginning of investigations, give students time to develop their own ideas.

investigation is just beginning, he thinks this is the time for him to listen and let students develop their own ideas. The wheels of ideas are turning and he notices that one group is debating whether four plus eleven is the same as or different than eleven plus four. These students are more focused on the order of the addends and not on the sums they yield.

Next the teacher watches a pair of students trying to accomplish the task with a more abstract approach. The students decide to abandon the random pulling of cards from the bag and place all four cards faceup on the table. They then try to write all the possible combinations of numbers by making

TEACHER REFLECTION

> Students need to feel comfortable sharing their ideas with the whole class. More time with this work will help them to prepare for our discussion.

When the work in pairs began, I realized that I had underestimated the time this task would require. It took a lot of time for students to collect their data. I recognized that we would not be ready to debrief our work today. I gave them a warning about this, telling them that we would return to the task another day. Telling the children this helped them to relax and to understand that this was a big investigation.

Students need to feel comfortable sharing their ideas with the whole class. More time with this work will help them to prepare for our discussion. It's not just one group of students that need this time. Seeing Cassandra and Craig's inclusion of the subtraction equations reminds me that all of my students need considerable time to process a task when it is at the right level of challenge. Both Cassandra and Craig are quite comfortable creating different equations during our morning number-of-the-day routine. Here, they were falling into a familiar pattern of response. Now that they know this task is somewhat different, they will look more thoughtfully at their data.

I can't wait to have a chance to talk as a class about this investigation. We did have to stop midstream, which was hard for some children, but I hope it will also break the momentum of pulling random cards and help them to refocus on what they have recorded. Carrying the work over to a second day will also give them additional practice time. Sometimes I feel for some of my students; there just isn't enough time to practice. Additional practice with an investigation feels great!

a list of equations. The teacher is pleased to see this change of strategy, but then realizes that their list also includes $11 - 5 = 6$ and $11 - 4 = 13$. The teacher acknowledges the pair's decision to write equations and then asks them to reread the directions.

"But, I thought we were supposed to find all the ways," Craig protests.

Cassandra points out her recognition of the error when she says, "Oops! It does say make a list of all the sums." Reluctantly, they erase their equations involving subtraction.

Take Action!
When necessary, redirect students in ways that allow them to take responsibility for their own learning.

Part II: Exploring (Day 2)

On the second day, procedures are reviewed and the children get back to work quickly. As the teacher circles the room, he hears a new kind of sentiment. "Wow! We got five plus eleven or eleven plus five a lot." "Let's make a list to see if we missed any." It is exciting to see how the children now refer to the information they gathered on the first day. Today, the students are looking more closely at their data, instead of just writing the random numbers they pull, along with their sums, on their lists. The teacher soon recognizes that the focus of the second day is more on the "Stop and Think" and "What Did You Learn?" stages of the investigative process. The teacher uses these phrases often as a way to remind students to reflect on their work during the problem-solving process.

"We already have this one" becomes a familiar mantra.

"We keep getting the same number!" Ezra declares, "I mean the same sum."

Energy is beginning to shift and the individual groups, regardless of the addends they are using, are starting to think in more generalized ways.

"Let's make a list," Lucinda suggests in her small group.

"I know! Let's look at what we have and then match them up," Iris suggests. Although this pair of students did not identify each of the six sums, their "matching" led to their affirmation of the commutative (order) property of addition and their recognition that each pair of numbers has one unique sum. (See Figure 4–3 on page 124.)

Part III: Summarizing (Day 2)

After a bit more time for investigation, the teacher suggests that the groups begin to wrap up their work and get ready to share. When the students gather they are excited to tell what they have discovered and want to know what others have done. The teacher begins by recounting the directions of the tasks; he wants to make sure that everyone remembers that each group only used four number cards. He hopes that the students will use their individual

Take Action!
Highlight common directions of tiered activities to support a joint discussion.

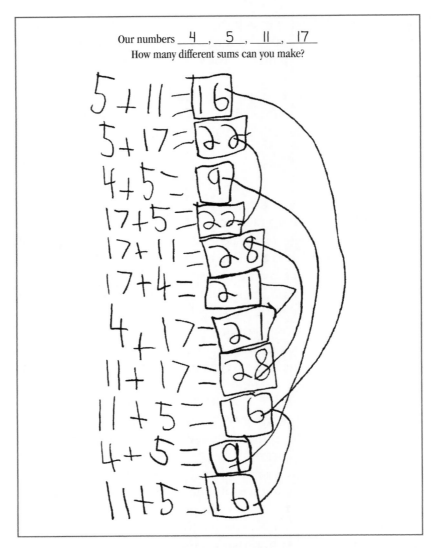

Our numbers __4__, __5__, __11__, __17__
How many different sums can you make?

$$5 + 11 = \boxed{16}$$
$$5 + 17 = \boxed{22}$$
$$4 + 5 = \boxed{9}$$
$$17 + 5 = \boxed{22}$$
$$17 + 11 = \boxed{28}$$
$$17 + 4 = \boxed{21}$$
$$4 + 17 = \boxed{21}$$
$$11 + 17 = \boxed{28}$$
$$11 + 5 = \boxed{16}$$
$$4 + 5 = \boxed{9}$$
$$11 + 5 = \boxed{16}$$

Figure 4—3. Iris and Lucinda match equations based on the order property of addition.

experiences with their different numbers as a way to connect with the bigger picture, or underlying mathematics in the problem. Two pairs, working with different sets of numbers, present their data when Sabrina suggests, "Everyone has four numbers, so everyone is going to get the same number of sums. We got six different sums, too. I bet everyone did."

Although many students could not make this dramatic leap, others were considering Sabrina's idea. At the beginning, every group agrees that they each got six sums. The teacher is not convinced that all the students believe that's the most sums they will ever get with their four numbers, no matter how long they keep trying, but it is a start and a validation of their hard work. Some students are clearly ready to examine this idea further and begin to offer conjectures regarding why there were six different sums.

"I think it's six. I mean you can't add twelve and twelve because there is only one of them," Jasper explains. He continues, "I can add the first number to the other three, but then the next one doesn't." Jasper is very eager to share this idea. He comes up to the board and writes his group's four numbers. Next, he draws a line from the twelve to each of the other numbers. He continues, connecting each number to each of the other numbers, and then announces, "See? It has to be six."

The teacher thinks this is a good place to stop. Some of the students are nodding eagerly while Jasper presents his reasoning, but other classmates are beginning to fidget or tire. The teacher recognizes that further consideration of this idea will need to be differentiated once again. But, all of his students experienced a meaningful investigation and found a preliminary way to convince themselves that they had found all the sums. Right now, however, it is time to shift the focus to another subject.

Later, the teacher thinks about the next challenge for the students who agreed with Jasper. Perhaps he might give them a set of five numbers or maybe another set of four numbers in which two of the number pairs have the same sum, such as 8, 9, 21, and 22. He could also save this task and reconsider it in the context of the money unit they will be working on next. It will be simple to translate this task to four coins in a hat.

This teacher created a common task for each group, but tiered the assignment based on readiness. The greatest number of students was in the middle, or blue, group, but the teacher thought it was important to develop tasks for students who were at different places on the learning continuum. In his reflection on the next page, he explains why he made the changes he did and what he thought about as he designed modifications for this task.

The story from this second-grade classroom demonstrates the effectiveness of tiered assignments. This is usually the case when teachers have a clear rationale for creating an assignment and make sure that the activities include mathematical ideas at varying complexities so all students can be challenged appropriately. In addition, the teacher made sure that the task could be approached from a variety of entry points and was thus accessible to all students. Finding the right combination of accessibility and challenge is the goal of a tiered approach.

Take Action!

Monitor whole-group discussions carefully and switch gears when several students can no longer focus on the topic.

The second graders in my class enjoy working together to learn math. They are an eager group and have already had a lot of experience talking about how they solve problems. They like to share their strategies, but I'm not always sure how much they learn from each other when we share. Some of the children seem to get overwhelmed if the numbers we are using are too big, whereas others find the work tedious if the numbers are too small. I find a great need to differentiate work on number concepts and operations, but have not always been successful when trying to keep the work relevant for all the children. I've played around with changing numbers in problems or giving practice packs that are designed to hit the target for a particular group of students. This works, but inevitably when kids are working on different assignments there isn't any real need to come together and share. I feel this can fragment the class and I don't want to do that.

I noticed a colleague working on a type of problem I had not seen before. The goal was to have children investigate what happens when you have a set of possible addends and ask them to add only two of them together at a time. The overarching goal of the problem is to have students generate a list of all the possible sums and then to consider what this means. I quickly recognized how this problem offers students a way to think algebraically, while they have a context for practicing the operation of addition. I wanted to give it a try.

> **In an attempt to make the problem accessible to all of my students, I tiered the directions and carefully selected the number sets with which each group would be working.**

In an attempt to make the problem accessible to all of my students, I tiered the directions and carefully selected the number sets with which each group would be working. It dawned on me that this type of problem lends itself to exactly the type of investigation we could focus on as a class, while differentiating the actual level of addition work. I believed that all of my students could take on the algebraic challenge that the problem suggests, as long as the numbers they use are within their operational range. I was thrilled to see how this played out.

From the onset, my class loved the playful way I picked two of the four number cards from the hat.

"It's like a magic trick!" one student exclaimed.

Although I want to dispel the idea of math being "magic," it was a fun place to start. I was momentarily stopped in my own tracks, however, when one student asked what *sum* meant. I guess I take it for granted that this word is part of the math vocabulary of second graders. In particular, the word added an interesting spin as one child offered, "Not *some*, like you are only going to use some of these cards, but *sum*, as in the total."

Another student said, "Think of it as finding how many."

After the students let me know they were comfortable with the task and the parameters I had set, they headed off to work in their assigned groups. I did feel a need to explain that some groups would be working with different sets of numbers. I did not tell them that I had also differentiated some of the outcomes listed on their Getting Started sheets. I felt I needed to differentiate this part to give more challenge for my stronger students while also giving more direction for those who are easily overwhelmed by the process.

Creating Tiered Assignments

So how do teachers create tiered assignments? As always, the first step is to identify the important mathematical ideas. In the following pages teachers use a kindergarten lesson example to walk through the creation of a tiered assignment. To help you become familiar with a variety of formats and characteristics of tiered problems, we present one tiered assignment at each of the other grade levels as well as consider another classroom vignette with video. Often, you will find that you can use some aspect of the task at your grade level.

Kindergarten: *Shape Puzzler* (A Tiered Activity) Consider kindergarteners studying geometric shapes, focusing on their abilities to identify and describe two-dimensional shapes, regardless of their orientation. Teachers can use a Shape Puzzler task to reinforce this particular content goal while also providing students with opportunities for critical thinking. The visual nature of the task helps to make it accessible to young learners, but it is easily adapted to all grade levels. The format can stay the same as the geometric focus shifts.

It often helps to begin with the middle level, focusing on what you would expect most of your students to be able to do. (We call this level, or tier, *blue*.) A Shape Puzzler card can then be developed for that audience. (See Figure 4–5; also available as Reproducible 12.) The blue card begins with *mips*, triangles with a three-line "tail." Triangles without the tail do not fit

Lesson Idea!

Focus: Classification of shapes

Domain: Geometry

Context: Puzzle problems

For a general lesson plan for these tiered tasks, see Lesson Idea 4.2, page 141.

See REPRODUCIBLE 12

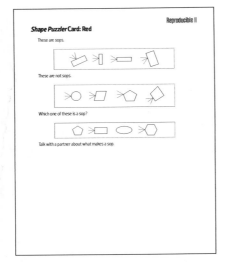

Figure 4—4. Red-tier *Shape Puzzler* for kindergarten (available as Reproducible 11).

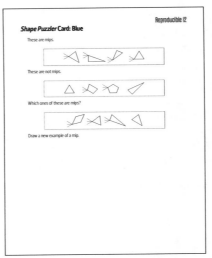

Figure 4—5. Blue-tier *Shape Puzzler* for kindergarten (available as Reproducible 12).

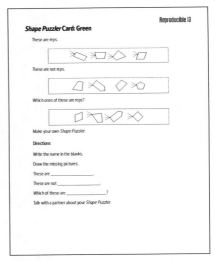

Figure 4—6. Green-tier *Shape Puzzler* for kindergarten (available as Reproducible 13).

the rule, nor do polygons with more than three sides even if they have a tail. Students are shown pictures of figures that are mips and pictures of figures that are not mips. After looking at these visual data, students are shown four new figures and are asked to identify those that are mips and to draw a new example of a mip.

Two other tiers can then be developed by adjusting the middle (blue) tier. For example, in a simplified version—red—the sop figures are composed of rectangles, a shape easier for students to recognize in different orientations because the angles are always right angles. All of the examples of nonsops have "tails," which help students to focus on the shape of the figure. Students only need to identify one sop, and its shape is in a standard position. Last, rather than creating a new example of a sop, students talk with a partner about what makes a sop. (See Figure 4–4; also available as Reproducible 11.)

In a more challenging version (green), reps are explored, which are four-sided figures with tails. (See Figure 4–6; also available as Reproducible 13.) There is great variety in the quadrilaterals shown, and so noting the similar characteristic of number of sides is more challeging. Students are then required to create their own Shape Puzzler task, providing the name and the drawings.

First Grade: Addition Facts In first grade, there is much attention given to addition with single-digit numbers. Students need to develop strategies for finding sums and then practice applying them to develop fluency. The Addition

See REPRODUCIBLE 11

See REPRODUCIBLE 13

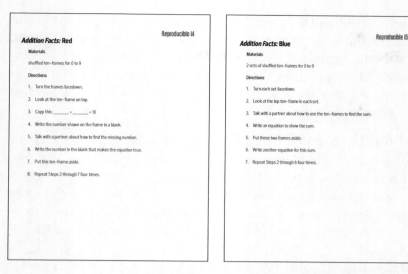
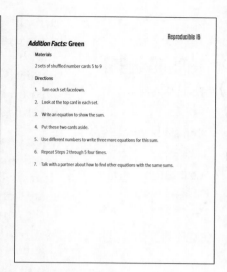

Figure 4–7. Tiered task for grade 1 (available as Reproducibles 14, 15, and 16).

Facts task is tiered according to the size of the numbers, but also by the inclusion or lack of visual models. (See Figure 4–7 and Reproducibles 14, 15, and 16.) Working with or omitting visual models changes a task's level of difficulty across the grade levels.

The red tier (Reproducible 14) focuses on facts to ten, an important building block for facts to twenty. The blue tier (Reproducible 15) involves facts to twenty. The ten frames (Reproducible 17), used for both the red and blue

See REPRODUCIBLES 14–16

See REPRODUCIBLES 17 and 18

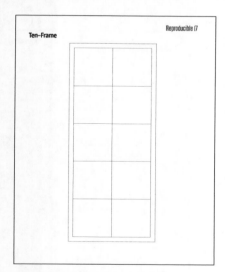

Figure 4–8. Ten-frames and number cards are for the first-grade red- and blue-tiered tasks, and the green-tiered tasks, respectively (available as Reproducibles 17 and 18).

tiers, help students think about using the Make-a-10 strategy, because students can visualize filling the empty spaces on one of the frames to make ten, and then identify the number that remains. Students at the blue tier are also required to write another fact for this same sum. At the green level, students use number cards (Reproducible 18), rather than ten frames. They also must identify three more equations for this same sum.

Third Grade: *Finish the Story* (A Tiered Activity)

Measurement and data is a key domain in grade 3. Among the standards are the expectations that students will tell and write time to the minute, compute time intervals, and estimate volume and mass using grams, kilograms, and liters. *Finish the Story* tasks combine these criteria by requiring students to fill in blanks in a story so that the measures make sense. (See Figure 4–9; also available as Reproducibles 19, 20, and 21.)

In the red tier (Reproducible 19), students can determine the time interval by counting by fives. Some students might note that the singular and plural nouns indicate where the 1 and 2, respectively, should be written. Students are able to choose the answer for which they provide an explanation. At the blue tier (Reproducible 20), the time interval is to the minute, and students must be able to estimate grams and kilograms to determine which number to place where. They are asked to explain a particular answer and to make a conjecture about something that happens next. At the green tier (Reproducible 21), the time interval is across the hour and moves from a.m. to p.m.

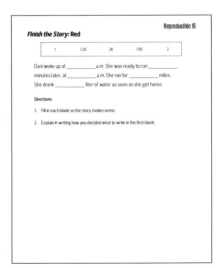

Figure 4–9. Tiered task for grade 3 (available as Reproducibles 19, 20, and 21).

Students must explain each of their responses and add a sentence to the story, which includes a reference to grams or kilograms.

Fourth Grade: *Hopping Robots* (A Tiered Activity)

The ability to generate and analyze patterns is an expectation for fourth-grade students. In the *Hopping Robots* task, students are asked to imagine a toy robot that hops along the number line, making a certain-size hop each time. (See Figure 4–10; also available as Reproducibles 22, 23, and 24.) At the red level (Reproducible 22), students imagine a 5-hopper robot that starts at zero and makes 15 hops. The task directs them to write the numbers where the robot lands and particular patterns to consider. At the blue level (Reproducible 23), students consider the same robot, but choose different start numbers and compare the results without specific suggestions to consider. At the green tier (Reproducible 24), students consider both a 2-hopper robot and a 5-hopper robot, with different starting numbers. In addition to looking for patterns, students are also asked to consider the relative impact of changing the jump number and the start number.

Lesson Idea!

Focus: Generate and analyze patterns

Domain: Operations and algebraic thinking

Context: Hopping robots

See REPRODUCIBLES 22–24

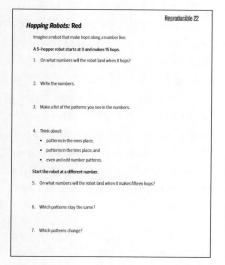
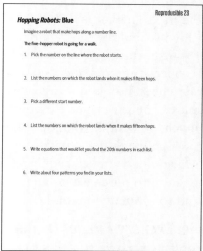
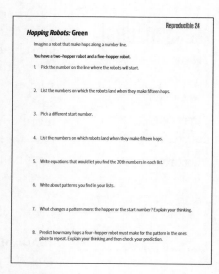

Figure 4–10. Tiered task for grade 4 (available as Reproducibles 22, 23, and 24).

Fifth Grade: *Real-World Connections* (A Tiered Activity)

Complex, more project-based tasks can also be tiered and often involve several areas of mathematics. During the *Real-World Connections* task, students conduct a survey, represent and interpret results, and compute costs related to the data. (See Figure 4–11; also available as Reproducibles 25, 26, and 27.) In the simplified

See REPRODUCIBLES 25–27

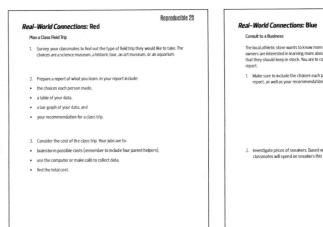

Figure 4–11. Tiered task for grade 5 (available as Reproducibles 25, 26, and 27).

Lesson Idea!

Focus: Collect and analyze data to solve a real-world problem

Domain: Measurement and data

Context: Plan a trip, make recommendations to a store, or plan a luncheon with kindergarten buddies

(red) tier (Reproducible 25), students plan a class trip. Four choices are provided for the trip to make the data more manageable. The computation will most likely involve multiplying to find the total admission fee and then adding the cost of transportation by bus. The blue tier (Reproducible 26) requires students to collect data to make recommendations to an athletic store about sneaker preferences. It does not restrict the data, and the computation is also more complex. The green tier (Reproducible 27) requires students to prepare for a luncheon with their kindergarten buddies. They are responsible for planning the lunch and the activities, and again, the choices are not limited. The task is far more complex, requiring students to decide on the quantities of food they need to purchase, to analyze the caloric and sodium content of the food, and to estimate the total cost of the food.

Third-Grade: *Mystery Puzzles* (A Tiered Activity)

Teachers can tier the quicker problems we give students to solve while emphasizing the CCSSM. Consider this example from a third-grade classroom. The teacher begins by presenting the following problem to all of the students:

$$\Phi + \Phi + \Phi + \Delta = 324$$

$$\Phi - \Delta = 76$$

$$\Phi = \underline{\quad\quad}$$

$$\Delta = \underline{\quad\quad}$$

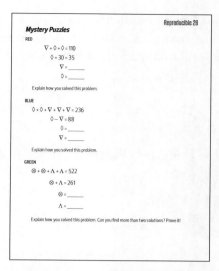

Figure 4–12. Tiered tasks for grade 3 (available as Reproducible 28).

She gives the students a moment to think and then encourages them to turn and talk to a neighbor. When the teacher thinks she has given them enough time to solve or come close to solving the problem, she invites a couple of students to share their thoughts about the specific values of the symbols. The teacher then tells the students that this is a mystery type of problem that can be solved by using their knowledge of addition and subtraction, along with their problem-solving skills. She further explains that sometimes mathematicians use symbols to represent specific numbers.

When the teacher is comfortable that the students have a basic understanding of this type of problem, she gives each student a problem to solve: red, blue, or green. (See Figure 4–12; also available as Reproducible 28.) In the red-tier problem, the second equation allows students to identify the value of one of the symbols easily. They can then work backward to find the other symbol's value. When solving the blue-tier problem, students discover that an infinite number of solutions are possible. When solving the green-tier problem, students need to use a combination of number sense, and guessing and checking to find the solution.

The teacher tells the students that they should first work independently, getting to know the problem and trying some initial ideas, then they can work with a partner to finish solving the puzzle and representing their solution. Knowing that the students will work at different paces, she adds, "When you solve the problem that I give you, you have two choices: you can select another problem to solve or you can write a similar problem yourself."

Lesson Idea!

Focus: Solve problems involving the four operations, and identify and explain patterns in arithmetic.

Domain: Numbers and operations in base ten

Context: Mystery puzzle problems with variables

See Lesson Idea 4.3, page 142.

Take Action!

Consider launching a tiered activity with a shared experience.

See REPRODUCIBLE 28

Take Action!

Be deliberate about identifying students to share their thinking.

The teacher circulates as the students work, asking questions and noting which students' thinking she wants to share and the order in which she wants them to do so. This careful planning allows students at all tiers to follow or participate in a joint debriefing.

▶ VIDEO CLIP 4.3

Mystery Puzzles (A Tiered Activity)

In this video clip we see excerpts from Mrs. Thompson's use of the tiered activity *Mystery Puzzles* with her third-grade class.

As you watch the clip, consider:

1. How are the students actively engaged in the mathematics?
2. What is the role of the teacher in this lesson?
3. What is the benefit of having students explain each other's thinking?
4. There are symbols in this lesson used as variables. The teacher and the student use the informal term *diamond* rather than the geometric term *rhombus* and the Greek letter π is called I-O rather than PHI. If you were teaching this lesson how would you balance the need to support students making sense of the problem and their use of precise mathematical language, both called for in the Common Core State Standards for Mathematical Practice?

Curriculum Compacting

Along with tiered tasks, some teachers consider *compacting* content for more ready learners. This strategy recognizes that some content can be accelerated or eliminated for these learners. What remains is a more *compact* version of the standard curriculum. The process is similar to all models of differentiation: key curricular ideas are identified, students are preassessed, and appropriate learning decisions are made based on that data.

Although compacting is often associated with gifted learners, it is important to remember that a variety of factors affect students' readiness. A student may have come from another school district or another country in which the material was already considered. Students' interests or family culture may have already provided significant learning opportunities within a particular content area. For example, Gwen is a third-grade student whose father is a carpenter and is in the process of remodeling their kitchen. Gwen often serves as her father's "assistant." She has been involved with making scale drawings of the new kitchen and measuring boards before her father cuts them with a saw. Also, her father lived in France until he came to this country for college and so he is comfortable with both systems of measurement (standard and metric). As a result, Gwen's exposure to standard and metric measurement, measuring tools, and ways to reduce errors of measurement is well beyond her grade level. Although other mathematical units are well suited to Gwen, measurement is one that can be compacted.

Although compacting can serve a variety of students, teachers are sometimes reluctant to eliminate content from the curriculum. As teachers learn from *this* teacher, outside support for compacting can be helpful.

TEACHER REFLECTION

Jamie seemed to walk in the door already knowing everything covered in our curriculum. Fortunately, my school system has been holding workshops on differentiated instruction. The presenter introduced me to the idea of compacting. I never thought about just eliminating some of the lessons. I was always trying to find a way for Jamie to be more involved, even if it was just to help others. I was disinclined to try compacting, but didn't know what else to do. I made an appointment with my principal and asked for her advice. She was supportive and encouraged me to try this approach.

Now, Jamie and I hold a mini-conference at the beginning of each unit. After the preassessment, we look at the list of the unit's lessons together. He sees me check the ones that he is still responsible for and watches me cross out some of the others. Jamie is an independent learner and, together, we identify projects that he can do in lieu of participating in the other lessons. The plan is also shared with his family. Jamie is so much happier now that we have begun to compact his learning. He now offers to help his classmates more readily and looks more engaged during our class discussions. It's as if a burden has been removed from both of us. We no longer just have to make the curriculum work; we can change it more than I realized.

> **Jamie is an independent learner and, together, we identify projects that he can do in lieu of participating in the other lessons.**

Extend Your Resources

Although the teacher in the previous Teacher Reflection has been successful with the compacting strategy, it does require you to monitor independent work and to have additional resources available. Teachers also need more resources for those students who need additional support. This need is felt particularly by some teachers who use nontraditional textbooks that have fewer practice exercises or problems. The following pages include ideas for extending your resources.

Share Materials with Teachers at Other Grade Levels

Exchanges with other teachers can be helpful. The goal is to provide mathematical materials equivalent to the multilevel classroom libraries for reading.

Multilevel Problem Decks

Take Action!

Acquire multigrade resources.

Multilevel problem decks can provide for the broad spectrum of readiness in grades 1 and 2. Grade-level decks can be purchased, and then teachers can redistribute the decks among themselves so that each class set contains cards for additional grade levels. If purchasing is not an option, problems can be found in old textbooks or in sample textbooks for each grade level. Cut out problems from lessons and paste them onto file cards of the same color. Then, cut out examples of more challenging problems often included in special boxes in texts and highlighted as brainteasers or some similar title. Paste these problems onto file cards of a different color. You may want to search for problems across two, three, or four grade levels. Label the cards from each grade level with a different letter or use some other identification scheme, then sort the problems by strand. So, for a particular strand such as geometry, your deck would consist of the following.

A Sample Multilevel Problem Deck for Geometry
- *Basic problems below grade level (color 1, A)*
- *Advanced problems below grade level (color 2, A)*
- *Basic problems at grade level (color 1, B)*
- *Advanced problems at grade level (color 2, B)*
- *Basic problems above grade level (color 1, C)*
- *Advanced problems above grade level (color 2, C)*

This organizational approach allows students at all readiness levels to have access to more advanced problems as well as basic ones at their grade level. Although the initial creation of the deck is time-consuming, teachers find that it serves their students well and can be used for many years.

Card decks can also be available to kindergarten students, but the limited number of readers makes this resource less useful. Some tasks cards, such as those involving patterns, are accessible to these young students. Some kindergarten teachers have found it helpful to combine pattern materials designed for preschool, kindergarten, and first-grade students.

Use Internet Resources

Technology also offers teachers many resources. If one or more computers are available in your classroom, Webquests, applets, and practice games can help meet a variety of readiness levels. A worthwhile site for ideas related to Webquests is http://school.discovery.com/schrockguide/webquest/webquest.html.

When children are learning new mathematical skills, they need to practice those skills. As you know, when practice is needed, the focus of the practice, and the amount of time that practice is appropriate vary greatly among students. Computer games often provide different levels of challenge. A game in which the focus is merely to practice should not be played for too long; after a skill is mastered, there is no reason to play the game. However, for the brief time when a practice activity is needed, a computer game can make it readily available within a motivating format.

Take Action!

Take advantage of technology.

Connecting the Chapter to Your Practice

1. What do you find most challenging about meeting different levels of readiness?

2. What methods do you have for transforming tasks so that they are more inclusive?

3. What concerns do you have about using tiered activities?

4. What Web tools do you use to help you support a wide range of learners?

Sum Investigations (A Tiered Activity)

To learn insights into how this lesson is carried out in a classroom, see page 120.

Recommended Grade: 2

CCSSM Correlations

- Add and subtract within 100 fluently using strategies based on place value, properties of operations, and/or the relationship between addition and subtraction.

- Explain why addition and subtraction strategies work, using place value and the properties of operations.

- Look for and make use of structure.

Time

Day 1: 30 minutes

Day 2: 30 minutes

Materials

- number cards 4, 5, 11, and 17 (use the blank cards in Reproducible 18 to create the number cards)

- chart paper

- hat (ideally, a black top hat)

- colored folders (red, blue, green)

- copies of task directions (Reproducibles 8, 9, and 10 or your own versions)

- blank number cards, four per each pair of students (Reproducible 18)

- paper bags, one for each pair of students

Preparation: Group Chart and Folders

Using a class roster, divide students into three color-coded groups: red is associated with the first level of the task, blue with the second, and green with the third. Within each group, pair students. Write these groups on chart paper. Next, use a paperclip to secure four blank number cards to each copy of tailor-made direction sheets (Reproducibles 8, 9, and 10 or your own versions). Place the sheets in the corresponding colored folders.

Directions

Part I: Introducing (Day 1)

1. Gather students in the meeting area. Show them four number cards: 4, 5, 11, and 17. Also, draw a picture of these number cards on chart paper.

2. Place the cards in a hat and shake it. Ask students, "If we pull out two of these numbers, I wonder what their *sum* would be? Can you help me find out?"

3. Invite two students to reach into the hat and draw one card. Ask students to talk briefly with their neighbors about the sum of the two numbers drawn.

4. Repeat Steps 2 and 3 one more time.

Part II: Exploring (Day 1)

5. Now share the color-coded group chart with students. Explain that they will pair with the person indicated on the chart and will get the colored folder that corresponds with their group color on the chart. Let the students know that directions for their task are in the colored folder. Tell each pair of students to grab a paper bag.

6. Before releasing students to their worktables, point out, "Because we do not have enough top hats, we will be using paper bags. I can't wait to see what you discover. Let's get started!"

7. As students work, circulate, checking in with pairs. Observe. What initial predictions are students making? Are students beginning to look more closely at their growing list of combinations and sums? Are they beginning to make general statements about why the repetition might be happening? What addition strategies are students using? How are they explaining their thinking?

Part II: Exploring (Day 2)

8. This task may take two days; give students enough time with the task so that they'll be comfortable with a whole-group discussion. On the second day, review procedures and allow students to get back to work quickly.

9. As students work, circulate again, this time noting what new discoveries are being made. Are students referring to the information they gathered on the first day? Are they looking more closely at their data? In what ways? Is students' thinking beginning to shift in more generalized ways?

10. After a bit more time for investigation, suggest that groups begin to wrap up their work and get ready to share.

Part III: Summarizing (Day 2)

11. Gather students together for a whole-class discussion. Recount the directions of the tasks; make sure that everyone remembers that each group used only four number cards.

(continued)

Lesson Idea 4.1 (continued)

12. Ask students, "Who found all the sums?" Have students present their data and discoveries. Ask key questions such as:

    - How did you decide you have all the sums?

    - What generalizations can you make about the sum of two numbers?

    - Who can explain what [student's name] just explained?

Extensions

- Give student pairs a set of five numbers instead of four.

- Give another set of four numbers in which two of the number pairs have the same sum, such as 8, 9, 21, and 22.

- Use the task in the context of a money unit; translate the task to four coins in a hat.

General Lesson Plan for a Tiered Activity

Preparation: Group Chart and Folders

Using a class roster, divide students into three color-coded groups: red is associated with the first level of the task, blue with the second, and green with the third. Within each group, pair students as needed. Write these groups on chart paper or use another management system for identifying groups. Next, place tailor-made direction sheets in the corresponding colored folders or distribute tasks to students.

Directions

Part I: Introducing

1. Gather students in a meeting area. Create and share a red-tier version of the task (or one between a red and blue tier) so that all students become familiar with the concept and format.

Part II: Exploring

2. Now share the color-coded group chart (or other management system) with students. Identify pairs in each group if applicable. Explain that the colored folders contain directions that correspond with their group color on the chart (or distribute copies of the task).

3. Circulate as the students work, asking key questions to probe student thinking. Make notes regarding possible misconceptions or notable strategies. Identify students to have share their thinking, noting the best order for them to do so.

4. After a bit more time for investigation, suggest that groups begin to wrap up their work and get ready to share.

Part III: Summarizing

5. Gather students together for a whole-class discussion. Recount the directions of the task, invite identified students to share their thinking, encourage student-to-student discussion, and ask key questions when appropriate.

Mystery Puzzles (A Tiered Activity)

▶ To learn insights into how this lesson is carried out in a classroom, see page 133. Also, see Video Clip 4.3.

Recommended Grade: 3

CCSSM Correlations

- Add and subtract within 1,000 fluently using strategies and algorithms based on place value, properties of operations, and/or the relationship between addition and subtraction.

- Make sense of problems and persevere in solving them.

- Reason abstractly and quantitatively.

Time

45 minutes

Materials

- chart paper with the problems prewritten

- a document camera or a smart board (for use when students share their thinking)

- copies of task directions (Reproducible 28 or your own version)

Preparation: Group Chart and Folders

Using a class roster, divide students into three color-coded groups: red is associated with the first level of the task, blue with the second, and green with the third. Make copies of the problems in Reproducible 28, cut so only one problem shows, and write the name of each student on the appropriate task.

Directions

Part I: Introducing

1. Gather students in the meeting area. Show them the following visual and ask, "Can we figure out what each symbol represents? Think and then turn and talk to your neighbor."

   Explain how you solved this problem.

   $\Phi - \Delta = 76$

   $\Phi = \_\_\_\_\_$

   $\Delta = \_\_\_\_\_$

2. When students have had enough time to solve or come close to solving the problem, invite a couple of them to share their thoughts about the specific values of the symbols.

3. Say, "This is a mystery type of problem that can be solved using your knowledge of addition and subtraction, along with your problem-solving skills. Sometimes mathematicians use symbols to represent specific numbers."

Part II: Exploring

4. Give each student a problem to solve—red, blue, or green. (See Figure 4–12; also available as Reproducible 28.)

5. Tell the students that they should first work independently, getting to know the problem and trying some initial ideas. Then, they can work with a partner to finish solving it and representing their solution. Say, "After you solve the problem that I give you, you have two choices: you can select another problem or you can write a similar problem yourself."

6. Circulate as the students work, asking questions such as:

   • What do you know?

   • What numbers might you try for the symbols?

   • What can you tell from the sum (or difference) of the numbers you guessed and checked?

   • Is there another student working on the same problem that you might talk to?

   • How do you know your solution is correct?

7. As you circulate, take notes regarding potential misconceptions and strategies used. Also identify which students you want to have share their thinking with the whole group and the order in which you want them to do so.

8. After a bit more time for investigation, suggest that groups begin to wrap up their work and get ready to share.

Part III: Summarizing

9. Gather students together for a whole-class discussion. Recount the directions of the tasks and say, "Although you may have worked on different problems, your job is to listen to how others solved their problem and to be able to explain their strategies. Ask questions to be sure you understand what is said."

(continued)

Lesson Idea 4.3 *(continued)*

10. Have students share in the order you selected. Stop occasionally to have another student explain the strategy that the presenting student used. For instance, ask:

    - How did [student name] start her solution?
    - What did [student name] try that did not work?
    - Who used a similar strategy as this?
    - Would you try this strategy next time?

11. Collect any mystery problems that the students created and say, "I will copy these for us to work on [tomorrow or next week]."

PART 2 Tools for Differentiation

. . . .

Overview

The chapters in Part 2 focus on strategies for making tasks accessible, challenging, and interesting for a variety of learners. Choosing tasks that have multiple entry points and finding ways to scaffold learners are key. Teachers must also remember that readiness is only one piece of the puzzle. The matching of tasks to learners also has to consider language, learning styles, and preferences. Providing students with choices can increase motivation and lead to greater success.

Chapter 5 Breaking Down Barriers to Learning

(continued)

Introduction

The term *universal design* originated in the field of architecture. This philosophy of design is committed to providing inclusive environments that work better for everyone: door levers rather than knobs, curbless showers, and doors that open automatically are examples. Door levers are easier to manipulate for older, arthritic hands and for anyone else carrying packages with only an elbow free for use. The idea is to build this way right from the beginning, rather than to retrofit spaces when special circumstances arise. So with this philosophy, all bathrooms would be built with wider doorways, not renovated when a family member needs to be in a wheelchair. In this type of environment, barriers to independent living are removed at the design stage. Access for people with physical disabilities is considered from inception, and everyone benefits from these decisions.

Many students face learning barriers in the classroom. Students' readiness levels are not always apparent, even when conscientious teachers observe their students closely and provide tasks designed to preassess learning. Sometimes there are barriers that keep students from accessing prior knowledge or from demonstrating what they have learned. When not attended to adequately and respectfully, language, learning styles, sensory preferences, and anxiety can keep students from reaching their full potential as successful mathematical doers and thinkers.

Known as *universal design for learning* (UDL), educators have begun to think about a teaching philosophy that embraces universal design. What would your curriculum plans look like if you designed activities that worked for everyone right from the beginning, rather than remediating or reteaching or, in architectural terms, retrofitting, when original plans prove unsuccessful or inadequate? In this chapter, we look at how barriers to learning can be removed through several lenses: attending to language, engaging multiple intelligences and multiple senses, reducing anxiety, and addressing learning challenges.

> "What would your curriculum plans look like if you designed activities that worked for everyone right from the beginning, rather than remediating or reteaching or, in architectural terms, retrofitting, when original plans prove unsuccessful or inadequate?"

Attend to Language

As with universal design, attention to language benefits all students. When teachers listen deliberately to their students and themselves, and attend deliberately to the language used, students are better able to access their previous learning as well as to understand more completely the tasks they are asked to perform. Like all language skills, learning the language of mathematics is an important goal for all students and can remove barriers to learning mathematical ideas.

Janella's Understanding of What It Means to Skip-Count

Let's begin with language and its impact on learning mathematics by thinking about a class of second graders. The students are working with laminated hundreds charts and transparent chips to explore patterns and skip-counting. The students choose a number and place chips on their charts as they skip-count by that number, then they choose another number and investigate that outcome as well. After a few numbers are explored, each child chooses a result to record by coloring in the numbers on which they land on a copy of the hundreds chart and by writing about the patterns they observe. After working for about thirty minutes, the children gather in the meeting area to discuss their findings. The teacher notices that Janella appears confused throughout the discussion. The teacher is somewhat surprised. Although Janella is often unclear on directions and has a more limited grasp of English than many of the other students, she usually does well when concrete materials are used. Today, she seems to be working successfully during the investigation, but once on the rug, she is silent and fidgety.

Later in the day, the teacher finds time to sit with Janella. The teacher asks her to use the materials and skip-count by twos. Janella sighs, looks concerned, and bows her head. With further prodding and her teacher's insistence that she just wants to listen to her thinking, Janella begins. She counts quietly, "One, two," and places a transparent chip on 3. Then she counts, "Four, five," and places another transparent chip on 6. She follows this pattern several more times, placing chips on 9, 12, and 15. Before long, the teacher realizes that Janella thinks that skip-counting by twos means to skip two and land on the next one. The teacher wishes she had said, "What numbers do you say when you count by twos?" The teacher comments on what a good job Janella did with keeping the pattern and acknowledges the sense Janella made of this task.

"I can see how you followed your pattern of skipping two numbers. I should have been clearer," says the teacher, and they work together to clarify the expectations of skip-counting by twos.

Fortunately, Janella's misconception was discovered because she cued the teacher to her confusion and the teacher followed up with her individually. It would have been easy for the teacher to have missed Janella's visual cues or to have been unable to find the time to follow up on her instinct that something was amiss. Janella might have submitted her work without identifying it as a "two pattern" and, when viewing the work, the teacher might have assumed that Janella had submitted a three pattern. The teacher wonders what language misconceptions others students might have.

Misconceptions involving language are sometimes hidden. Children may pretend to understand or be able to submit work that can be deemed correct despite their literal interpretations, misperceptions, and confusions. Children who are learning English or who have language difficulties may be reluctant to communicate their thinking. Note that in the previous scenario, the teacher first made sure to make sense of Janella's work and to compliment her for following her pattern consistently. She also took some responsibility for the confusion. This stance helped Janella feel more comfortable and to be open to clarification.

Sometimes it is difficult to separate language difficulties from mathematical ones. Consider the following interaction between Ross, a kindergartener, and his teacher.

Take Action!

Provide a specific compliment to help make an unsure student comfortable in sharing his or her thinking.

Ross' Understanding of *What Is One Less Than?*

Ross is being interviewed by his kindergarten teacher late in the spring. "What is one less than six?" the teacher asks.

"One," he replies.

His teacher then asks, "What is one less than three?"

Again, Ross replies, "One."

Next the teacher asks, "If you have three raisins and eat one of them, how many do you have left?" As she says this she points to imaginary raisins on the table and pretends to eat one of them.

Immediately Ross responds, "Two."

When asked about six in the same problem format, Ross correctly identifies five as the answer. The teacher is not sure whether the real-world model or the gestures were essential for Ross to understand what to do, or if he just didn't understand the phrase *one less*. She wonders if Ross thought he was supposed to name the number that was less, one or six. She was pleased that he was able to answer the questions about the raisins and that she could work with Ross to connect real-world ideas with abstract mathematical language.

Take Action!

Use context and gestures to increase comprehensible input.

Classroom examples like this one emphasize the important role of language in the teaching and learning of mathematics. For some students, talking about mathematical ideas can help to solidify concepts and develop confidence. Occasionally, students have a minor difficulty or misunderstanding that can be addressed easily. For others, language can be a significant barrier, one that keeps them from grasping new ideas or from demonstrating what they know.

Students who are confident in their thinking are often more willing to expose their misconceptions because they are less concerned about having a different perspective. Consider Mabel, a third-grade student, in the following conversation.

Mabel's Understanding of the Word *Plot*

Mabel has collected data on the number of aunts each of her third-grade classmates has. After collecting the data, she represents the information with Unifix cubes. The teacher reminds her to show the data in a line plot.

With surprise in her voice Mabel asks, "Does each aunt have to be in the story?"

The teacher is taken aback at first, but then realizes that Mabel is associating the word *plot* with creative writing. The teacher pauses and then says, "Plots are about stories. Graphs can tell stories, too. A line plot is a way to tell the story of your data." Because Mabel was comfortable asking a question immediately, the teacher could address the misunderstanding right away. The teacher knows that Mabel is a strong student in both language arts and mathematics, and is reminded that even students such as Mabel can miss the nuances of mathematical language.

It is helpful to connect to students' other languages. Sometimes, as is the case with Spanish names for three-dimensional figures, the non-English terms provide greater insight into the terms. Consider what this fifth-grade teacher decides to do.

"It's Easier When You Say It in Spanish!"

A fifth-grade teacher in a dual-immersion school has noted the confusion her students have about the names of three-dimensional shapes. One day, a student whose primary language is Spanish says, "It's easier when you say it in Spanish. It's backward in English." Several students agree and, when the teacher asks other teachers, she learns that they have heard similar remarks as well. In English, we say *rectangular prism*; in Spanish, we say *prisma rectangular*. By saying *prisma* first, students may think immediately about a three-dimensional shape. Conversely, when *rectangular* is said first, students are more likely to think first about a two-dimensional figure. The teachers decide to teach everyone the names for prisms in Spanish first and then later introduce the terms in English.

It is common to hear teachers' concern about their students who are struggling to learn the language necessary to be successful in mathematics. The mathematics vocabulary of elementary classrooms has increased dramatically in recent years, and both teachers and students are sometimes challenged to use correct terms as they communicate their understanding of concepts. As one fifth-grade teacher explains, "These students have so many mathematical words to learn. When I went to school, I had never even heard of a right triangular prism."

Although language has always been important, today the relationship between language and mathematics is even more prominent. Mathematical tasks are often presented within language-rich contexts. The once familiar phrase *Show your work* is now often replaced with *Explain your thinking*. Students are expected to discuss their mathematical ideas and to build on the ideas of others. These approaches to mathematics necessitate careful attention to mathematical vocabulary and to the language of mathematical reasoning so that these barriers to learning can be ameliorated.

> **Mathematical tasks are often presented within language-rich contexts. The once familiar phrase *Show your work* is now often replaced with *Explain your thinking*.**

Create Interactive Word Walls

Some teachers invest a great deal of time creating word walls in their classrooms so that students have constant access to the vocabulary related to current topics. At the beginning of the school year, one group of teachers begins with words already posted on the wall and, as the year unfolds, adds more terms. Many of these teachers, however, find that several of their students do not refer to the word walls, even though doing so is beneficial. They discover that the word walls didn't work because they were a teacher initiative that did not involve the students.

The following year, these same teachers have their students participate in the creation of the word walls. Students choose words they wish to define

See also Word Banks in Chapter 6, page 203.

Take Action!
Create interactive word walls.

and illustrate, and then post their work beside the word strips. The teachers also have students play word games. For example, one teacher takes down the definitions and illustrations, leaving the words. Then, she reads a definition or shows an illustration and a student finds the matching word. The teacher repeats this process until all the words are matched. Taking time to do this several times a year keeps the word wall interactive. This level of involvement seems to have made the word walls more meaningful, and students consult them more regularly.

Use Several Approaches to Ensure Language Is Understood

The language of mathematics is both complex and subtle. It takes considerable experience for children to become comfortable with it. Even a mathematical term that has been discussed for several days can be more challenging than teachers realize. Students develop a deep understanding of mathematical language only through several approaches that develop mathematical concepts and connections. Sometimes, when the nature of the activity changes, less than complete understanding is revealed.

Teachers must pay significant attention to language issues. The number of English language learners in public schools has increased by 51 percent from 1998 to 2009 (National Clearinghouse for English Language Acquisition 2011). Before students are asked to complete mathematical tasks, teachers need to make sure that the language of the task is understood. The following is a list of ways teachers can do this.

To Ensure That the Language of a Mathematical Task Is Understood:

- have students read the task repeatedly, as in a choral reading format;
- encourage students to dramatize word problems;
- ask students to summarize the task in their own words;
- preview specialized vocabulary;
- have vocabulary lists available when students write about their ideas;
- use pictures, models, and gestures to clarify ideas whenever possible;
- have students try out their thinking in pairs or small groups before speaking in front of the whole class;
- make sure that symbolic notation is mapped carefully to everyday situations and concrete models;

- speak slowly and avoid idioms and contractions; and
- pose problems in familiar contexts that students will recognize.

Identify Language Objectives Related to Mathematics

In some districts, teachers are expected to identify one or more language goals for each math lesson. Language objectives should explain how the student will learn the content using the language skills of listening, speaking, reading, and writing. Examples of language objectives related to mathematics are provided in the following list.

Language Objectives Related to Mathematics

- Read your partner's math reflection.
- Listen to the story for examples of when telling time is important.
- Restate a classmate's mathematical idea.
- Talk with a partner about whether a square is a rectangle.
- Participate in a small-group discussion about the use of measurement tools.
- Read and summarize orally another student's definition of a factor.
- Post an example on our electronic bulletin of how to use a fact you know to find a fact you do not know.
- Write the steps you used to solve the problem.

Pay Attention to Cognates, Different Meanings, Homophones, and Similar Sounds

Cognates

Focusing on cognates (words with a common origin) can be helpful, especially for students who are fluent in Spanish. Up to 40 percent of English words have a related Spanish word (Gomez 2010).

Words with More Than One Meaning

Teachers also need to pay attention to particular terms that may be problematic. For example, many mathematical terms, such as *face*, *plot*, and *difference*, have a different meaning in everyday usage. Examples of words found in the elementary curriculum that have different everyday and mathematical meanings include the following:

angle	mass
count	odd
difference	one
edge	plot
expression	point
face	range
factor	ruler
fair	set
graduated	side
height	table
identity	volume
left	yard

Homophones

Homophones, or words that sound the same but have different spellings and meanings, can be similarly problematic. Again, special attention should be given to these terms, and humorous examples can be helpful. One teacher tells her students about the following conversation and asks them to figure out what happened.

Two patients walk out of a doctor's office at the same time. One patient asks, "What was your weight?" The other replies, "Five minutes." "Oh," says the first. "Mine was one-hundred thirty pounds."

Examples of mathematical words with everyday homophones include the following:

cents/scents	sum/some
eight/ate	symbol/cymbal
hour/our	week/weak
one/won	weight/wait
pi/pie	whole/hole
plane/plain	

Similar Sounds

Some everyday words sound similar to mathematical terms, including *cents/sense*, *half/have*, *quart/court*, *sphere/spear*, and *tenths/tents*. Teachers should enunciate these words carefully, record them when they are first introduced, and listen deliberately to students' pronunciation of them.

The Research: The Impact of Test Language on Success

Teachers must also remember not to make assumptions about students' mathematical knowledge that may merely be based on the understanding of English. Abedi and Lord (2001) conclude that the language used in test items has a significant impact on success. Fernandes et al. (2010) did follow-up interviews of students who had not answered a meaurement question correctly on the National Assessment of Educational Progress. They found using the following techniques revealed deeper understanding:

- Avoid complex syntax such as if–then clauses.
- Break problems into subproblems to avoid cognitive overload.
- Place concepts in familiar contexts.

Fernandes et al. (2010) encourage teachers to use these techniques in interviews as well as to incorporate these strategies throughout their teaching.

Provide Sentence Frames

Bressor et al. (2008) provide numerous detailed lesson plans in their series *Supporting English Language Learners in Math Class, Grades 3–5*. They strongly recommend the use of sentence frames such as:

A _____ has _____ sides and _____ angles.

They suggest that teachers differentiate the frames they provide for students whose language is at the beginning, intermediate, and advanced levels, and develop a mini-lesson in which students use the frames with familiar content. Furthermore, they recommend that each lesson have a math goal along with a related language goal. They offer a particularly helpful planning template for teachers (Bressor et al. 2008, 180). (See Figure 5–1 on page 158.)

> See *Supporting English Language Learners in Math Class, Grades 3–5* by Bresser et al. (Math Solutions, 2008)

> **Take Action!**
> Use lesson templates that emphasize the importance of language.

<table>
<tr><td colspan="3" align="center">Lesson Template</td></tr>
</table>

Lesson Template

Math Goal

_____

_____

Language Goal

_____

Key Vocabulary

_____   _____   _____

_____   _____   _____

_____   _____   _____

Materials

_____   _____   _____

_____   _____   _____

Sentence Frames That Support the Language Goal

    Beginning:

    _____

    Intermediate:

    _____

    Advanced:

    _____

Activity Directions for the Minilesson (including opportunities to talk)

1.
2.
3.

Activity Directions for the Main Lesson (including opportunities to talk)

1.
2.
3.
4.
5.

Writing Prompt

Figure 5–1. Lesson template developed by Bressor et al. (2008).

Tap Into Multiple Intelligences

Along with language, students differ greatly in the ways they prefer to explore mathematical ideas. Howard Gardner (1999) emphasized the differences among students' thinking when he developed his theory of multiple intelligences. Eight intelligences are usually considered.

Gardner's Eight Multiple Intelligences

1. Linguistic
2. Logical–mathematical
3. Spatial
4. Bodily–kinesthetic
5. Musical
6. Interpersonal
7. Intrapersonal
8. Naturalist

When lessons and activities do not tap into different ways of knowing, barriers result. Because limited knowledge and facility with basic facts can also become a barrier to success with more complex computations, let's consider the goal of learning basic facts through the perspective of multiple intelligences.

Attitudes about how best to learn these basic facts have changed in recent years. Most experienced teachers first learned their basic facts through memorization accompanied by timed tests. One hundred facts were presented on a single sheet of paper, and they and their fellow students were given three to four minutes to complete the items. Often, this ritual was repeated on a weekly basis. In between, they might have studied the facts for one number—for example, the seven's table—or practiced with flash cards. There was little or no instruction on conceptual models that could be linked to these facts or on ways to make connections between one fact and another.

Today's teaching tends to place more emphasis on conceptual understandings to support the learning of basic facts. Building on known facts is emphasized. For example, to find 7 + 8, students might decompose the 8 to form 7 + 3 + 5, and then find 10 + 5. When developing subtraction fact knowledge, many students are taught to think: What do I add to nine to get twelve? Similarly, for division, students might think: What do I multiply by five to get forty-five? The CCSSM also emphasize algebraic thinking, applying the properties of the operations to fact knowledge. Through physical models and drawings, students are expected to recognize and then use their understanding that the order of the addends and factors can be changed without changing the sum or product—that is, the commutative property. The distributive property of multiplication also is emphasized, allowing students to find 6 × 8 by thinking (3 × 8) + (3 × 8).

So is this a better approach to learning basic facts? The answer is not simple. Placing an emphasis on conceptual development is definitely a better way to learn the meaning of the operations and making connections among them. In the previous approach, students often memorized the facts without ever developing an understanding of the operations. They also developed strategies that can be applied to greater numbers.

Fact strategies may not be the best way, however, for *all* students to learn their facts. Such strategies often assume a logical–mathematical intelligence that may not match students' strengths. This is not to say that strategies should not be taught; rather, strategies should be part of a diverse approach designed to reach all intelligences. Also, fact strategies should be taught in ways that incorporate several ways of learning. Possibilities for addressing

> Fact strategies may not be the best way, however, for *all* students to learn their facts. Such strategies often assume a logical–mathematical intelligence that may not match students' strengths.

students' multiple intelligences while they learn basic facts are summarized here:

Ways to Address Students' Multiple Intelligences While They Learn Basic Facts

Linguistic
- Read a book and then make up basic fact story problems related to the characters in the story.
- Talk about fact strategies.
- Write poems with basic fact rhymes.

Logical–Mathematical
- Create fact strategies.
- Make generalizations (identity, zero property, commutative property).
- Practice with puzzles, such as magic triangles with each side having the same sum or product.

Spatial
- Find patterns on the hundreds chart.
- Make visual models to match fact cards.
- Make triangle fact cards to connect addition and subtraction as well as multiplication and division.
- Use area models to demonstrate the distributive property.

Bodily–Kinesthetic
- Dramatize story problems and fact strategies.
- Use counters to model problems.
- Have students walk or hop along number lines to model equations.

Musical
- Create songs about facts.
- Relate rhythmic patterns to facts.

Interpersonal

- Practice with fact buddies.
- Discuss fact strategies in groups.

Intrapersonal

- Set personal fact goals.
- Keep a journal about fact strategies.

Naturalist

- Find examples in nature of things that come in fours, fives, and so on.
- Categorize facts that best fit particular strategies.

Let's look at multiple intelligences at play in three mathematics classrooms. In the first classroom, a third- and fourth-grade class, teachers see students at work at various stations or centers, their tasks tapping into various intelligences. In the second classroom, a second-grade teacher uses just four stations or centers and has students consider their own multiple intelligences to make a choice regarding which center to visit. In the third classroom, a first- and second-grade class, teachers see how stations focused on various intelligences can give the teachers an opportunity to work with small groups of students without pulling them from the classroom.

Third- and Fourth-Grade Combination Class: Multiplication and Division Basic Facts

Students are working at various workstations with both multiplication and division basic facts (the basic structure can be applied easily to addition and subtraction). Often, such activities tap into more than one intelligence; in this case, the primary intelligence is listed for the station.

Intrapersonal Intelligence: Playing Multiplication Games on the Computer Individually

Among the many small groups is a cluster of three students working on computers. They are each playing a game that provides basic practice with multiplication facts. Chips, hundreds charts, and drawing materials are available for use. The game allows the user to choose the level of difficulty for each round. The less complicated levels focus on the factors zero through five and provide more time between examples. Mike has decided that he is ready for a more complicated level today, and he is excited about it. He notes his personal goal in his journal.

Musical Intelligence: Composing a Song About Multiplication

Gil and James are writing a song about multiplication. Their words follow the melody of "ABC," a song first made popular by the Jackson 5:

ABC, easy as one times three.

My mama is studying with me.

Oo, ah, I want to know the answer to

two times three.

Oo, ah, I know the answer is six,

because three plus three that six mix.

The teacher notes that the boys connect multiplication to repeated addition and to create a song that they are enjoying sharing with others. She is certain that they know this fact, however, and wants to push them further without negating their hard work. After noting how pleased they seem with their song, she asks them to see if they can modify it a bit to connect to eight times three. They begin this new task enthusiastically as she moves to another writing group.

Linguistic Intelligence: Writing Poems About Multiplication Facts

Brenda and Jill are among a group writing poems about multiplication facts. They have been building other facts from the square number facts that they know. Their poem follows:

Multiplication is really cool.

It helps you at work and at school.

We know our squares. They're just fine.

Seven times seven is forty-nine.

Add one more seven to the mix.

Eight times seven is fifty-six.

As Jill describes, "It's a poem to help you. It shows how we get one fact from another." The girls return to their poem throughout the day. They change it a bit during snack time and look at it again during recess. They are quite proud of their work and ask the teacher if they may have a class bulletin board for "cool fact poems." The teacher agrees and several other poems are added during the course of the week.

Spatial Intelligence: Working with Arrays

Niki and Lucinda are among pairs of students who are also exploring how known facts can help to find other facts. They have pictures of arrays and a straw. When Niki chooses the 4-by-7 array, it is Lucinda's turn to place the straw in a vertical or horizontal line to separate the array into two parts. When Lucinda places the straw, two arrays result: 4 by 4 and 4 by 3. (See Figure 5–2.) The girls record the product of each new array formed and then use addition to find that $4 \times 7 = 28$. When they finish this example, Niki explains to Lucinda that they are using the "distribution" property.

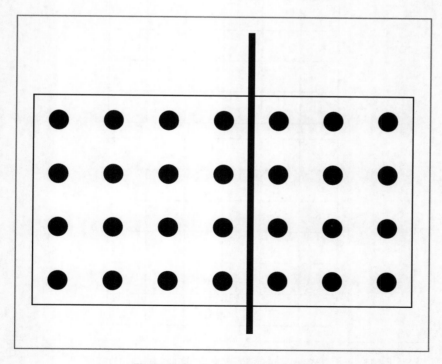

Figure 5–2. Array-and-straw result.

Bodily–Kinesthetic Intelligence: Playing the Board Game

Multiplication Threesome

Tina, Jared, Lori, and Tommy enjoy playing board games. Today they are playing *Multiplication Threesome* to practice their facts. The game boards are blank partial multiplication tables. The products are written on tiles and turned over. On each turn, a player picks up a tile and places it correctly on the board. The first player to place a tile that shares three complete sides with other tiles is the winner. Tina and Jared are working with factors five through nine while Lori and Tommy focus on two through six. (See Figure 5–3.)

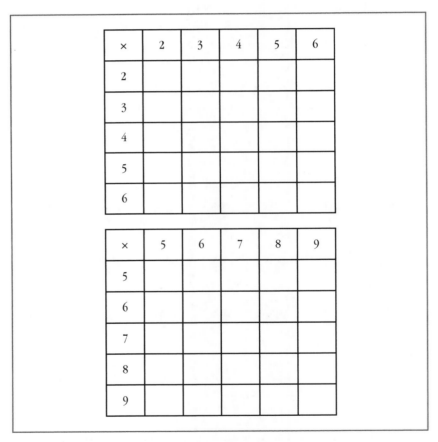

×	2	3	4	5	6
2					
3					
4					
5					
6					

×	5	6	7	8	9
5					
6					
7					
8					
9					

Figure 5–3. Two levels of board games for practicing multiplication facts.

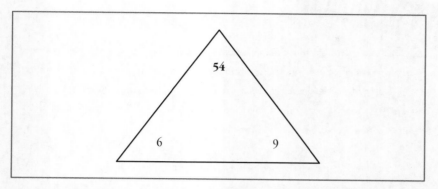

Figure 5–4. Triangle fact card showing all three numbers in a fact family.

Interpersonal Intelligence: Exchanging Triangle Fact Cards

Janet and Cassandra are connecting their multiplication and division facts. Together with their teacher, they have each identified ten facts that they want to practice. They then make their own fact cards for these examples. The teacher has shown them how to make triangle fact cards. (See Figure 5–4.) Triangle fact cards help students to connect the three numbers. The goal is for them to identify the correct number, no matter which one is missing. The two girls exchange fact cards and take turns covering up one of the corner numbers for their partner to recall. As the teacher checks on them, she hears Janet giving Cassandra a hint. "Think about ten times six," Janet suggests when Cassandra struggles with nine times six.

For another example of a multiple intelligences activity in a fourth-grade classroom, see the activity *Graph Your Intelligences* in Chapter 8, page 270.

See *Graph Your Intelligences*, Chapter 8, page 270.

Second-Grade Class: Choose Your Center

Ms. Cocuzzo, a second-grade teacher, returns to her second year of teaching with an interest in tapping into students' multiple intelligences. She is particularly drawn by the notion of having students evaluate their own best ways to learn and to take responsibility for their own learning by choosing instructional opportunities accordingly. She identifies four intelligences that she believes will tap all of her students' strengths (linguistic, spatial, musical, and interpersonal) and creates a station or center for each one. Her reflection captures this interest and gives more details.

This year, one of my goals in teaching second grade is to think about how I can learn more about my students and involve them in setting goals for themselves. I went to a workshop last summer and was intrigued by multiple intelligences. If I learn more about my second graders' intelligences, how can I use this knowledge to plan lessons?

> **If I learn more about my second graders' intelligences, how can I use this knowledge to plan lessons?**

Last year was my first year of teaching and what I loved the most was when the children were having fun while learning. When they said they were bored or refused to do an activity, I wondered why. I followed the curriculum and spent hours thinking about different ways to make the lessons interesting. I never thought about developing lessons best suited to their intelligences. I knew that some kids liked to move a lot and others liked music or reading books, but I didn't know what way each of my students thought they learned best. I wondered if anyone ever asked them.

This year I started the year by interviewing each student and asking them about their interests and what they liked best about school. I used this information in my planning. I learned that there were four multiple intelligences that stood out for most of my students: linguistic, spatial, musical, and interpersonal. With this understanding, I wanted to offer my students a choice of how they thought they would learn best.

In second grade, students need to add and subtract to twenty fluently, so I designed four activities best suited to their multiple intelligences and then asked them to take responsibility for making decisions about how they wanted to learn about doubles. The students understood that learning about doubles would help them to learn their basic facts. I posed four questions to the whole group on posters:

1. Do you like to read and create your own stories about memorable characters?
2. Do you like to write, sing, or listen to music?
3. Do you like to work with a partner and play games?
4. Do you like to see patterns and pictures when you're thinking about learning math?

I then said, "If you answer yes to any of the questions, then that is the activity for you." The children loved choosing their own activity and were more motivated than usual to stick with the task. They could write a story about a character using a double combination, sing a song about doubles, play a game, or see a pattern on dominoes of doubles. They were doing activities that worked best for them and it was great to see.

By considering multiple intelligences in my lesson design, I provided an opportunity for all students to shine and to do their best work in a style that's comfortable for them, where they could feel successful. I am hopeful that the more they learn about themselves as learners, the more they will be supported in achieving their goals and taking responsibility for their own learning.

VIDEO CLIP 5.1

Tapping Into Multiple Intelligences: Choose Your Center

In this video clip we see Ms. Cocuzzo carry out her lesson plan designed to tap into the multiple intelligences of her second graders. Read Ms. Cocuzzo's reflection above before watching the video.

As you watch the clip, consider:

1. What do you notice about how Ms. Cocuzzo structures the lesson to incorporate multiple intelligences?
2. How is Ms. Cocuzzo giving students choice? Why is this important?
3. Though the students are involved in different activities, they are all focused on the doubles strategy. What do you see as the advantages of this instructional structure?
4. In your classroom, how have you found ways to support your students' multiple intelligences?

First- and Second-Grade Combination Class: *Facts I Know!*, *Making Progress*, and *Too Hard Right Now*

A teacher in a combination first- and second-grade classroom has her students engaged in a variety of activities focused on addition. When the teacher believes that the students are working and engaged, she calls a specific small group to meet with her at a table at the back of the room. The students are aware that their goal is to become confident in their abilities with addition

> ### Lesson Idea!
> **Focus:** Addition facts
>
> **Domain:** Operations and algebraic thinking
>
> **Context:** Sorting facts and self assessment
>
> See Lesson Idea 5.1, page 181.

facts as an extension of the other practice work they have been doing. The teacher also wants these students to feel more comfortable and flexible with numbers. She believes that efficient retrieval of these facts will help achieve these goals.

The teacher has created a set of fact cards for these students and she asks that the children bring the cards to the table. During the past few weeks, the students have sorted their fact cards into three labeled envelopes: *Facts I Know!*, *Making Progress*, and *Too Hard Right Now*. Initial conversations centered on the purpose of knowing addition facts and ways to learn them. Time was also spent deciding how to label each envelope. Today the group is meeting to discuss and honor the progress these students have been making with moving more cards into the first two envelopes.

As you learn from her reflection that follows, this teacher has thought long and hard about how to approach basic facts in a way that supports differentiated learning, particularly for students who may not naturally link one fact to another.

TEACHER REFLECTION

> I don't want to overmanage development of this skill, but rather encourage children to begin to take ownership of their learning of basic facts.

I've tried various approaches and activities throughout the years to encourage my students to learn their basic addition facts. I don't want to overmanage development of this skill, but rather encourage children to begin to take ownership of their learning of basic facts. I've noticed over time that my strongest and most self-assured math students have basic facility with number facts. Sometimes facts have been learned through memorization, but mostly it seems to me that these children just feel comfortable playing with numbers and building a repertoire of known facts or ways to know them. I wanted to let all of my students in on what seems to be their secrets. I want to give all children an opportunity to work with facts as individual pieces of knowledge or offer children an opportunity to analyze the facts by chunking or grouping them in some meaningful way.

Using the envelopes to sort the fact cards is one step in this process. I also ask my students to think together about the necessity of basic facts; I begin to help them see facts as a tool that can help them in the future. I recognize that many of my students are still developing the idea of what it means to add, and thus memorizing basic facts may feel too premature, whereas other students delight in reciting facts they know. Even my kindergarten colleagues tell me that some of their students are eager to share that two and two is four and five and five is ten. It seems to me that using the facts that are "easy" to know or recall can be the stepping-stones to future success in this area. The challenge is to have all students be able to identify facts "they know" and take pride in this knowledge first. Then, over time, we can help them increase the number of known facts.

Using the envelopes as benchmarks for learning is a tangible way for this teacher to help her students take ownership of their learning. It also allows for variability in the manner in which students make strides in learning their addition facts. The teacher moves slowly with the children, establishing the idea that each individual student makes his or her own decisions about what is too hard right now, is something that is currently being worked on, or is established and can be called up with ease.

There are times when the students in the small group all agree that a fact is easy to recall, as in 1 + 1 or 2 + 2, or the opposite, that 7 + 6 is one of the hardest. Then again, one child comments, "That one is easy for me, because six and six is twelve and one more is thirteen." Individual strategies are always acknowledged while trying not to make one idea more celebrated than the next. A strategy that works for one student, or many, more than likely does not work for all. The goal is to increase student learning and facility with addition facts, not to cause children to feel inferior about their ideas.

Initially, when the students look at the fact cards and talk about what they notice, they sort the cards in a variety of ways. Some children group them by common addends—for example, all facts with an addend of 5. Other students put facts together that had the same sum. Other students put all of the double facts, such as 6 + 6, together. The idea is to tap into what makes sense for each child and not to set an explicit way of organizing the cards. The teacher also makes preliminary decisions about how to group students for this work and how many of the basic fact cards to use at one time.

The notion of using the labeled envelopes is the next step; students talk as a whole class about how to sort the facts. They are asked to think about

> Individual strategies are always acknowledged while trying not to make one idea more celebrated than the next. A strategy that works for one student, or many, more than likely does not work for all.

this in the same way that they might choose a book for reading. They are used to the idea that some things are easy, that some things feel ready to be worked on, and that some things feel too hard. Selecting reading texts in this way is familiar to this class and it is another example of where differentiation is tightly woven into the fabric of the classroom environment. These first- and second-graders assume that everyone is not working on the same ideas in the same way.

In the small group, students are asked to review the cards in their *Facts I Know!* envelope first. They begin by working with the cards on their own. When they feel comfortable, they ask a classmate if they want to review together. Some pairs compare cards and talk about how they know the fact; others like to "test" each other. Next they look at the cards in the *Making Progress* envelope. Students are encouraged to think about the facts they know to help them with this next set.

Ricardo shares, "Wow! I can move these cards! When we were using our cards the other day I tried to think about all the cards that use a four. I first added two, because I know all the ones with a two and then I added two more, since I already know this. So, it's really like eight plus four is eight plus two is ten and ten and two makes twelve. I'm not super fast, but I know I know them!"

"This one used to be too hard for me," Miranda offers while looking at 3 + 8. She continues, "I know I can count up, but counting on eight took too long and sometimes I missed one or counted too many. I might get ten or twelve as the answer. I made a challenge for myself to just remember that three and eight make eleven. I kept saying it over and over in my mind." The notion that once something was too hard and now it is not is a very powerful step in learning. Seeing the cards as fluid, and that movement from one envelope to another is a form of progress, is another tangible aspect of this activity.

Engage Multiple Senses

Although multiple intelligences identify eight intelligences, multiple senses focus on the senses: visual, auditory, and kinesthetic. Both types are important in differentiating your instruction. Being strategic and mindful of the purpose of the activities in which you ask your students to engage helps them to make powerful instructional choices. Having some control over their learning helps children to be more powerful learners. As you learn from the teacher reflection on the next page, when you try to remember something, it is helpful to have several senses engaged.

The integration of multisensory activities in the classroom is essential, regardless of whether it is related to memory. Technology provides myriad ways to offer visual, auditory, and kinesthetic learning experiences to your

Last summer I read *Differentiation through Learning Styles and Memory* by Marilee Sprenger [2003] for a course I was taking. It really made me think about memory. One part of the book that really struck me involved not being sure about whether we have turned off something. I can't remember if it was an iron or a stove in the example, but I remember the suggestion was to use all of the senses. Our eyes can see the dial move and our fingers are touching it, but we are not using our auditory memory. Just saying something like, "I am turning the iron off now" can really make a difference! I began to think more about how I could improve my ability to remember things. I started looking at the keypad when I wanted to memorize a telephone number. Making a visual pattern of the numbers was much easier for me than just remembering what I heard the information operator say or what I saw in a phone book.

Next I began to think about my students and how challenging it is for some of them to learn their basic facts. I wondered if I was including enough alternative ways for them to practice their memory skills. This year I have made practice time more varied. The students have more of a choice in how they practice, and I try to make sure that, over time, visual, auditory, and kinesthetic memory are involved. It seems to be helping. Just yesterday, Willy asked me if we could add another practice time to our week!

> "This year I have made practice time more varied. The students have more of a choice in how they practice, and I try to make sure that, over time, visual, auditory, and kinesthetic memory are involved. It seems to be helping.

students. The prevalence of smaller and less expensive phones, e-readers, tablets, and computers increases the likelihood that students have access to these tools in school or at home. The following are examples of ways teachers can include technology to provide multisensory learning.

Technology-Based Ways That Provide Multisensory Learning

- Tap into some students' interest in games that can motivate students to practice skills and perform efficiently.
- Use e-books that are interactive.
- Take advantage of tool programs such as the Geometric Sketchpad, which allows students to manipulate objects and note what changes and what stays the same.

- Explore Web sites such as the National Council of Teachers of Mathematics' *Illuminations*; these sites provide activities and lesson plans that involve dynamic mathematical models.
- Find ways for students to connect mathematics to real-world situations with information available on the Internet.
- Connect students to videos that explain mathematics in different ways and allow students to play and replay the video at their own pace.

Reduce Anxiety

Anxiety can be a barrier both to learning and to demonstrating what has been learned. Mathematics anxiety has received much attention in recent years. Although early studies focused on adults, mathematics anxiety is now recognized as beginning early and being difficult to change after it is established. This anxiety is a major contributor to limiting the number of mathematics courses taken later in life. As a result, many people take only required mathematics courses, which can greatly limit career options. It seems essential, then, that teachers begin to address this learning anxiety during the elementary years.

Although mathematics anxiety is not completely understood, experts recognize it as a specific anxiety, one that generalized anxiety alone cannot explain. Those afflicted experience a severe dread of the subject, and tension that interferes greatly with their ability to work with numbers or to perform mathematical tasks in front of others. It can interfere with working memory to the point that new information cannot be stored or cannot be retrieved during a test. As one fifth-grade student explains, "I usually get a stomachache the morning of a test. I get all sweaty when the test is handed out. By the time I get my copy, my mind is totally blank." Family attitudes, social factors, teacher judgments, and negative classroom experiences can all contribute to mathematics anxiety (Geist 2010). The following pages provide suggestions for helping to reduce mathematics anxiety.

Family Math Nights

Ideally, parents, teachers, and other school personnel work together to prevent the occurrence of mathematics anxiety in the first place. For example, family math nights help many parents recognize that learning and doing mathematics can be enjoyable. The evenings can also be structured so that those parents who have their own mathematics anxiety are comfortable identifying themselves. Follow-up conversations can help them to understand the importance of not modeling or perpetuating negative attitudes for their children.

School Math Displays

Schools should be sure to project a positive attitude about mathematics. Most schools have ample displays of students' writing and artwork. Walls are often lined with posters related to books. Less often, visitors, students, and teachers are greeted with a colorful and dynamic display related to mathematics when entering a school building. Even a colorful bulletin board for "Numbers in the News" can help connect mathematics to the real world and make it more meaningful.

"Safe" Classrooms

So what about your classroom? It is clear that difficulty learning mathematics and low achievement in mathematics contribute to anxiety. There is also evidence (Beilock et al. 2010) that girls in grades 1 and 2 are more likely to experience math anxiety and to develop the belief that boys are better at math than girls if their female teachers experience math anxiety. Clearly, teachers must make sure that they have the opportunity to develop confidence in their own mathematical abilities.

Teaching mathematics in a rote, context-free manner makes it more difficult to learn and may result in more students suffering from anxiety (Popham 2008). Providing rich contexts allows more students to relate to the subject and often suggests entry points to problems being explored. Small-group work may be less threatening than whole-class discussions, and concept building, rather than rote rules that can be forgotten easily, help empower students' faith in their ability to do mathematics.

Math Talk and Anxiety

Overemphasizing oral explanations and justifications can increase anxiety in some students. Such students develop a great fear of doing mathematics in front of others, just as having the teacher walk near may cause some students to freeze. As one first-grade student put it, "I hate when it is my day to do the attendance chart. I get so scared I can't count right." A fourth-grade student expressed similar feelings, "I just can't do it and they all know it. How can I try it in front of them?" Students who feel this way may benefit from writing and rehearsing explanations first, and then reading them to the class. Also, some students may perform better when creating explanations with a peer who will report to the group.

Anxiety Management Training

If you think one of your students suffers from mathematics anxiety or appears to be developing attitudes and behaviors rooted in being anxious while learning mathematics, you may want to talk with his or her parents and your school's guidance counselor. The Mathematics Anxiety Scale (Chiu and Henry 1990) can be administered to children in grades 4 through 8. In most cases, classroom interventions are not sufficient. Anxiety management training usually also involves breathing exercises, visualization techniques, "I can do it" mantras, and desensitization. Working with parents and other professionals, teachers can work to reduce any future concern in this area.

Additional Ways to Reduce Anxiety

The following list presents other ways to reduce mathematics anxiety:

- *Self-talk:* Promote self-talk, which is when students verbalize what they are doing by using statements such as "First I am going to . . ." to focus their attention and to help them believe that they do know what to do. This is sometimes called *anchoring*.

- *Help students recognize what they* can *do:* Build confidence by helping students recognize what they *can* do. Use questions such as, "What do you know about this?" Keep samples of their work so that they can see their improvement over time.

- *Provide a variety of tools:* Keep number lines, hundreds charts, and calculators available so that students can use these devices to ensure accuracy.

- *Use multiple sources of assessment:* Use multiple sources of assessment and deemphasize high-stakes testing. Understandably, teachers are under much pressure from all of the attention given to mandated tests. It is important not to share this pressure with the students. Test anxiety correlates highly to mathematics anxiety and vice versa.

- *Encourage journal writing:* Have students keep a journal in which they can record their feelings about mathematics. Use journal prompts such as the following:
  - When we start a new topic in math, I feel . . .
  - When I am asked to explain my thinking in math, I feel . . .
  - When I am asked to come to the board in math class, I feel . . .

  Teachers and students must be aware of these feelings to reduce them.

- *Limit timed activities:* Limit activities that are timed. Time is one more pressure that can add greatly to anxiety.

- *Choose partners carefully:* For some students, choosing partners carefully may mean being in a group that works at a slower pace. For others, it may mean the need to work with the same partner throughout a unit.

- *Let students set personal goals:* When students set their own objectives, it gives them a greater sense of control, which in turn lessens anxiety.

- *Integrate mathematics with other subject areas:* Some students feel more comfortable performing mathematical tasks when they are related to an area of their strength or interest. A student interested in the Civil War may enjoy constructing a time line of that period whereas a student whose favorite subject is science may be interested in collecting and analyzing data related to an experiment. Students also tend to develop more positive attitudes toward mathematics when it is perceived as connected to their world.

Address Learning Challenges

Barriers, both visible and invisible, are very real for many students. The list of diagnosable learning disabilities seems to be growing as we learn more about how the human brain functions and what happens if an area is underdeveloped or functioning in a unique way. For many students, the level of engagement and pace of learning in their elementary classroom is overwhelming. Although this book is not a resource about specific learning disabilities, we would be remiss not to take to heart the physical, emotional, and intellectual challenges of many students as they try to navigate the precarious terrain of mathematics. It is important that teachers develop theories regarding students' needs and recognize that different students require different adaptations (Tapper 2012). As teachers strive to get to know all of their students, they can also recognize that no one classroom teacher can fully differentiate the mathematics curriculum for each and every student every day. Teachers need to be able to use all of the resources available to craft programs and meaningful experiences for each student. The following pages present insights into resources that can be helpful when tackling learning challenges.

> See *Solving for Why* by John Tapper (Math Solutions, 2012)

Distinguishing Barriers

In *Teaching Inclusive Mathematics to Special Learners, K–6,* Julie Silva (2004) offers many techniques and insights that can help teachers better meet these students' needs. Being able to distinguish what barriers might be present for a student is the beginning of goal obtainment, and Silva's book offers many evaluation forms to help us make these differentiations. Strategizing with colleagues and working collaboratively with assistants, tutors, remedial staff, and special educators is essential. In many ways, each educator has a critical piece of the puzzle and, when all the pieces to the puzzle are assembled, the whole child can be seen more clearly.

The Role of Tutors

As students advance in the elementary grades, parents who are able to do so sometimes seek tutors for their children. Tutors get to know your students in a different way and see them work in a different environment. Ideally, tutors are in communication with classroom teachers, and insights gained from their sessions can inform classroom practice. Consider the following reflection of an experienced tutor.

TUTOR REFLECTION

For almost twenty years, I have been working privately with math students in grades K–12. Throughout the years, I have learned a lot about how children learn and what prevents them from learning. Most of my relationships with my students begin with a phone call from panicked parents requesting help for their children. Typically, the parent just received a report card and realizes that the child is struggling in mathematics. Nine times out of ten, the child is resistant to working with me. The opportunity to receive tutoring is viewed negatively, more or less a punishment for not performing well. So my work begins with building trust and helping the student to feel comfortable with me. The goals for tutoring are to build confidence, to help the student to learn the necessary math at grade level, and to sustain the learning beyond the tutoring session.

One student I tutored was in the fifth grade when her mother called me. She described her daughter as a very social child who can memorize everyone's telephone number, but is unwilling to memorize her multiplication facts. Her daughter was failing math. Sure enough, Beanna did not know her facts and she also was very weak in subtraction. As she explained, "Well, you see, when I was in first grade, I was absent for two weeks and that is when the teacher taught subtraction, so I never learned it." So since first grade, Beanna has carried this problem with her. Even though she had developed her own method of subtraction, she continued to view it as something that she missed and would never master. As for the multiplication facts, it turned out that Beanna was unable to provide products in the speedy way she

> "The goals for tutoring are to build confidence, to help the student to learn the necessary math at grade level, and to sustain the learning beyond the tutoring session."

was being asked to perform in class. She actually had a good understanding of multiplication concepts, but would freeze every time the phrase *timed fact test* was mentioned. Conversations with her teacher helped to limit these tests and, within a couple of months, Beanna was able to retrieve the facts in a reasonable amount of time.

Another girl, Karen, struggled with algorithms for addition and subtraction. In second and third grade she spent hours learning these skills and finally mastered them on a rote level. Then, fourth grade came and, when she was learning how to multiply, she forgot how to add and subtract. She would get so frustrated that she would literally hit herself in the head, asking for her brain to remember. After she felt comfortable with multiplication, her addition and subtraction skills returned. Then, along came long division and she forgot how to multiply.

> She would get so frustrated that she would literally hit herself in the head, asking for her brain to remember.

I once heard a story that I shared with her about driving. We all can feel very comfortable driving our cars with the radio on and chatting with passengers until we hit a torrential downpour. Suddenly we need to turn off the radio and we can't talk. It takes all of our energy to concentrate on just turning the wheel and staying straight on the road, skills that are usually performed without thinking. I told Karen that I thought she needed to concentrate so hard on learning a new skill, that sometimes a skill that was once fairly rote became difficult if not impossible to remember. I think the story calmed her and made her feel less strange. She became more patient with herself and, as she relaxed, she found it easier to remember previous skills. I also talked with her teacher. He agreed that while she was mastering a new skill, she could work with a partner when multiple skills were needed.

In both examples on which the tutor reflects, conversations between the tutor and the students' teachers were critical. Helping students doesn't always go so smoothly. Some students present more complex learning profiles and, of course, many students do not have access to private tutoring. Teachers need to be sure they are using all school resources available to them.

Child Study Teams

In many schools, child study teams (CSTs) are formed as a venue for teachers to voice concerns about the lack of progress a student is making. Teachers are encouraged to share trepidations, raise questions, review student work, and share anecdotes about what is happening in class. Ella's teacher was able to take advantage of this support and used the CST in her school as an opportunity to focus more fully on Ella's mathematical profile and to collaborate with fellow educators about her continued concerns. In preparation, she completed a form about Ella's strengths and weaknesses, and answered a few guiding questions for the pending conversation. In addition, the teacher made copies of some of Ella's current math work. Although Ella may not ever know that a meeting focused on brainstorming possible ways to help her make progress in mathematics took place, her teacher wanted to be sure that she represented Ella in a fair and respectful manner. She also made sure

TEACHER REFLECTION

I see the CST as a great opportunity to tap into resources to serve Ella more fully. Although my school does not require parent permission for this meeting to take place, I wanted Ella's mom to know that I continue to have concerns with Ella's grasp of mathematics, and I wanted to see if it is was possible to have her receive additional support. Ella's mother agreed that this meeting would be helpful.

At the CST meeting, I was able to place Ella's case in the center of a circle of professionals who were all willing to share their expertise to help her. I appreciated that our principal set the stage by reminding all of us that we needed to be respectful of each other's ideas and that teaching, like learning, can make one feel vulnerable. I didn't realize how personally I was taking Ella's struggle in math until my principal said this. I was worried that one of the other teachers might question my style of teaching and profess to know more than I did. Thankfully, this did not happen. I shared my views about how I see Ella as a learner—her strengths and weaknesses, understandings and confusions—and how I thought she was feeling as a student. We reviewed progress reports from her previous teachers and, in fact, her last year's teacher was able to be a member of the CST. We concurred on so many levels as we both shared stories about Ella's learning profile.

I prepared two questions for the meeting. One was, "Why is Ella so

> "I didn't realize how personally I was taking Ella's struggle in math until my principal said this. I was worried that one of the other teachers might question my style of teaching and profess to know more than I did."

successful in language arts and yet seems to be struggling in mathematics?" We agreed that we all felt this was true, but we were not able to answer why this was happening. Our math specialist agreed to come and observe Ella and to take her out of the class for a few sessions to see if she could pinpoint any specific holes in Ella's understanding of mathematics. We reminded ourselves that, last year, Ella went through a series of tests that yielded no finding of special needs, but we also wondered what type of testing was done that looked specifically at mathematics. Our math specialist agreed to review the tests to check for this level of detail.

As the CST meeting proceeded, I could feel a sense of relief pass over me. It felt so good to share this responsibility with other professionals. Prior to the meeting, I wasn't sure I wanted to bring up my other question, but I felt secure enough at this moment to ask, "Is there anything in my style of teaching, expectations, or the curricular decisions I make that is creating these confusions for Ella?"

The special ed liaison for my grade level responded thoughtfully, "Do you have any specific thoughts about this yourself? This must have been hard for you to ask. I'm not sure I would feel comfortable opening myself up in this way. I would be happy to come and observe Ella if you feel I can help at all."

I really appreciated that no one made any quick judgments. I was afraid that they thought my class was not very structured or that I didn't follow the curriculum the way they interpreted it to be. At that moment, I really did feel like a member of a team.

to contact Ella's mother. Although the teacher had been reporting to Ella's mother consistently about her concerns, and Ella's mom had concurred, the teacher wanted to make sure that she had permission to go ahead with the next step of bringing her concerns about Ella to the school's next CST meeting.

In the weeks that passed after the CST meeting, Ella's teacher found that the follow-through from the group discussion added to her feeling of inclusiveness. The math specialist worked with Ella and pinpointed an instructional level at about the range first described by the teacher. In conjunction with the in-class observations by the special education teacher, it was agreed that Ella would truly benefit from a tailor-made remedial program targeted at her current level of proficiency, and that it would be too much of a stretch for Ella's teacher to take this on alone. Because the staff had been discussing the discrepancy in remedial reading and math services, it was agreed that a pilot program would be developed around Ella's needs. Ella would work with a tutor–teacher for twenty minutes, three times a week, on specific mathematical skills. It was also agreed that this opportunity would be offered to other teachers in the event that they had a student with a similar profile that had not been discussed at a CST meeting. Working together, the math specialist, tutor, special education liaison, and classroom teacher developed and implemented a program of intervention for Ella. It's exciting to think what can happen when barriers are acknowledged and time, effort, and resources are used to put services in the best place to support learning.

Increasing Instructional Support

More and more schools are looking at ways to increase instructional support in mathematics. Coaches now work more closely with teachers and students on assessment, curriculum design, implementation, and direct teaching. Some school systems are hiring assistants and tutors who focus on mathematics; special education staff, who often have stronger backgrounds in literacy learning, are beginning to augment their mathematical skills. Many schools, however, still find that budget limitations keep all staff members from participating in professional development opportunities in mathematics or from receiving curriculum materials. To remove barriers as successfully as possible, schools *must* provide these opportunities and materials to *all* professional staff and be committed to success in mathematics for all. Teachers must nurture open channels of communication with parents, specialists, assistants, tutors, and their students. They need to be willing to take risks, ask questions, examine their beliefs and behaviors, and make accommodations so that everyone achieves success.

> To remove barriers as successfully as possible, schools *must* provide these opportunities and materials to *all* professional staff and be committed to success in mathematics for all.

Connecting the Chapter to Your Practice

1. Consider a student in your class who has a language barrier. How will changing the way you teach to accommodate his or her barrier also be helpful for other students?
2. Reflect on a time that you have experienced anxiety. How did it affect your learning?
3. How would you describe your own learning in terms of multiple intelligences and preferred senses?

Facts I Know!, Making Progress, and Too Hard Right Now

Recommended Grades: 1 and 2

CCSSM Correlations

- Add and subtract within twenty.

Time

45 minutes

Materials

- sets of basic fact cards for each student
- envelopes, three for each student

Directions

1. Ahead of time, decide how to group students and how many of the basic fact cards to use at one time.

2. Have students sit together in their groups. Give each student a set of fact cards. Ask the students to talk in their groups about how they might sort the fact cards. Encourage them to sort the cards in a variety of ways; however, do not set an explicit way of organizing the cards (some students might group the cards by common addends whereas others might sort by common sums, for example).

3. Gather students together for a whole-class discussion about how to sort the facts. After collecting their ideas, ask them to think about this in the same way that they might choose a book for reading—the idea that some things are easy, that some things feel ready to be worked on, and that some things feel too hard.

4. Display the following three labels: *Facts I Know!, Making Progress,* and *Too Hard Right Now.*

5. Give each student three envelopes and have students return to their desks or tables. Tell them to write one of the labels on each envelope and ask them to place the fact cards accordingly in their envelopes. Over time, have students revisit each of their envelopes to review the fact cards first on their own and then together in their small groups. Some students might want to compare cards and talk about how they know the fact whereas others might like to "test" each other. Encourage students to think about the facts they know to help them with the next set of cards.

(continued)

Lesson Idea 5.1 *(continued)*

6. As students review their fact cards, remind them that they can move the cards from envelope to envelope as appropriate and as they become more comfortable with each fact. To note their growth, students can write the number of facts in each envelope, crossing these numbers out and correcting them as they change. Encourage students to share strategies regarding how they get better at learning their facts.

Chapter 6

Scaffold Learning

(continued)

Introduction

Scaffolds, a term related to architecture and construction, are temporary structures that remain in place as long as they are needed. The scaffolds are not permanent. Workers use scaffolds to get to parts of buildings that would otherwise be inaccessible.

Similarly, teachers use scaffolds to support students' learning. Training wheels are used when a child is first learning how to ride a two-wheel bike. These extra wheels allow children to ride successfully—something that would be impossible without the added support for balance. These wheels are removed when the child establishes his or her own sense of balance and is ready to ride without them.

When teachers make scaffolding an integral component of their teaching, they develop a coaching style aimed at helping all students reach their potential. As teachers provide direct modeling, group work, and tasks broken into mini-tasks, and access through students' areas of strength, they are scaffolding learning (Holton and Clark 2006). The challenge for teachers is to identify which students need what kind of scaffolding and when.

Too often, scaffolding is associated with less ready learners. Scaffolds are appropriate for more ready students as well. If a task is really a challenge for them, then they, too, need some initial form of support. In fact, Barger (2009) lists "Explain new material" first among her list of ten ways to support gifted students. As you will see in the reflection (page 186), until teachers push their more advanced students, they may not recognize their need for assistance.

Saye and Brush (2002) suggest two categories of scaffolding that they refer to as *soft* and *hard*. Soft scaffolding is the scaffolding that a teacher provides informally while circulating around the classroom and responding to questions, giving feedback, and encouraging task commitment. Hard scaffolding is more proactive and requires more planning. The terms *soft* and *hard* may suggest that one is more important than the other. To the contrary, teachers need to provide both; they need to develop the skills and habits that hone expert moves in reaction to what occurs in the classroom, as well as bring scaffolding to their plans and learning extensions.

Students can also provide scaffolding for one another. In this chapter, we consider scaffolds that involve asking questions, adapting reading strategies for math, having students collaborate, making connections, and using graphic organizers. These scaffolds support learning by making the work more accessible for all students as they pursue tasks, make choices, and solve problems.

> Too often, scaffolding is associated with less ready learners. Scaffolds are appropriate for more ready students as well. If a task is really a challenge for them, then they, too, need some initial form of support.

> Soft scaffolding is the scaffolding that a teacher provides informally while circulating around the classroom and responding to questions, giving feedback, and encouraging task commitment. Hard scaffolding is more proactive and requires more planning.

I used to think my top students could just work independently no matter the task at hand. When I started to differentiate more and give them more difficult assignments, I found that they also needed my attention. It made me wonder whether I had ever been truly pushing their thinking or asking them to be in the domain of uncertainty that is often part of learning. I seemed to have believed that only students in my class who struggled would ever be vulnerable as learners. I now think I have viewed feeling vulnerable as weak or bad as opposed to a temporary place of discomfort that can truly help learners move on to new ideas, information, and understanding. I no longer think of my job as to ensure that no one struggles, but rather to ensure that everybody has the opportunity to struggle just the right amount.

> I have viewed feeling **vulnerable** as weak or bad as opposed to a temporary place of discomfort that can truly help learners.

Ask Questions

 VIDEO CLIP 6.1

Asking Questions

This video clip presents a medley of questions teachers ask on a day-to-day basis in their classrooms.

As you watch the clip, consider:

1. What do you notice about the types of questions the teachers are asking?
2. How can these questions foster students' critical thinking?
3. In your own classroom, what types of questions do you ask that require students to go beyond their comfort level and deepen their understanding?

One of the ways that teachers support scaffolded learning in the classroom is by asking questions. It is important that their questions require students to go beyond their current comfort level and understanding. Frequently, teachers pose simple questions at a level of thinking that requires only the recall of information—for example, "What do we call a figure that has eight sides?" By analyzing the questions asked, teachers can make sure that they are inviting students to engage in more complex and deeper levels of thinking.

> By analyzing the questions asked, teachers can make sure that they are inviting students to engage in more complex and deeper levels of thinking.

Using a Cognitive Taxonomy to Analyze Questions

One way to analyze the questions to ask is to use a cognitive taxonomy (see "Revised Bloom's Taxonomy"). Using this taxonomy, teachers categorize the questions asked or tasks provided to make sure that students are exposed to all cognition levels.

Revised Bloom's Taxonomy

The work of Benjamin Bloom is closely associated with cognition. His taxonomies were first published during the 1950s. His cognitive taxonomy describes six levels of cognition: knowing, comprehension, application, analysis, synthesis, and evaluation (Bloom 1984). A group led by one of Bloom's students, Loren Anderson, recently updated Bloom's work (Anderson and Krathwohl 2001). The group made four changes in the revised taxonomy. They:

- changed the names of the categories from nouns to verbs,
- renamed three of the categories,
- reversed the order of the top two categories, and
- made the taxonomy two-dimensional.

The authors used verbs because they believe that this form of speech reflects more accurately the active nature of learning. They renamed Bloom's first category, knowledge, to *remember* because the term better describes a form of thinking. Comprehension is now identified as *understand*, and synthesis as *create*. They reversed the order of the last two categories because they believe that creating is more complex than evaluating. The following lists the six categories of the revised taxonomy along with associated tasks.

Revised Bloom's Taxonomy and Sample Activities

Remember: Sample activities include identifying, telling, listing, naming, and reciting.

Understand: Sample activities include explaining, summarizing, paraphrasing, retelling, and showing.

Apply: Sample activities include demonstrating, illustrating, solving, dramatizing, adapting, and incorporating.

Analyze: Sample activities include comparing, categorizing, and deducing.

| Evaluate: | Sample activities include judging, predicting, assessing, and estimating. |
| Create: | Sample activities include generalizing, inventing, formulating, transforming, and producing. |

For practice, try categorizing the level of thinking of each of the following questions or tasks. Note that more than six examples are listed and thus some levels are repeated. This repetition is intentional to make sure that final choices involve more than a simple process of elimination.

Analyzing Questions Task

While referring to Figure 6–1, categorize each of the following questions or tasks by level of thinking:

1. How else can you explain what Chad is saying?
2. Which estimation of the dog's weight do you think is best? Why?
3. Invent a new way to multiply these expressions.
4. What is the name of this part of the fraction?
5. Which strategy do you think is best? Why?
6. How does Sally's method compare with Janet's?
7. How many of these numbers have a 6 in the tenths place?
8. What number do you think will be next in the pattern?
9. What is a story you could dramatize for seventy-two divided by six?
10. Tell how rectangles and squares are the same and different.

You can find the generally agreed-on levels listed at the end of this chapter.

Although six different categories are provided, they are not always discrete. For example, evaluating a pattern to predict what comes next requires that you first analyze the elements in the pattern that have been provided. Similarly, to dramatize a story for seventy-two divided by six, students must first remember and understand information about the equation that they can apply. Because of this overlap, it is sometimes difficult to distinguish one level from another. One way to simplify thinking about these levels is to

LEVELS OF THINKING						
TYPES OF KNOWLEDGE	Remember	Understand	Apply	Analyze	Evaluate	Create
Factual						
Conceptual						
Procedural						
Metacognitive						

Figure 6–1. Revised Bloom's taxonomy.

think about them in pairs—remember and understand, apply and analyze, and evaluate and create—and then focus on the dominant level of a task. Regardless of the exact organization of the question, the goal is for the students to be engaged in more complex levels of thinking.

Perhaps the greatest change is the addition of the knowledge dimension, making this cognitive taxonomy two-dimensional. The knowledge dimension identifies the four types of knowledge discussed in Chapter 3: factual, conceptual, procedural, and metacognitive. The six levels of cognition intersect with the four types of knowledge as summarized in Figure 6–1.

See **CHAPTER 3**

We do not suggest that you complete the chart in Figure 6–1 as you make your daily plans; rather, we hope you use it as you reflect on planning across a unit or year. So, for example, when we consider procedural knowledge, we think across the levels of thinking from remembering a taught procedure for addition to creating a new procedure to use. Similarly, when analyzing, we can think about analyzing, over time, all four types of knowledge.

Since its inception, some people have viewed Bloom's taxonomy as linear, and assumed that students could only move to the next level after they mastered those that precede it. Other educators saw this view as problematic and believed teachers held back students from potential learning opportunities because such teachers believed students would not succeed in more advanced mathematical work until they achieved less complex skills. No doubt, all teachers can think of students for whom the opposite was true; students who, by their very nature, engaged in analytical thinking even though they found it difficult to remember basic factual knowledge and thus did not perform well on certain types of tests. Seeing this taxonomy as more fluid can help you challenge and serve your students more effectively.

Questions That Support Complex Thinking

You can support more complex thinking through questions that serve as prompts and cues designed to activate, not simplify, thinking. Xun and Land (2004) suggest questions or prompts to support procedures, elaboration, and reflection. Examples of such questions follow.

Questions That Support Complex Thinking

Procedure
- What procedure could you follow?
- Have you checked your steps?

Elaboration
- Is there another example you could give?
- What could you add to your explanation so that a friend can understand what you mean?

Reflection
- Why do you think a table would be helpful?
- How do you know you met your goal?

Wait Time

Sometimes teachers ask demanding questions and then backpedal when students do not seem ready for the challenge. Too often, teachers jump in after only two or three seconds, without giving students time to collect their thoughts. Waiting longer can yield surprising results.

Adapt Reading Strategies for Math

Today's reading instruction places an emphasis on reading strategies. This instructional focus asks even very young children to be aware of what is happening as they read, and offers them a variety of ways to identify an unknown word as they come upon it in the printed text they are trying to comprehend. These good-reader strategies are explicit. They are talked about during reading instruction and are modeled by the teacher. Reminding readers of these strategies is a way to scaffold instruction. Teachers need to make a similar cadre of strategies explicit for use when working with new mathematical content and tasks. Possible strategies, listed in the form of questions, follow. Note that the key words *connect*, *try*, and *wonder* are used as cues to aid students as they take on this learning stance. Their use makes the learning process more transparent.

Possible Math Strategies

- *Connect:* What do you know about this situation?
- *Connect:* Have you ever solved a problem like this? How might that experience help you now?
- *Connect:* Are there materials in our classroom that can help you?
- *Try:* Can you make a drawing to help you?
- *Try:* Would a list or diagram help?
- *Try:* Will it help if you make an estimate?
- *Try:* Are there numbers you could put together or separate to make the problem easier?
- *Wonder:* What would you do if the numbers were smaller?
- *Wonder:* What might your friend do to solve this problem?

VIDEO CLIP 6.2

If It Works in Reading . . .

In this video clip we take another look at Ms. Cocuzzo supporting her students in sharing what they learned during their work at centers (for a more thorough look at the entire lesson see Video Clip 5.1: Tapping Into Multiple Intelligences: Choose Your Center). The student, Mary, has just finished writing a poem; Ms. Cocuzzo is especially interested in the strategies Mary used to complete this task.

As you watch this clip, consider:

1. What are the reading strategies that Ms. Cocuzzo is highlighting?
2. What strategies do you currently use in literacy that you would like to try in math?
3. How could these strategies help students deepen their math understanding?

This morning I heard myself say, "What would a good reader do here?" I paused for a moment and wondered: Do I have a similar phrase when a student is stuck solving a math problem?

Asking my students to think about what a good reader does has almost become a mantra in my classroom. I model good-reader strategies when tackling a new word or making sense of what is happening in a story, and I have tried to make the process of reading come alive and be more accessible to the students in my class. From the first day of school, my goal is to help them become proficient readers and writers, and I have found it to be very effective to show them what I mean by being a good reader and writer. They are learning steps that they can rely on every time they come to an unknown word or begin to lose sight of what they are reading about. They are learning to stop, think, reread, and read through the word; think about character motiva-

> **Have I been this inclusive during math class if I have not made everyone aware of effective learning strategies when they run into trouble like they do when reading?**

tion; note the significance of the setting; and much more. They know what I mean by a *strategy* and think about what sounds right, looks right, and, most important, makes sense as they read. But today I stumbled as I thought: Do I give the same opportunities and models in math? I think the Common Core Mathematical Practices indicate that students develop this kind of thinking.

I see the strategies we use in reading and writing as a way of sharing tips that have been effective for other readers and writers that have come before. It's as though I have now given this newest group of students membership cards in the readers and writers club. Everyone gets a lifetime membership—not just some of us. Have I been this inclusive during math class if I have not made everyone aware of effective learning strategies when they run into trouble like they do when reading?

Making reading strategies a part of learning for all of my students has given all of us a common language that then allows everyone the opportunity to help each other. I love it when I hear one child turn to another and ask, "What's this word?" and the other child responds, "Remember, stop and think. What makes sense?" I'd love to hear this same type of interaction in math class. Also, I want to be sure that my students know that many of the same tools available to them in reading are also available to them during math lessons.

Have Students Collaborate

The teacher in the previous reflection should remind you that by giving students developmentally appropriate tools and strategies, they have more opportunities to hone their skills both independently and collectively. Furthermore, when teachers view every member of the classroom as a learner *and* a teacher, there are many more people in the room who can help others learn. Many teachers recognize the powerful possibilities that can arise when student peers take on the teacher role, which allows for reciprocol scaffolding (Holtan and Clarke 2006). To help students engage in such behavior, teachers structure situations strategically that support peer teaching and learning.

> Many teachers recognize the powerful possibilities that can arise when student peers take on the teacher role, which allows for reciprocol scaffolding (Holtan and Clarke 2006).

 **VIDEO CLIP 6.3** . . . .

Fostering Collaborative Student Partnerships

In this video clip we see teachers reflecting on student partnerships as well as students collaborating on various tasks.

As you watch the clip, consider:

1. How is each collaborative partnership being fostered?
2. How are partners supporting each other's mathematical thinking?
3. How do you foster partner collaboration in your classroom?

Extend Your Learning: For more insights on students working in collaborative partnerships, see Video Clip 2.2: Partners Working on an Open-Ended Task.

. . . .

Whole-Class Discussions and Small-Group Work

Too often in the past, mathematics instruction has focused exclusively on students working independently, without support. Most of the time was spent working silently on the completion of seat work. Little or no assistance was given. At the end of a week or unit, each child took a test to determine what was learned. Fortunately, learning mathematics is no longer viewed as something that is done in isolation. Whole-class discussions and small-group work provide opportunities to share ideas and talk about what has been learned. These groups in and of themselves are a form of scaffolding. Many learners can do more when the classroom environment is communal. Help from a peer and collaboration with others are viewed as integral parts

See Chapter 8

of the learning process. For a closer look at grouping students and whole-class work, see Chapter 8.

Peer Partnerships

When teachers engage in think/pair/share debriefings, they are using peer partnerships to scaffold learning. The thinking time may just be a few moments of silence, or students might be encouraged to make a drawing, build a model, or jot down some notes before talking with their partners. Talking in pairs can help some students clarify their thinking or gain additional ideas. Sharing happens between two sets of pairs or as a whole group.

Sometimes a simple, "Turn to your neighbor and whisper your prediction" is enough to form partnerships. Direct modeling of how to work in pairs helps more efficacious peer partnerships to develop. Ideally, partners develop a sense of trust, a sense of responsibility to help one another, and a commitment to do their best individual work. Partners also need practice in learning to strike a balance—that is, to be as helpful as possible without becoming overzealous and doing work for someone else.

The Research: Working Collaboratively

Acccording to the research of Gillies and Haynes (2011), students taught how to work collaboratively on common tasks are more successful on tasks that require higher order thinking. They suggest students be taught how to:

- present their thinking,
- negotiate different points of view, and
- develop criteria for presenting arguments.

As a teacher, you need to model these behaviors and make sure students know that these skills are valued.

Sometimes, when more independent work is preferred, teachers suggest that math partners sit across from one another rather than in the adjacent position usually preferred for reading partners. Materials can be placed between the students. The amount of shared text is much less than when reading a story, and placing written directions between partners often is adequate. Depending on seating flexibility, you may want students to read tasks side by side first and then assume their working positions. The following list summarizes other strategies that you can use to foster collaboration among partners.

Strategies to Foster Collaborative Partnerships

- Give partners more than one problem to solve, but only one pencil. Have the partners trade the pencil between problems so that they take turns being the recorder.

- Have pairs alternate between the tasks of (1) recording the work—list, picture, or computation—and (2) writing the explanation.

- Direct students to complete work and written explanations separately and then exchange their products for feedback, the same way they might trade stories they have written.

- Assign one pair of students to work with another pair after work has been completed. Have each pair rehearse the presentation of their work to the other pair, in preparation for a presentation to the larger group.

- Have individual students describe their work to their partner. The partner then presents the work to the larger group.

Early during the year, teachers can help students practice how to be helpful to their partners by asking such questions as, "If your partner didn't know nine times eight, what hint could you give to help?" Over time, a list of partner behaviors can be posted on a chart so everyone can see it.

How to Support Your Partner in Thinking About Mathematics

- Ask questions.
- Don't tell answers.
- Give hints.
- Respect each other.
- Listen attentively.
- Each take responsibility for learning.

I have been trying to find more effective ways for my kindergarteners to develop skills and the right attitudes for working collaboratively by giving them practice in supporting each other while working in pairs or small groups. One way I have chosen to do this is to set out more games that provide practice, rather than giving them worksheets to complete independently. I have found that playing a game together naturally elicits conversation, which in turn supports learning.

Just the other day, Carmen, Brian, Rachel, and Ezra were playing the commercial board game *Hi Ho! Cherry-O*, produced by Milton Bradley. I wanted to hear their conversation, but I also knew from experience that if I got too close, they would try to pull me into their play. I tried to be unobtrusive, but still hovered nearby.

As I watched and listened, I saw them take turns, find ways to reconcile if they did not agree about the rules, and support each other if someone made a counting error. They were also beginning to show more compassion when one child, Ezra, spun the icon of the tipped-over cherry basket three times in a row. This meant that he had to return all of his cherries to his tree three times.

"Why do I always get that?" Ezra bemoaned.

Carmen tried to console his friend. He said, "Any of us could get it, but I think it's not fair that you have it lots of times."

"I think it's better to get it three times together than to get it once, then get more cherries and then spin it again," Rachel added.

I was very impressed by this interaction, and in particular by Rachel's sense that to take away all from none was better in this game than taking away all from some. I am not sure she realized the mathematical power behind her statement, but I was quite taken with her thinking.

I have also been impressed with the carryover of this type of work. Today I noticed Brian standing by our class survey board. He seemed to have a plan, although he was not really doing anything. "Brian," I asked, "what are you thinking about?"

"Oh, I'm waiting for Ezra. He's going to read the survey question for me so I can write my name. I know he's a good reader, and he won't tell me how to answer. He lets me figure out my own idea." This simple interaction made

> "
> As I watched and listened, I saw them take turns, find ways to reconcile if they did not agree about the rules, and support each other if someone made a counting error.
> "

Make Connections

Making connections is another way to scaffold learning. Students learn more easily when they connect what is to be learned to something they already know. Two ways to do this are outlined next.

KWL Charts

The fact that students learn more easily when they connect what is to be learned to something they already know is one of the reasons that KWL or KWHL charts are popular. By completing the K or *know* section of the chart, students are establishing their own understanding of the topic. They are also providing their teacher with preassessment data. By declaring what they *want to learn* (W), they are providing input to their curriculum. When they complete the *how* section (H), students are able to indicate how they would like to learn more about the topic. The final section (L) allows them to summarize what they *have learned* and to reconnect to their original knowledge base by comparing the columns. An initial chart that fifth-grade students generated for geometry is shown in Figure 6–2 (p. 198). Their teacher encourages them to identify what they want to learn in the form of a question. She believes that the question format helps students to recognize the investigative nature of learning.

The Real World

Making a connection or an analogy to something that is already known or is within a familiar real-world context helps students make sense of new ideas and gain access to curriculum that would otherwise be too difficult. One fifth-grade teacher, particularly concerned about the lack of connections her students are making among fractions, decimals, and percents, feels that "they are doing what I call 'school math,' but not making any connections to their own life and, therefore, not really internalizing the mathematics they are learning." She decides to work with the students to create a blog about

KNOW	WANT TO LEARN	HOW	LEARNED
Right, acute, obtuse	Why were names chosen?	Look online.	
Acute is less than 90 degrees. Obtuse in more than 90 degrees.	Who invented the protractor? When were angles first measured?	Look online.	
2D is flat and 3D is popping out.	How do the shapes fit a soccer ball?	Try to make one or take it apart.	
There are lots of shapes in math, art, and the world.	What shapes are used most?	Take a walk through the city.	
Parallel lines don't touch. Perpendicular lines form right angles.	Why don't parallel lines touch?	Find pictures of parallel and perpendicular lines.	

Figure 6–2. KWHL Chart for geometry.

real-life connections and these topics. Titled, "Don't Be a Fool; Do Math out of School," the blog is created in Google Drive so that all students can contribute if they wish. Students are given points for homework if they add an example to the blog that shows how fifth graders think about fractions, decimals, and percents outside of class. Examples students have provided to similar collections over the years include the following.

Student Contributions to a Blog on Real-Life Connections to Math
(Blog Title: Don't Be a Fool; Do Math out of School)

- *Don't be so hard on yourself if you are playing baseball and get a hit 1 out of every 3 times at bat, or about 33 percent of the time. You are doing as well as a professional baseball player.*

- *If you order pizza with your friends or family to be delivered to your house, you need to know decimals to figure out the money, and percents to figure out the tip. You don't want to rip off the guy delivering the pizza. He might make your food gross.*

- *When you leave for school, check out the weather forecast. If it is more than a 50 percent chance of rain, be ready to get wet.*

- *My older brother never understood decimals when he was in school. When he was getting gas the other day he didn't have enough money to pay his bill, so my mom had to talk to the gas station owner.*
- *It is easy for me to figure out how I do on a practice spelling test at home. I can do it in my head. For example, $\frac{18}{20}$ is the same as 90 percent.*

The list of examples expands throughout the unit. Most important, students refer to it when there is an example that is relevant to their work. Furthermore, as students sign their contributions, each idea identifies a "peer expert" to contact for more information.

Use Graphic Organizers

Graphic organizers—visual representations that provide a prompt or an organizing framework for retrieving, storing, acquiring, or applying knowledge—are also a way to scaffold learning. They are often used in the teaching of language arts, social studies, and science. They also have a prominent role in the teaching of mathematics. The more that teachers use both linguistic and nonlinguistic representations in their classrooms, the more they can help their students learn and remember. Graphic organizers often contain both linguistic and nonlinguistic features. These organizers also can offer teachers valuable assessment data (Zollman 2009).

> The more that teachers use both linguistic and nonlinguistic representations in their classrooms, the more they can help their students learn and remember.

As can be seen from the examples of graphic organizers in the following pages, these visual tools can be powerful models for conceptual development or simple ways to illustrate a particular task or process.

Concept Maps or Webs

Concept maps or webs are a way to graphically present relationships among ideas. The maps help students develop a framework for what they already know and provide a model that they can make more elaborate as their learning increases. The main concept can be written at the top or in the middle of the map. Rays or arrows then span outward from that main idea. As the rays fan out, the ideas generally move from more general to more specific.

Students can investigate concept maps in a variety of ways. Some teachers provide a physical template for a map, with some of the topics identified, then students add real objects, pictures, or words to the diagram. One

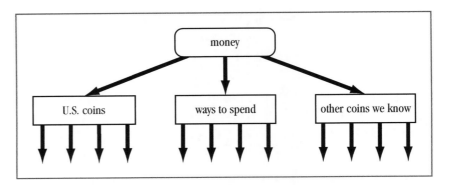

Figure 6–3. A concept map for money.

Lesson Idea!

Focus: Connecting ideas about fractions

Domain: Numbers and operations, fractions

Context: Making a concept map

See Lesson Idea 6.1, page 222.

Take Action!

Let students take the lead in an investigation.

Take Action!

Work with small groups to allow each student to be an active participant.

teacher gave a group of second-grade students beginning a unit on money a map template and some written words to position in the headings. After the group placed these words, students chose their own examples to write under the arrows. (See Figure 6–3.)

Webs tend to be more free-flowing than concept maps and can be used to brainstorm what students know. Computer software tools are available that are designed to help K–5 students create their own graphic organizers.

Fourth-Grade Class: *What We Know About Fractions*

One fourth-grade teacher knows that the students can complete models that she offers them and that they understand the purpose of concept maps and how they are structured. Now she wants them to gain a deeper understanding of how webs are made from scratch. She thinks the best way to do this is to have students brainstorm ideas and then categorize them. During this process, she is careful not to impose too many of her own ideas or organizational strategies; she hopes to encourage the students to think about what they know and how their ideas are related.

The teacher is working with a group of six students at a table. For two days, each student in the class will participate in such a group. The teacher prefers to work with groups rather than the whole class so that she can better access the students' thinking. She also wants to make sure that each student participates in this initial process. The students are coming to the end of their unit on fractions and the teacher is hoping that this activity will help them to solidify and connect the ideas they have explored. She comes to the table with a stack of blank index cards and a larger card with the words *What We Know About Fractions* written on it. She says, "I'd like you to think about what you know about fractions. We've been working with fractions for quite a while now and I'm curious about how you think about what you have been learning."

Jack begins by saying, "It's about pieces of a whole."

The teacher gives him an index card and asks him to write that down while Champei adds, "Like a pizza." Champei is also handed an index card to record her thinking.

Nate offers, "There's a numerator and a denominator." This comment stimulates additional information about these components of a fraction and, before long, the following comments have been recorded:

Students' Ideas About Fractions

- *The denominator is on the bottom and the numerator is on the top.*
- *The higher the numerator the more the pieces.*
- *The smaller the denominator the bigger the pieces.*
- *Fractions are numbers.*
- *You can compare fractions by thinking about whether they are close to 0, $\frac{1}{2}$, or 1.*
- *When the numerator and denominator are the same, it's a whole.*
- *You can write a fraction on the number line.*

The teacher is pleased to see the students building on each other's thinking and doing so without her intervention. Following this burst of ideas there is a bit of a lull. The teacher waits patiently and then Dominique says, "I know that two-fourths is one-half." Once again, a flurry of similar ideas is offered. This time, several students make drawings to illustrate their thinking. Before long, two other important terms are included in the conversation: *mixed numbers* and *equivalent fractions*.

Then Benito says, "I know how to add and subtract them."

The teacher says, "Each of you write down something you know about adding and subtracting fractions."

Another lull follows, but at this point the teacher decides to trigger their thinking a bit. She asks, "When do we use fractions?" There is an immediate chorus of "Pizza!," then *musical notes*, *cooking measurements*, and *measurement data* are also identified and recorded. As each idea is presented, the

Take Action!

Allow some lulls in discussions. Wait to see whether a student ignites a new direction in thinking.

Take Action!

Ask questions to trigger student thinking about an idea that has been omitted.

teacher asks the student to explain his or her thinking to make sure that the other students understand it.

After each student has recorded four to six ideas, the teacher decides that they are ready for the next step in the process. She asks, "How might you sort the ideas you have brainstormed? Do some of your cards go together?"

Champei says, "I'll take the ones with pictures that show the different names for fractions." Cards are passed around and discussions are held about exactly where each one belongs. When this sorting is completed, the students have placed the cards in four groups. The teacher asks them to describe each group and then to write labels for the groups on larger index cards. The labels *Special words*, *Ideas about numerators and denominators*, *Ways we use them*, and *The same* are chosen. During the labeling process, it's decided that they also need to write *Numerator* and *Denominator* on index cards so that these ideas can be in the special words pile.

Students are then asked to review the classroom's graphic software tool and discuss how labels can be created and arrows can be drawn from one to another. There are two computers in the room and the teacher sends three students to each computer with the challenge of making a concept web for fractions. She tells them they can use the ideas that they have discussed already or create new ones. The students are eager to get to work. After the teacher is confident that they are settled and comfortable with the webbing tool, she calls up another group.

Venn Diagrams

Venn diagrams are another example of a graphic organizer. They are often introduced in the primary grades and are used to sort shapes. Students in the upper grades can also use them to sort shapes or names of shapes, perhaps with labels such as *Quadrilaterals*, *Has right angles*, and *Has parallel lines*. The structure of the diagram allows students to note similarities and differences among the individual items as well as relationships among the categories. For example, if the labels are *Rectangle* and *Square*, the diagram would highlight the fact that all squares are rectangles.

In the intermediate grades, terms and ideas related to factors and multiples can be used with these diagrams. (See Figure 6–4.) Note that the three rings are enclosed in a large rectangle, which helps some students better identify the region outside all of the rings as a relevant area.

Take Action!
Take advantage of technology.

Take Action!
Think about related misconceptions when designing a graphic organizer.

202   How to Differentiate Your Math Instruction

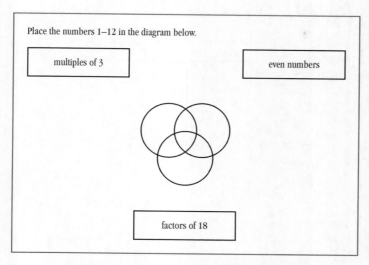

Figure 6—4. Completing a task using a Venn diagram.

Word Banks

A word bank is a graphic organizer that focuses on mathematical vocabulary and supports students' written work. When designing a task, a teacher may choose to scaffold the students' ability to explain their thinking by providing a bank of words at the bottom of the assignment sheet. (See Figure 6–5.)

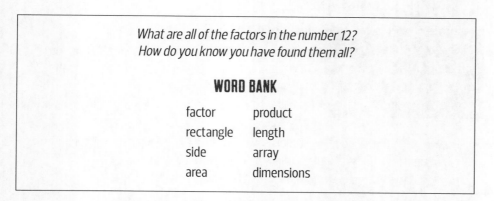

Figure 6—5. A task with an accompanying word bank.

Some teachers prefer to include this organizer but leave the bank empty. (See Figure 6–6 on page 204.) The teacher using this format asks the students to brainstorm and record words in the bank before they begin the task. Note that this form also provides further scaffolding for questions that require students to make comparisons.

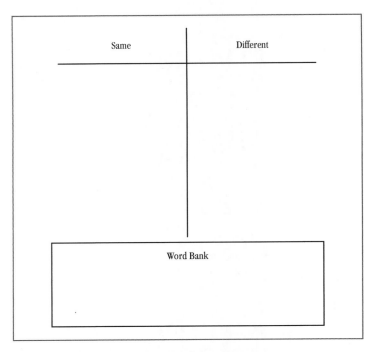

Figure 6–6. An alternative word bank template.

 **VIDEO CLIP 6.4** . . . .

Using Word Banks

In this video clip the math coach Mr. Geiger is working with a small group of fifth-grade students.

As you watch the clip, consider:

1. What strategies is Mr. Geiger using to foster communication?
2. Do you agree that supporting students with vocabulary development will support them in expressing their understandings of mathematics? Why?
3. How does this work support the Mathematical Practice of attending to precision?

. . . .

As teachers struggle with how to help their students respond effectively to open-ended response questions in mathematics, more teachers are considering word banks. When examining student responses, they find that, too often, students lack the vocabulary to be able to address questions adequately. As you learn from the following reflection, students familiar with word banks can apply that knowledge to other tasks.

This year I have explored the use of open-ended questions with word banks. Today I assigned the problem, *Why is 2 the only even prime number?* No word bank had been provided, but one of my students drew a picture of herself with a word bubble overhead. In the word bubble were the words *prime, even, odd, composit[e], factor,* and then the student began her response on another page. (See Figure 6–7.) The student showed just how powerful this technique can be. Because of her familiarity with word banks and the emphasis on vocabulary, she created her own word list. After the student formed her list, she was able to begin writing about her mathematical thinking. What a great connection!

> "No word bank had been provided, but one of my students drew a picture of herself with a word bubble overhead."

Figure 6–7. One student's drawing suggests thinking of a word bank.

Vocabulary Sheets

Another graphic organizer is a vocabulary sheet. One second-grade teacher has students complete a sheet whenever a new term is introduced. The sheet purposely asks for the students to create and record their own definitions, rather than use one provided by the teacher or text. This teacher believes strongly that students need to make their own connections with a term to internalize its meaning. Using a blank space rather than lines for the example

Reproducible 29

Vocabulary Sheet

New word: ____________________

My definition: ____________________

____

____

____

Examples

Used in a sentence:

____

____

Figure 6–8. A graphic organizer used to support the learning of new mathematical terms (available as Reproducible 29).

REPRODUCIBLE 29

portion of the form allows students to choose to draw pictures or to write words. (See Figure 6–8; also available as Reproducible 29.) Students place each new sheet in the back of their mathematics binder and practice their alphabetizing skills by keeping the sheets in order. They can refer to the forms easily whenever they need to be reminded of the meaning of one of the terms. They are also encouraged to add to their pages as their understanding of the terms deepens.

Problem-Solving Supports

You can design several graphic organizers for students to use when solving problems. Let's take a closer look at a few of them next.

Icons for Problem Solving

Some teachers use a series of icons to remind students of the steps in problem solving. (See Figure 6–9.) As a first-grade teacher explains, "A text we used a few years back had a four-step model of problem solving that was

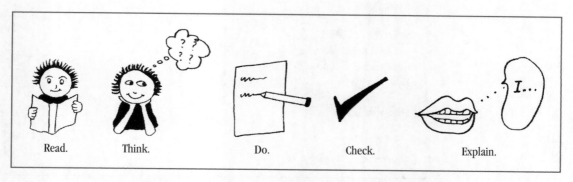

Figure 6–9. Icons for problem-solving steps in a first-grade classroom.

adapted from the ideas of George Polya. My current curriculum does not include this idea and I missed it. I found that it helped organize some of my students and, in particular, helped them to remember to check their answers. Now that we put so much emphasis on students explaining their thinking, I added a fifth stage, *Explain*."

Structured Scaffolds

Some teachers present problems in a way that organizes a student's work graphically. One example is a structured form that requires a number of steps to be completed. (See Figure 6–10.) Sometimes students need a less structured form, with the problem presented

> It's important that scaffolds, even simple ones, be removed or modified as the student progresses.

There are some bicycles and tricycles.
There are 7 wheels.
How many bicycles are there?
How many tricycles are there?

Facts:	Drawings:
Computation:	Answer:

Figure 6–10. A structured scaffold.

Marcia has 15 pencils.
She gives Brenda some pencils.
Now Marcia has 7 pencils.
How many pencils did Marcia give to Brenda?

Show your work:

Answer: _____ pencils

Figure 6–11. A less structured scaffold.

at the top and a clearly designated place to record the answer. (See Figure 6–11.) Such graphics can scaffold students through the problem-solving process, but should not be used with all problems or be implemented for any length of time. It's important that scaffolds, even simple ones, be removed or modified as the student progresses. Remember, the goal is for the problem-solving process to be organized by the student and that the student—not the teacher—take responsibility for deciding whether making a drawing would be helpful and for remembering to identify the answer within the work.

Multiple-Response Scaffolds

Forms with spaces for multiple answers scaffold student work. For example, if students are asked to name all possible combinations, a table can be provided that indicates how the data are to be organized and can provide space for the number of answers the student is to identify. (See Figure 6–12.) Again, such multiple-response scaffolds should only be used with students who would otherwise be unable to work with a more open-ended presentation. Students can use this problem (without the scaffold) as an opportunity to create their own methods for deciding whether they have identified all the correct responses. But for some students, this task is too overwhelming at first. The scaffold, or response template, provides a systematic way for them to give the problem a try, and the structure can help students who find the empty page, or the requirement to find multiple answers, too intimidating.

Key Word Scaffolds in Problem Solving

The importance of providing only those scaffolds that are needed and to lessen or remove them as soon as possible cannot be overemphasized. It is also important to use scaffolds that support robust concepts. Too often, students

The Homespun Bakery sells muffins in packages of 2, 4, 6, or 8.
How can you buy a dozen muffins?
For each way you find, record how many of each package to buy.

Packs of 8	Packs of 6	Packs of 4	Packs of 2	Check total

Figure 6–12. A scaffold for a problem with multiple responses.

who reach the intermediate grades and still experience difficulty with choosing the correct operation to solve a word problem have been told to focus on key words. For example, words such as *take away* and *left* would be viewed as cues for subtraction whereas *together*, *in all*, and *total* would cue addition. Teachers sometimes provide additional scaffolding by hanging a poster in the classroom that identifies key words for each operation, and students might be asked to underline these words in word problems.

This approach is problematic for several reasons. For one, no list of key words can be exhaustive. For another, a term such as *total* could indicate addition or multiplication. Also, as word problems become more realistic and less "canned," such terms may not even appear. Furthermore, this approach assumes that subtraction would be used to solve a word problem such as the following:

Chad has 14 stamps from South America.

He gives 6 of them to his friend Eduardo.

How many stamps from South America does Chad have left?

Some students would determine the answer by adding up from six. For these students, subtraction is not involved. So what would it mean to identify *left* as the key word that maps to subtraction? This reductionism asks students to look for specific words, rather than the underlying conceptual meaning of the context.

The Research: Key Words in Problem Solving

Researchers have identified four categories of addition and subtraction problems. These categories are highlighted in the CCSSM: adding to; taking from; putting together, taking apart; and comparison. The glossary of the CCSSM document provides an example of each problem situation (2010, 84). It also reminds teachers that any one of the three numbers within the associated number sentence may be missing in the problem structure. Too often, problems focus on the number "in all" or the number "left."

Although limiting initial exposure to similar problem structures may be seen as strategic planning on the part of a teacher and an appropriate scaffold, teachers must remember to provide appropriate challenges as well. Otherwise, teachers are limiting the conceptual models of joining and separating that their students can build. We prefer to expose students to a wider array of word problems and use manipulative models, dramatizations, drawings, and peer conversations to support investigations with less familiar structures. Consider the following teacher reflection about the need for continued attention to varied problem structures.

TEACHER REFLECTION

I used to think addition and subtraction word problems were the exclusive purview of the primary years. I assumed my students had mastered these skills. By that I mean that they understood the meanings of these operations. As we explored fractions and decimals, I would just create basic addition and subtraction problems as a way for them to practice their new computational skills. Without realizing it, I was writing problems that always asked students to identify the number in all or the number that was left.

One day, I was talking with my friend who teaches second grade and she mentioned how much trouble her students experienced when the first number in a word problem was missing. As she talked, I began to wonder about my students. I decided to be more intentional about the kind of problems I was giving students. I created several fraction and decimal problems in which the start or change number was unknown, not the result. All of a sudden, my students were

Graphic organizers can also be introduced at all grade levels to connect problem structures. Note that although the action may vary, each *adding to* and *taking from* word problem shares a similar schema in that there are two distinct sets that make up the whole. (See Figure 6–13.) Arrows can be added to the graphic to show the action of adding to or taking from situations. (See Figure 6–14 on page 212.) Over time, students can connect problems to this graphic organizer, adding numbers or drawings to make the connection meaningful. Note that, as with triangle fact cards (see Chapter 5, page 164), any one of the three numbers may be missing.

See **CHAPTER 5**

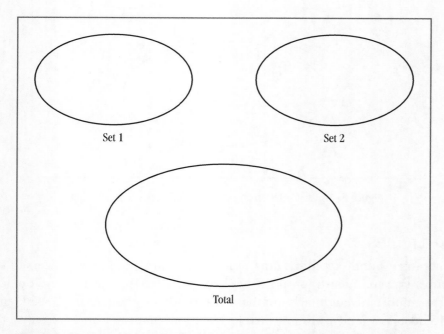

Set 1   Set 2

Total

Figure 6–13. A graphic organizer for adding to and taking from word problem structures.

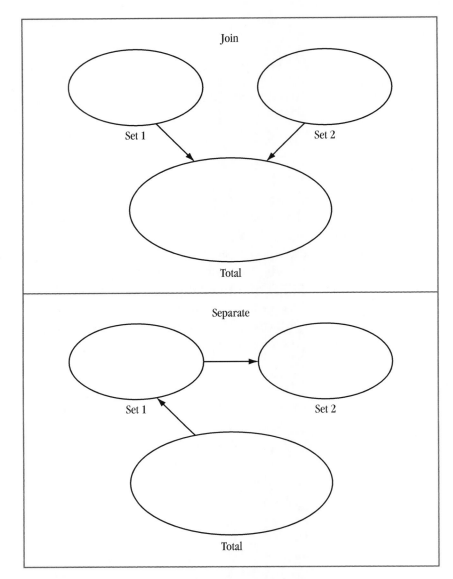

Figure 6–14. A graphic organizer with arrows added to show action.

Ten-Frames

It Makes Sense! Using Ten-Frames to Build Number Sense by Melissa Conklin (Math Solutions, 2010)

Ten-frames, hundreds charts, and number lines are graphic organizers of the number system. A ten-frame is a 5-by-2 array used to support the development of the important landmark numbers 5 and 10 (Conklin 2010). (See Figure 6–15; also available as Reproducible 17.) Note that the frames organize the numbers in a systematic manner. One more dot or chip is added from left to

How to Differentiate Your Math Instruction

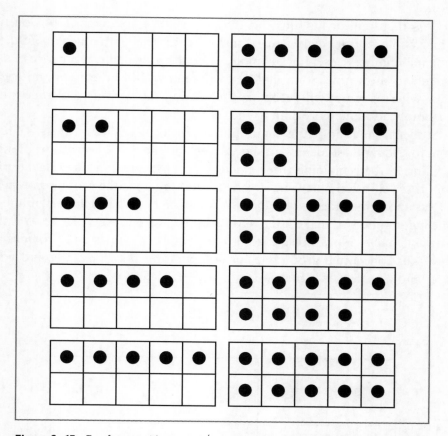

Figure 6–15. Ten-frames with counters (a ten-frame is also available as Reproducible 17).

See Reproducible 17

right in the top row until that row is complete, then one is added from left to right in the bottom row. This sequence shows that each counting number is one more than the previous number, and it anchors each of these numbers to five and to ten. Students can order ten-frames, match them to numerals, determine their numbers without actual counting, develop visual images to anchor number quantities and concepts, and respond to questions such as, "How many more than five is this?" and "How many more are needed to make ten?" If appropriate, have some children begin with a five-frame, which shows only one row and the numbers 1 through 5. Some teachers also use the frames to highlight the visual images of even and odd numbers.

Although students can explore many activities with completed ten-frames, some teachers prefer to work with blank arrays or frames. Originally, a child may "show eight" by placing chips, one at a time, while counting to keep track. Over time, children might recognize eight as three more than five or two less than ten, or may just be able to visualize how eight looks on the frame. While working with a ten-frame, teachers can learn much about their students' number sense. For example, after showing eight, teachers can ask students to show nine. Some children will remove all of the chips and begin again, whereas others will recognize the relationship between eight and nine, and simply add one more chip to the frame.

Students can represent greater numbers by using two ten-frames. To find 7 + 6, for example, students can show seven and then count on six, beginning by filling in the remaining three places on that frame and then placing the other three chips on a new array. The frames organize the grouping-by-tens process and help students recognize the number 10 as a benchmark number. Splitting numbers to make a ten—for example, recognizing that 8 + 5 is the same as 8 + 2 + 3—can result from work with ten-frames and provides an important conceptual grounding for computation both mentally and with paper and pencil. (See Figure 6–16.)

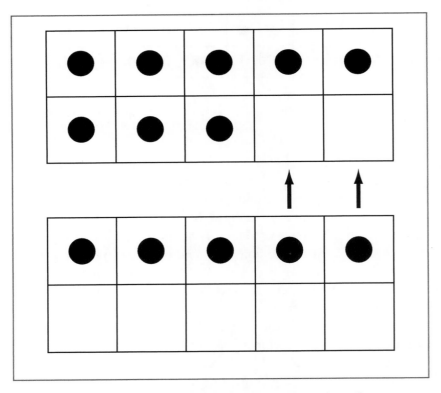

Figure 6–16. Ten-frames and splitting numbers to use the Make–a–10 strategy.

Hundreds and Thousands Charts

Hundreds charts and thousands charts are graphic organizers of the number system. They emphasize the way the number system is based on grouping by tens and can help to build number relationships. The hundreds chart is one of the most important tools teachers can manipulate to help students think about the base ten number system and to build a mental model of the mathematical structure of it (Conklin and Sheffield 2012). Students recognize the pattern of counting numbers in both the ones and tens places by using the structure of the hundreds chart. The thousands chart continues the ten-to-one ratio between tens and hundreds, and hundreds and thousands. It is often assumed that students recognize these patterns by the time they have completed the primary years. For students experiencing difficulty, however, it is often these basic concepts that can be missing or not yet internalized.

Students can create a hundreds or thousands chart with a blank board and number tiles. Once created, a handful of tiles can be removed and then the missing numbers identified. A similar process can be followed using a pocket chart and file cards. Similar *Missing Number* tasks also can be presented without the materials. (See Figure 6–17 for examples of two tasks.)

> *It Makes Sense! Using the Hundreds Chart to Build Number Sense* by Melissa Conklin and Stephanie Sheffield (Math Solutions, 2012)

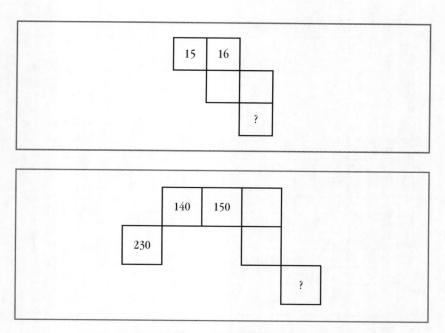

Figure 6–17. *Missing Number* tasks.

Beginning with 1

1	2	3	4	5	6	7	8	9	10
11	12	13	14	15	16	17	18	19	20
21	22	23	24	25	26	27	28	29	30
31	32	33	34	35	36	37	38	39	40
41	42	43	44	45	46	47	48	49	50
51	52	53	54	55	56	57	58	59	60
61	62	63	64	65	66	67	68	69	70
71	72	73	74	75	76	77	78	79	80
81	82	83	84	85	86	87	88	89	90
91	92	93	94	95	96	97	98	99	100

Beginning with 0

0	1	2	3	4	5	6	7	8	9
10	11	12	13	14	15	16	17	18	19
20	21	22	23	24	25	26	27	28	29
30	31	32	33	34	35	36	37	38	39
40	41	42	43	44	45	46	47	48	49
50	51	52	53	54	55	56	57	58	59
60	61	62	63	64	65	66	67	68	69
70	71	72	73	74	75	76	77	78	79
80	81	82	83	84	85	86	87	88	89
90	91	92	93	94	95	96	97	98	99

Growing up

91	92	93	94	95	96	97	98	99	100
81	82	83	84	85	86	87	88	89	90
71	72	73	74	75	76	77	78	79	80
61	62	63	64	65	66	67	68	69	70
51	52	53	54	55	56	57	58	59	60
41	42	43	44	45	46	47	48	49	50
31	32	33	34	35	36	37	38	39	40
21	22	23	24	25	26	27	28	29	30
11	12	13	14	15	16	17	18	19	20
1	2	3	4	5	6	7	8	9	10

Figure 6–18. Three organizational structures for a hundreds chart.

As with ten-frames, observing how a child uses a hundreds chart can be helpful. For example, when determining 7 + 15, many students place their fingers on the 7 and then count up fifteen, touching their fingers to each of the next numbers they encounter as they move to the right and then do their return sweep to the row below—the same routine they follow when reading in English. Others may recognize that fifteen is composed of one ten and five ones. With this awareness, they may begin on the number 7, slide their finger down one row to 17, and then count on five.

Not everyone agrees how a hundreds chart should be organized (see Figure 6–18 for three different organizations). The first chart shows the number representing the next decade at the end of each row. You can then view the number 34, for example, as three complete rows of ten and four more in the next row. Advocates of the second model argue that this placement emphasizes the importance of zero and that the tens digit is the same throughout the row. Furthermore, if you draw a vertical line down the middle of the chart, numbers on the right side round up to the next decade (when context is irrelevant), and those on the left round down. Critics of this format express concern for the lack of cardinality. That is, the fourth number is three, not four, and thus the starting point for children is confusing. If you believe it is more natural to think of numbers as growing bigger, you will prefer the third chart with the numbers that are less on the bottom and the numbers that are greater on the top. These differences point out the importance of thinking about the graphic organizers to use.

Number Lines

A number line supports a different conceptual model of numbers, one to which fractions, decimals, and negative numbers can eventually be added. It highlights the continuous nature of numbers. In the upper-elementary years, it is important to extend traditional number lines so that students visualize the placement of zero, negative integers, and rational numbers.

Number lines can also be shown with hatch marks only. Some tasks help students match a base ten or digital representation of a number with a ones (or linear) model. When the longer hatch marks at the tens are included, they can be used to simplify the counting process. Students can use the marks to count ten at once. Such tasks help to support the concept that ten is both one ten and ten ones. (See Figure 6–19.) Teachers can make a large number line that can be rolled out on the floor, to extend the task to hundreds, tens, and ones. Although these are tasks teachers expect students to master at the primary level, not all students do so.

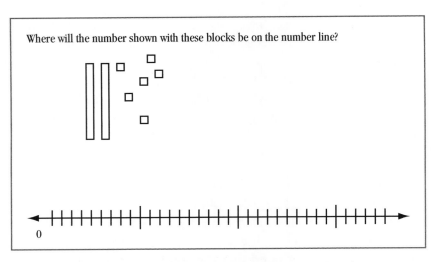

Figure 6–19. A task with a number line that uses hatch marks.

Lines can also be shown without either numbers or hatch marks. Open number lines are simply lines, perhaps with one or two numbers identified. They can be an excellent tool for developing a sense of the relative position or size of numbers. Tasks can provide teachers with a glimpse into students' understanding of the relative magnitude of one hundred and one thousand. (See Figure 6–20.)

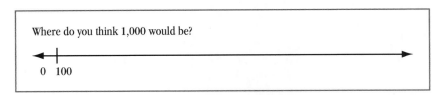

Figure 6–20. A task focused on the relative magnitude of one hundred and one thousand.

Students find it helpful to use open number lines to organize their addition and subtraction strategies. For example, to find 235 + 78, students may use tens and hundreds as benchmark numbers and keep track of their work on an open line. This visual organizer allows some students to understand and remember the sequence of their steps; it gives them the tool they need to manage their thinking. Such a model would not be appropriate, however, for students who are confused or uncertain about the relative value of numbers, because students are unlikely to draw the open lines to scale.

The open number line does allow students to compare their representations and perhaps make new connections or discoveries. Sammy and Manuela

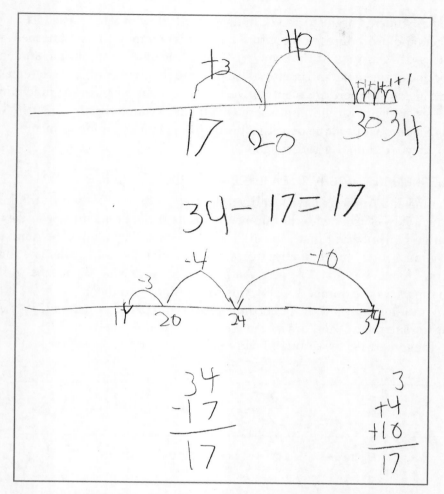

Figure 6–21. Use of an open number line to organize an addition strategy.

are each using an open number line to represent their thinking for 34 – 17. (See Figure 6–21.)

When they compare their work, Sammy exclaims, "Look! Yours is backward!"

Manuela looks and replies, "Yes, but we used the same numbers. Subtraction and addition must be alike, but backward."

Self-Created Graphic Organizers

It is also important to give students opportunities to create their own graphic organizers. Students are likely to remember graphics they create themselves. One teacher leads what she calls a *What Makes You Stuck?* conversation.

She has students brainstorm vocabulary words they mix up, basic facts they forget, and procedures that confuse them. It is common to hear another student say, "I get stuck on that one, too!" After the discussion, she has students pick one of the ideas and create a visual image that will help them to remember. She knows there are plenty of verbal cues such as rhymes or mnemonic devices students can use, but she wants them to think visually, as well. She tells them to work alone or with a partner to create a graphic so memorable that they would never forget again.

Johanna and Anthony's Self-Created Graphic Organizer

Johanna and Anthony have identified the fact $7 \times 8 = 56$. They start thinking about a 7-by-8 array with the number 56 inside it, but decide they would have trouble remembering that as well. Then Joanna says, "Look. The numbers are all in a row. I mean, it goes five, six, seven, eight, but the order is wrong. I won't remember that." At first, Anthony is not sure what she means and so Johanna says the numbers again, this time pointing to them.

Anthony says, "Wait," and thinks for a moment. He then adds, "Let's just rewrite them," and draws the diagram shown in Figure 6–22.

Johanna says, "Awesome! I can remember that!"

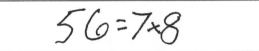

Figure 6–22. Student-generated graphic to remember $7 \times 8 = 56$.

Deidre and Madigan's Self-Created Graphic Organizer

Deidre and Madigan have identified different concerns but are working together to help one another develop a graphic tool. Their teacher has taught the students in this class how to ask helping questions, and they have been using this kind of partnership since the beginning of the year. Deidre announces, "My problem is area and perimeter. I never remember which is which. Mr. S. gave me a diagram with them labeled, but I have to use it every time."

Madigan tells Deidre to get the diagram. When she returns with it, Madigan asks, "What about this diagram works for you?"

Madigan thinks and then replies, "They're both on the same picture."

Then Madigan asks the second question she has learned to include, "What makes it hard?"

Deidre pauses longer this time, but then says, "I confuse the words." Together, they brainstorm what would help Deidre remember. They decide she should draw the diagram shown in Figure 6–23.

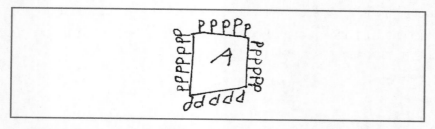

Figure 6–23. Student-generated graphic to distinguish area and perimeter.

Connecting the Chapter to Your Practice

1. What are the best practices you use in literacy that you could also use in math?

2. As you create scaffolds to support mathematics learners, how do you consider breaking down the scaffolds for the learner to gain independence?

3. What are some terms or concepts that your students often confuse or forget?

Answers for the *Analyzing Questions* Task (page 188)

1. *understand*
2. *evaluate*
3. *create*
4. *remember*
5. *evaluate*
6. *analyze*
7. *remember*
8. *evaluate*
9. *apply*
10. *analyze*

What We Know About Fractions

To learn insights into how this lesson is carried out in a classroom, see page 200.

Recommended Grade: 4

CCSSM Correlations

- Extend understanding of fraction equivalence and ordering.

- Build fractions from unit fractions by applying and extending previous under-standings of operations on whole numbers. Look for and make use of structure.

Time

20 minutes

Materials

blank index cards

larger card with the words *What We Know About Fractions* written on it

larger blank index cards

Directions

1. Gather a small group of students (about six or so) around a table. Have a stack of blank index cards on hand. Show students the larger card with the words *What We Know About Fractions* written on it.

2. Ask students, "I'd like you to think about what you know about fractions. We've been working with fractions for quite a while now and I'm curious about how you think about what you have been learning."

3. As students present their ideas, ask them to explain their thinking to make sure that the other students understand. Then, give the students an index card to record what was said.

4. If no one brings up something related to computation, suggest that each student write down something they know about computing with fractions.

5. Provide wait time as needed for students to generate more ideas. Trigger students' thinking with questions such as, "When do we use fractions?"

6. Continue until each student in the group has recorded four to six ideas, then ask, "How might you sort the ideas you have brainstormed? Do some of your cards go together?" Allow cards to be passed around, and encourage discussions about exactly how each card should be grouped.

7. When the sorting is completed and the cards are all in groups, ask students to describe each group and then to write labels for the groups on larger index cards.

Extension

If a graphics software tool is available, discuss how labels can be created and arrows can be drawn from one label to another. Send some of the students to computers with the challenge of making a concept web for fractions. Tell them they can use the ideas that they have discussed already or create new ones. Use this opportunity to gather another group of students and repeat the lesson.

Chapter 7 Support Choice

(continued)

Introduction

Our society places value on making choices. Making a choice involves self-expression, which is a form of creativity. Depending on your access to technology, it may be possible for you to choose the ringtone on your phone, the music on your playlist, and the exact time at which to watch a movie. Parents may be able to choose among charter, virtual, hybrid, and traditional schools for their children. Choice is also a way teachers are able to differentiate their instruction.

Choice is highly motivating and is one way that students can take responsibility for their own learning (McCombs 2006). Although having more choices is frequently associated with growing older and being able to handle responsibilities, choice for students often diminishes as they advance through the grades (Otis et al. 2005). Time to make choices is a common practice in preschool and kindergarten classrooms. Teachers honor their students as learners by allowing them to make choices. So how do teachers make room for and how do they structure choices for students to make across the grades?

> Teachers honor their students as learners by allowing them to make choices.

As you learn from the teacher reflection that follows, opportunities to make choices does not mean that students can do anything they want. Rather, students can be given choices among tasks, with each choice designed to support the instructional goals in the classroom.

TEACHER REFLECTION

I began my career as a kindergarten teacher. I used to marvel at the way my students focused during choice time and how activities during that time led to exciting new areas of study. These young students were used to making decisions about what materials to use, much as they did at home with toys. Choice time allowed them to do something they really cared about, to have some control of their learning environment. When I became a fourth-grade teacher, I quickly realized that choice time was not something that was built into the schedule at this level. I missed the comfortable way I was able to interact with students during this time and I worried that I was giving my older students the subtle message that I didn't have confidence in the decisions they would make. *(continued)*

In response, I decided to offer project time for the last hour of Friday afternoons. It worked well for a couple of weeks and then slowly things began to deteriorate. Too many students were getting off task and, as a result, behavior problems started to increase. After some reflection, I realized that the projects weren't really connected to what we were studying. No wonder the students began to think of this time as a different kind of recess. I decided to decrease the time to thirty minutes and to make this a time for math games. Both changes helped and, over time, I developed different levels of each game to be sure that student readiness was addressed.

Now that I have been teaching at this level for quite a few years, I have found a number of ways to provide choices for my students to make. I look for times when they can choose their own partners, find their own workspace, or decide which task to do first. At the beginning of the school year we spend a lot of time establishing routines and expectations for making decisions. We discuss what it means to make a good choice, and students know they will be held accountable for their selections. I now incorporate choice into my curriculum on a frequent basis. In this way, students recognize choice as part of our classroom practice, rather than as a sign that it is time to fool around.

> "I have found a number of ways to provide choices for my students to make. I look for times when they can choose their own partners, find their own workspace, or decide which task to do first . . . we discuss what it means to make a good choice, and students know they will be held accountable for their selections."

The teacher in the previous reflection offers several ideas to think about when considering choice in the classroom. Having autonomy, making decisions, making good choices, selecting materials, and navigating the classroom are ideas that provide teachers with a framework for thinking about how to design and implement choice in the classroom. There are managerial implications around time, work habits, disposition for learning, behavior, and ways to monitor student progress that require teachers' attention, as well.

Being offered a choice implies the need for reflection and self-direction. Many children are adept at this; many are not. Holding class meetings and individual conversations are strategies used frequently to support students' growth in this area. It is the establishment of expectations, trust, accountability, and security that can support even your youngest students as they make choices in their classroom. As teachers get to know their students as individuals,

> "It is the establishment of expectations, trust, accountability, and security that can support even your youngest students as they make choices in their classroom."

and as students get to know themselves as learners, teachers can encourage, direct, redirect, and applaud their efforts. All of this must happen within a full and lively classroom that changes in atmosphere and mood throughout the day and the course of a year.

Childhood is a journey toward independence and self-discovery. Parents and teachers alike recognize that children need predictable structure, clear expectations, and innumerable opportunities to explore, practice, make mistakes, and learn. Teachers (and parents) also recognize that children need the time and room to practice decision making as well as learn how to compromise. In many ways, offering choices requires more preparation than merely directing students, but the gains are worth it. Students need to learn how to take increased responsibility for their own learning (Zimmerman and Schunk 2001), and making choices provides powerful opportunities for doing so.

There are a variety of choices you can offer your students.

Choices You Can Offer Students

- Which topics to study
- Which tasks to complete
- What materials to use
- With whom to partner
- Where to work
- How long to work on a particular task
- The order in which to complete assignments
- How to represent and present ideas
- How to demonstrate what is understood

Letting your students make such choices can have a positive impact on their learning and their self-esteem. The extent to which this potential impact is realized often depends on the ways in which teachers structure and organize choice in the classroom. In this chapter, consider centers, math workshops, projects, menus, Think Tac Toe, RAFTs, and learning stations as ways to organize and manage classroom choice as you strive to meet individual needs.

Key Ways to Manage and Organize Classroom Choice

- Centers
- Math workshops

Centers

Most kindergarten classrooms contain a variety of centers; grade classrooms may have centers as well.

Centers Typical in Kindergarten (K) and Grade (G) Classrooms

- Block area (K)
- Art center (K)
- Dramatic play area (K)
- Writing center (K, G)
- Classroom library (K, G)
- Listening center (K, G)
- Technology center (K, G)
- Sand or water table (K)
- Math center (K, G)

Sometimes, a predesigned activity is set up at a particular center. Sometimes, the work at centers is entirely open-ended for students. Just the sheer nature of the materials available, or the name of the center, designates the direction of the work. With younger students, everyone may work at a center at once, during a choice time. In later years, opportunities to work at centers are more likely tied to a specific management plan that allows for some choices to be made when work is completed or as part of a rotation that allows teachers to work with small groups.

Mathematical activities can be pursued in any of these centers. Some teachers manage center time with a work board. This graphic organizer uses icons to help establish which centers or activities are available, and it can also be used to monitor how often students are taking advantage of the choices offered. Students can place their nametags on the board to indicate that they will be starting at a particular center. Many teachers limit the number of children that may work at any one place. After the maximum number of spaces has been filled, other students wait for another day or another time. The work board is a visible reminder of what students are expected to do.

Consider this reflection from a kindergarten teacher as she wonders how to encourage the block area as a choice for all students.

TEACHER REFLECTION

One focal point for my students is the block area. I know for many students that this is what coming to kindergarten is all about. They cannot wait to dig in and build. I can think of so many students throughout the years who would have been happy to stay in the block area all day, every day.

I am a staunch advocate of the block area. There, students learn to share, negotiate, and cooperate. Almost hidden from them is the amount and kind of learning that is taking place. They learn about shape, balance, design, height, length, width, weight, symmetry, trial and error, how things take up space, what to do if a block they want is not available, and so much more. The language development alone is awe inspiring. In what they know as play, learning abounds. It is certainly an opportunity I want for all of my students.

This is one reason the block area is also so frustrating to me. Time and time again I see it dominated by the boys in my class. I know I need to address this for the sake of both girls and boys. I want all students to see the block area as a possible choice, but many—mostly girls—do not choose to spend any significant time there.

I asked my fellow kindergarten teachers about this. They were all too familiar with the situation I described. We agreed to set some time at a team meeting to talk about this. During our discussions, we realized we ended up talking a lot about the management of choice time. We want our students to make choices, but—all too often—preferences take over and children have a hard time breaking away from favorite centers. Also, some children avoid trying new experiences.

> We want our students to make choices, but—all too often—preferences take over and children have a hard time breaking away from favorite centers.

(continued)

One of my colleagues told me he struggles with this every year. He said he wants to give his students choices, but he feels he is not honoring this if he makes them go to another area during choice time. We all acknowledged his feelings, but then went on to say that maybe we are not doing our students any favors if we do not manage this in some way.

In the end, we agreed to try an experiment. We thought of a way we could use the block area as part of one of our new math units. We decided to structure an activity in the block area so that all students would have to take a turn. We called them *building teams* and gave each group of four students a specific task and time limitation for their work. The task was to design a three-story building by using no more than twenty-four of the assorted wooden blocks. We also gave them a 24-inch-by-24-inch paper mat to help organize their building. Their building could not extend beyond this area.

When I set up this activity in my classroom, I could not believe the excitement that ensued. Some children had a hard time working as a team, but for the most part everyone worked very well. By requiring everyone to work in the block area, I had given permission to girls to become builders and architects. I was thrilled.

Math Workshops

For more on math workshops, see also *Math Games for Independent Practice: Games to Support Math Workshops and More* by Jamee Petersen (Math Solutions, 2013) and *From Reading to Math* by Maggie Sienna (Math Solutions, 2009).

Some teachers use *math workshops* as a term to describe the kind of activity that occurs when students are given some choice in the mathematical ideas they investigate. The name, as opposed to something such as *free choice*, emphasizes that everyone is expected to work. In literacy learning there are writing workshops during which students may be writing about what is important to them in the same authentic way that writers do. Such workshops may also be a time to work on specific writing skills such as elements of grammar and punctuation. Writing workshops also suggest an ongoing process, one that begins with an original draft and then continues through a revision process.

Math workshops also can be designed to support authentic mathematical investigations while providing opportunities for skill development and expectations for work of high quality. Supporting students in making choices during a math workshop that is focused on learning a math concept is best implemented when teachers are clear about their expectations and hold students accountable for their own learning.

Perhaps the students are studying patterns, and pattern blocks, color tiles, attribute blocks, and interlocking cubes are available to construct models. There are a variety of ways to build choice into this workshop experience. Students could be working on the same goal (for example, further developing their computational fluency), but choose the specific task they wish to engage in to reach the goal, the specific materials or model they will use, and the particular area of fluency on which they will focus, along with the appropriate level of challenge.

Groups could also be assigned to specific tasks based on readiness. They also would expect to be held accountable for their work, perhaps through responding to prompts in their journals or completing exit cards. Some students could be expected to generate patterns, some to create rules for patterns that already exist, and others could be asked to generate models for specific generalizations such as: The number of total blocks is equal to three times the number in the first row, minus five. Reports of their investigations can be developed and can be peer evaluated and revised, much as would be expected in process writing. Even when assigned a task, students could still choose a partner with whom to work, the material to use, and the ways in which the work is to be represented.

In this work with patterns, students would choose their own materials. Easy access to materials is one of many managerial strategies that support learning. As students learn to use mathematical materials and come to expect them to be available for use, the students are also developing the good work habits and positive behaviors that are indicative of successful, independent learners. Ironically, we find primary students often have more choice in material use than upper-level students. Materials in primary classrooms are often housed in open bins or plastic tubs at a level that makes them easily accessible to young students. In upper-grade classrooms, however, materials may be stored on out-of-the-way shelves, or in file cabinets or closets. Teachers must find places in their classrooms to store materials that suggest students are free to use them as needed. Everything should be reachable, labeled, and easy to maintain (see Chapter 8 for a complete discussion of classroom space).

There are many ways that teachers support accountability. One fifth-grade teacher, Ms. Loguidice, spends time at the beginning of a workshop making

> Materials in primary classrooms are often housed in open bins or plastic tubs at a level that makes them easily accessible to young students. In upper-grade classrooms, however, materials may be stored on out-of-the-way shelves, or in file cabinets or closets. Teachers must find places in their classrooms to store materials that suggest students are free to use them as needed.

See CHAPTER 8

sure that students have a clear understanding of the goal of the workshop. She presents students with a list of choices, and gives them time to decide on which they will choose. To further reinforce ownership and reflection, she then asks students to turn to a neighbor and identify their choice and why they made it.

Though the specific tasks are new, students are familiar with the format of these activities. Their familiarity will allow them to work independently of the teacher while she spends time with a small group and then checks in with students. She reminds students, "I will be meeting with a small group as you are working on these tasks. If you have questions, remember to ask three peers before coming to me." At the end of the workshop time she asks students to reiterate the goal and to complete an exit card.

Workshop Choices

1. Problem Posing (Students write story problems for a given equation.)
2. Problem Decks (Students use the operations to solve problems.)
3. Tic-Tac-Toe Products Game (This game is also called Pathways.) (Students change a factor to get a new product and try to get six products in a row.)
4. Close to Game (Students arrange digits to create an expression with a sum or difference closest to a target number.)

 VIDEO CLIP 7.1

Focusing on the Goal in a Math Workshop

In this video clip we see the teacher Ms. Loguidice facilitating a math workshop with her fifth graders.

As you watch the clip, consider:

1. What do you notice about the students taking responsibility for their own learning?
2. In your classroom, what opportunities do you have for students to take ownership for their own learning?
3. What structure do you have in place to ensure students focus on learning the goal(s) of the lesson?

Projects

One way to allow your students to pursue their own interests is to involve them in projects. Projects provide learners opportunities to apply concepts and skills as students wrestle with significant ideas and in-depth study, while applying their mathematical thinking to real-world situations. Some teachers find it helpful to provide a specific time line for a project. For example, a fifth-grade class that was making math games for a third-grade class visit had specific tasks and deadlines that had to be met along the way. (See Figure 7–1.) The articulation of these tasks helped the students to break down their project into daily goals, and allowed the teacher to identify easily those pairs of students who were falling behind the intended schedule.

Other teachers allow for more open-ended projects and thus require students to complete a contract for their topic and plans. (See Figure 7–2 on page 236; also available as Reproducible 30.)

REPRODUCIBLE 30

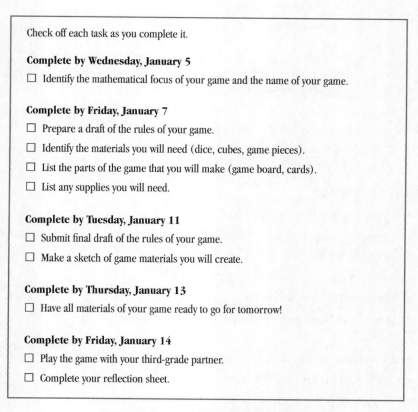

Check off each task as you complete it.

Complete by Wednesday, January 5

☐ Identify the mathematical focus of your game and the name of your game.

Complete by Friday, January 7

☐ Prepare a draft of the rules of your game.

☐ Identify the materials you will need (dice, cubes, game pieces).

☐ List the parts of the game that you will make (game board, cards).

☐ List any supplies you will need.

Complete by Tuesday, January 11

☐ Submit final draft of the rules of your game.

☐ Make a sketch of game materials you will create.

Complete by Thursday, January 13

☐ Have all materials of your game ready to go for tomorrow!

Complete by Friday, January 14

☐ Play the game with your third-grade partner.

☐ Complete your reflection sheet.

Figure 7–1. Checklist for project deadlines.

Figure 7–2. A project contract (available as Reproducible 30).

There are a variety of project ideas that are appropriate for students, including the following.

Math Project Ideas

- Create a mathematics board game.
- Create a poster titled "Everything You Wanted to Know About One Hundred."
- Make a digital book about your favorite number.
- Design an Estimation Olympics.
- Interview three adults about how they use mathematics at work.
- Learn about card tricks that depend on mathematics.
- Plan a $100 trip to the grocery store.
- Organize a group to make 1,000 origami cranes.

- Find out about number systems without a zero.
- Explore toy cars and ramps.
- Build a birdhouse.
- Investigate mathematics and secret codes.
- Investigate how mathematics helps artists.
- Make a model of a pencil for a giant.
- Make a sand clock.
- Pick and follow a stock portfolio.
- Start a school store.
- Summarize the life of a famous mathematician.
- Tutor a younger student in mathematics.

You may want to have students brainstorm their own ideas and then add some other ideas from this list. If your students are not familiar with mathematical projects, you might want to give them a few examples to prompt their thinking.

Across Grades: A Vocabulary Poster Extravaganza

Projects can also be shared across grade levels. As a way to enhance vocabulary development before a statewide standardized test, one math coach helped a school create a Third- through Fifth-Grade Vocabulary Poster Extravaganza. After a few meetings to organize the vocabulary poster event, the teachers agreed all of the classes would get together to generate a list of mathematical terms to be included, then each student would choose a word from the list. On posters, students would define the words, make illustrations, and then write about how they might use these words in real life. The work on the posters would be done in class. Each word could be used only once. At the end of the event, they would have a scavenger hunt involving their posters, which were hung in the hallway.

Marco's Poster and the Word *Equal*

A fifth-grade student, Marco, chose the word *equal* to define. He was confident he knew the definition, but was surprised when he looked it up in a math dictionary in his classroom. After reading the definition he asked, "What does it mean 'to have the same value or meaning?'" (So far he had written *7 + 3 = 10* and *3 × 5 = 15* on the sketch of his poster.) He asked a classmate about this definition who explained, "Well, words can have the same meaning."

So, Marco wrote *baby = infant* on his sketch, added *no = opposite of yes*, and then showed his sketch to his teacher. His teacher paused uncertainly, then said, "I think we better check a math dictionary." Together they found that, mathematically, *equal* refers to a relation between numbers. Marco's real-life connection was, "Sometimes in real life we use *equal* to mean *the same as*, but in math it is all about numbers!" Marco's teacher made a note to talk with her school's math coach about this new idea.

Polygons Poster

Two fourth-grade girls couldn't decide which word they wanted to define and asked if they could work together. The teacher agreed and they chose the word *polygon*. They, too, began by looking up the definition, which they wrote neatly at the top of their poster. They then made a list of all of the polygons they knew: triangle, square, rectangle, rhombus, trapezoid, pentagon, and hexagon. They drew pictures of each polygon and created a Venn diagram to show how the shapes related to each other, given the labels *Shapes that have parallel lines* and *Shapes that have four sides*. For their real-life connection, they drew a picture of a math teacher with a talk bubble that said, "You need to know polygons if you want to be a math teacher!" Their teacher wondered, "Did this mean they didn't see a need for anyone else knowing the names of shapes?"

As the project progressed, the teachers took note of misconceptions and used them to individualize instruction as well as to point out common errors to their students. The school's math coach found it particularly valuable to have a shared experience among the three grades. As she explained, "Often, I see learning happening in pockets, but not as a continuum. Having all the grades working on this project demonstrated to both the teachers and the students that vocabulary would continue to be important and to be a shared responsibility across the grade levels."

Menus

Within a menu format, several activities are listed and, just as if you were in a restaurant, you can choose what to order. A special menu board can be used or the work board can be reorganized to list menu options. During the span of a week, students may be encouraged to try each item on the menu. A recording sheet can be used to keep track of students' daily choices.

The items on the menu are presented and modeled over time. When first introduced, a game or activity may be explored by the whole class. Familiarity with menu choices may also be developed in small groups or with individual students. These students are then given the responsibility to share their menu experiences with their classmates. It is amazing how quickly an entire class can learn an interesting new game, even if it is introduced formally only to one student.

Kindergarten: Geometry Menu

One kindergarten teacher decides to create a geometry menu for her students so that they have more opportunities to identify, draw, and describe two- and three-dimensional shapes. She identifies five activities for the menu.

Lesson Idea!

Focus: Identify and describe shapes

Domain: Geometry

Context: Menu choices including a feely box, art project, and sorting activity

Activities for a Kindergarten Geometry Menu

Feely box	Create two identical "feely boxes," one for each group of students, filled with four to six three–dimensional shapes. Label each box top with the names of a shape along with its picture. Students work in triads. One student reaches into the box and describes the shape that he or she feels. (Students are reminded not to look, but rather to connect the kinesthetic feedback to what they know about shapes as they describe what they feel.) The other two students listen, discuss their ideas, and then choose a picture on the box to identify the block described.
Art project	Place templates of triangles, squares, rectangles, and circles of different sizes with the art materials. Ask students to trace one or two shapes using the templates and integrate those shapes into their drawings.
Books	Collect appropriate shape books and place them in a milk crate in the library area for the children to explore.
Sorting	Collect a variety of pictures of common objects in the shapes of spheres, cylinders, and rectangular prisms (using flyers from grocery and sports stores) for children to sort.
Block area	Include the block area as a menu choice so that students can relate this favorite activity to geometry.

The teacher is confident that the children will readily understand the choices involving the template, book, and block area. She will introduce the feely box during morning meeting on Monday, and the sorting activity on Tuesday. She makes a menu chart for each student so that they all can remember the various choices and keep track of which ones they have selected to

REPRODUCIBLE 31

do. (See Figure 7–3, Reproducible 31.) Students are told that they must make three different choices before returning to an activity explored already.

How choices are organized is a reflection of a teacher's style and classroom management preferences, coupled with the students' needs. Many teachers add a have-to element to the choices offered. In this way, teachers make certain expectations more explicit for students. In some classes, teachers require students to start or complete one or more of the have-to items before moving on to other choices. In the younger years, these must-make choices are sometimes identified with a star and are referred to as *I care items*. This phrase lets children know that the teacher cares that these items are chosen.

Ms. Corpas, a kindergarten teacher, creates menus with two boxes to check by each choice listed. After a student checks both boxes, indicating that the activity has been chosen twice, a new activity must be chosen. Ms. Corpas also provides differentiated activities within each menu choice. When the students receive their menus, there are colored stickers on them. The stickers determine the just-right activities for each student.

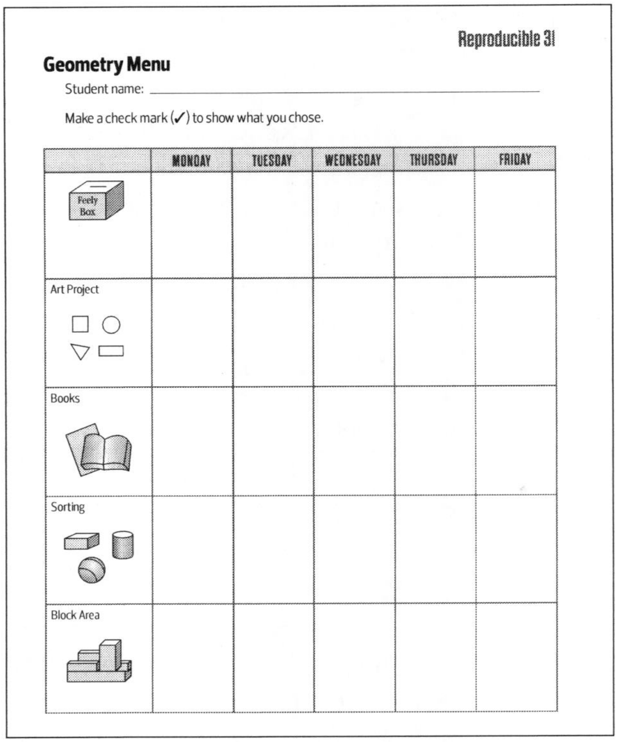
Reproducible 31

Geometry Menu

Student name: ______________________________

Make a check mark (✓) to show what you chose.

	MONDAY	TUESDAY	WEDNESDAY	THURSDAY	FRIDAY
Feely Box					
Art Project					
Books					
Sorting					
Block Area					

Figure 7–3. A menu chart that students can use to record daily choices (available as Reproducible 31).

For example, on one menu Ms. Corpas lists *Scoop and Count*, an activity that requires students to scoop buttons and count them. For this activity, there are two jars with buttons. The students use the container that has their color sticker on it. The color of the sticker determines whether the student uses one hand or two hands to scoop out buttons to count. One jar holds small buttons and the other, large. Students working on counting up to ten will scoop one handful of large buttons, students capable of counting up to twenty will scoop two handfuls of large buttons, and students who can count accurately to thirty-two or higher will scoop two handfuls of small buttons.

VIDEO CLIP 7.2

Working Within a Math Menu: *Scoop and Count*

In this video clip we see the teacher Ms. Corpas set her kindergarteners up for work within a math menu. We then see her interacting with the children at the *Scoop and Count* center (one of the activity choices on the menu).

As you watch this clip, consider:

1. What is the teacher's role when students are engaged in making choices within a math menu?
2. What is the role of the students?
3. How can you use the idea of choice to meet the needs of your students and close the achievement gaps that may exist in your classroom?

Extend Your Learning: See Video Clip 3.1: Giving Students a Choice of Their Challenge for further insight on how Ms. Corpas sets up her students to work with a math menu.

Lesson Idea!

Focus: Use of mathematics in the real world

Domain: Numbers and operations in base ten, measurement and data

Context: Menu choices including noting measures given in flyers, measuring items, writing problems and stories, and creating an estimation guide

REPRODUCIBLE 32

Third Grade: Measurement Menu

One way to organize menus is around a target sum. If the target sum is one hundred, choices worth 20, 30, or 50 points can be offered. Point values are assigned based on the challenge level of the tasks. A measurement example for third grade is provided in Figure 7–4 (also available as Reproducible 32).

Fourth Grade: Math All Around Us Menu

Carol Tomlinson (2003) provides menus with required features. Main course listings must be completed, one or two side dishes must be chosen, and

Reproducible 32

Measurement Menu

Student name: ____________________

20 points

- Get a flyer from a supermarket or a sports store. Cut out items that list a measure in liters, grams, or kilograms and make a collage.
- Measure the lengths of 5 items in your classroom that are shorter than $6\frac{1}{2}$ inches. Measure to the nearest half-inch. Make a list of the items and their measures.

30 points

- Write two story problems about liters, grams, or kilograms.
- Measure the lengths of 5 items in your classroom that are between $4\frac{1}{4}$ inches and $8\frac{1}{2}$ inches long. Measure to the nearest quarter-inch. Work with a partner to create a line plot using the lengths of all the items you each measured.

50 points

- Go through your kitchen or visit a supermarket. Make a guide that shows examples of items with their measures given in liters, grams, or kilograms that would be helpful to use as benchmarks. Use drawings and words to show how to use these items to estimate other masses or liquid volumes.
- Write a story about a scientist or designer who has to measure the perimeters of items very carefully. Include the measures of 5 real items in your story.

Figure 7–4. 100-Point measurement menu for third grade (available as Reproducible 32).

Reproducible 33

Menu: Math All Around Us

Student name: ____________________

Main Course *(You must do each one.)*

- For 1 week, keep a list of all the ways you use mathematics outside of school.
- Interview 2 adult neighbors or relatives about the ways they use mathematics when they are at work. Share your information with your team. Together, make a visual summary of your combined data.
- Create your own character. Write and illustrate your own version of *Math Curse*. Make sure your story contains at least 10 math problems, and attach an answer key.

Side Orders *(Complete two.)*

- Write about how mathematics is used in your favorite sport.
- Read 3 stories in the newspaper. Make notes about the ways mathematics is used in the articles or how knowing mathematics helps you to understand the articles.
- Reread *Math Curse* and solve 6 of the problems in the story.
- Make a photo display of geometry in our world.
- Choose 1 of the real-world math Web sites that have been saved as favorites and write 4 problems to put in our real-world problem box.

Desserts *(Do one or more if you are interested.)*

- Read a biography of author Jon Scieszka and coauthor/illustrator Lane Smith at www.kidsreads.com/series/series-warp-author.asp.
- Make up a song called "These Are a Few of My Favorite Uses of Math."

Figure 7–5. A menu that requires completion of main course items, designed for fourth-grade students (available as Reproducible 33).

Lesson Idea!

Focus: Use of mathematics in the real world

Domain: Numbers and operations in base ten, measurement and data

Context: Menu choices, including identifying ways mathematics is used outside of school, in the lives of adults, in sports, and in news stories as well as creating stories, illustrations, photo displays, and songs

desserts are optional choices that students particularly interested in the topic may wish to complete. A fourth-grade teacher wants to create such a menu. To begin, the teacher thinks about her key question for the menu and identifies it as: How is mathematics used in the real world? She then notes the following key objectives that she has for her students.

Menu Objectives for Math All Around Us Menu

- Identify ways in which mathematics is used in your daily life.
- Identify ways in which mathematics is used in various careers.
- Collect, describe, and organize data.

She decides she will introduce the topic by reading *Math Curse* (Scieszka and Smith 1995) to her students. This popular book is an amusing story of a day in the life of a young girl who wakes up and finds everything in her life to be a math problem.

The teacher then thinks about how to create a menu as a follow-up to the story. She identifies three activities that focus on her objectives, and includes them within the main course section. She thinks of side dishes as ways to reinforce these ideas, so she includes six options that focus on specific applications of mathematics. Last, she creates two desserts, activities that she thinks her students might enjoy doing, but that she doesn't think are essential. (See Figure 7–5; also available as Reproducible 33.)

REPRODUCIBLE 33

As needed, the teacher can easily tier the menu for less or more ready students. For example, writing only one page of an original version of *Math Curse* could be required, or a specific time of day, such as breakfast, could be identified to help students focus. For more of a challenge, students could interview several adults and create their own visual summaries of their data.

Homework Menus

Researchers debate the value of homework (Cooper et al. 2006). One teacher found that homework was more effective when she began to incude choice. When creating a menu format, she reversed Tomlinson's stucture (2003). She gave choices for the main course and required the dessert. She used the dessert portion for problems that would help students retain skills throughout the year and be ready for her state's standardized test without taking a lot of instructional time for test prep right before the test. She called it *dessert* to put a positive spin on it. Her reflection gives us insight into her thinking and how this new way of organizing homework worked for her and her students.

TEACHER REFLECTION

I used to assign homework problems recommended in the textbook we used. It saved me a lot of time. One year, some parents often asked me about the purpose of particular problems that their children had been assigned. Sometimes I could give a reason, but many times I had no other rationale than that the curriculum authors suggested the problems.

(continued)

The next year, I decided to make readiness-tiered homework menus. It was a daunting task, requiring me to complete every homework problem in every unit on top of my usual lesson planning. I felt that it would be worthwhile, however, because once I had created the homework menus, I could reuse them each year with only minor adjustments. I viewed it as a long-term investment of time.

My menus had three parts: information on where to find the problems (which unit, what page, on so on), three "main course" options, and a "dessert." For the main courses, I solved all the problems that the authors suggested for a particular lesson and then divided them into three categories. I created the following descriptions for each option that I thought would help my students make choices.

Key to Options

Option A	"Today's lesson was kind of a stretch for me. I think I get it, but I need more practice to feel comfortable."
Option B	"I got it today. I feel confident that I can do more of what we did in class, plus push a little beyond that."
Option C	"I really understand this. Give me a challenging way to apply what we did in class."

So an assignment might look like this:

Homework pp. 90–96

What homework is best for you tonight?

Option A	Option B	Option C
3–12	4, 6, 10, 11, 12, 30–34	11–13, 33–38

And now for dessert . . . short and sweet!

How many 15s fit in 100?

What does the remainder mean?

As I solved the next week's problems over the weekend and divided them into these categories, I gained a lot of insight into the curriculum and strengthened my own understanding of the math concepts I was teaching. I also discovered that I could include some problems in more than one category. This meant that there was always overlap between at least two and sometimes all three of the menu options. I hoped this would show the students that I didn't have them pigeonholed into rigid boxes of ability or knowledge.

I used the dessert part of my menu as a daily opportunity for cumulative review. That year, our math department began giving us packets of released problems from our state standardized test, organized by our curriculum units. They also gave us the flexibility to use the packets in whatever way we chose. I decided to include a short problem from the packets related to a concept from a previous unit on each menu. This kept the students thinking about the material that we had studied in depth in the fall all the way into the spring (state test time!). It was also an opportunity to expose my students to "test language," which was different from the language used in our curriculum.

I allowed the students to choose the option they wanted to tackle, and they enjoyed this autonomy. In my introduction to the students, however, I included the caveat that I would redirect anyone whom I thought should be regularly choosing a more challenging or more supportive option.

> In my introduction to the students, however, I included the caveat that I would redirect anyone whom I thought should be regularly choosing a more challenging or more supportive option.

One time, a student who normally chose Option C told me, "I was really busy last night, so I chose Option A." Rather than skipping his homework entirely on a busy night, this student knew that he could quickly solve a different set of problems than he normally chose, so that he would still be able to turn in his homework. I realized that having a degree of control over his homework made it more likely that he would get it done. Another student who wanted an extra challenge solved *all* the problems from A, B, and C every night—by choice!

Of course, there was a period of adjustment when I began using the menus. After we got used to the routine, though, things went well. In the end, I came away with a greater feeling of ownership over our packaged curriculum. My prediction that it would take a lot of time to solve and sort all the problems in the curriculum was accurate, but I ended up with a tool for daily differentiation that I could use again and again, as well as a deeper understanding of my math curriculum. And the parents? The parents were very appreciative of the homework menus.

Think Tac Toe

Think Tac Toe and RAFT are two other formats for organizing choices for students. A Think Tac Toe board is a 3-by-3 matrix with nine cells, resembling the familiar tic-tac-toe game board. It can be organized in a variety of ways. For example, rows could offer increasingly more challenging tasks and students could choose a row at the right level for them.

Kindergarten: *Counting Think Tac Toe*

A kindergarten teacher created the example shown in Figure 7–6 that focuses on counting (also available as Reproducible 34). She expects students to complete one of the tasks in each row. The tasks in the first row of this example are to be completed in the classroom. In the second row, the tasks are to be completed in the school; each choice is similar, but they include a range of difficulty. Tasks in the third row are to be done at home.

When working with emerging readers, it is important to make time to read a Think Tac Toe as a class or, when possible, to pair students so that

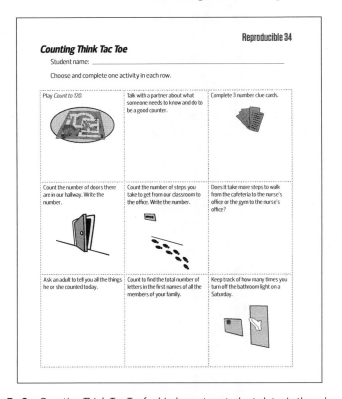

Figure 7–6. *Counting Think Tac Toe* for kindergarten students later in the school year (available as Reproducible 34).

one member of the team is a stronger reader. Icons can also be helpful. Even in the upper grades, to support all students having access to the mathematics, teachers provide opportunities for learners to make sense of the problems before starting a Think Tac Toe.

Fourth Grade: Multiplication Think Tac Toe

Think Tac Toe

In this video clip we see excerpts from beginning to end of Ms. Anderson working with her fourth graders on the Think Tac Toe shown in Figure 7–7.

As you watch the clip, consider:

1. How does the teacher help students to make sense of the problems in a Think Tac Toe choice board?
2. Why is this important?
3. In your own classroom, what strategies do you use to support students making sense of problems?

Extend Your Learning: To see the partners who summarize what they did actually work through the problem, watch Video Clip 2.2: Partners Working on an Open-Ended Task.

Choose and complete one activity in each row.

Draw a picture that shows a model of 7 × 35. Make connections between your drawing and how you use paper and pencil to find the product. Discuss your ideas with a friend.	Your brother multiplied 64 by 8 and got the answer 4,832. What could you show and tell your brother to help him understand why his answer is wrong?	Write directions for two different ways to find the product of 92 and 25 when you use paper and pencil.
Place the numbers: 3, 4, 6, 15, 20, and 30, so that the product of each side is 360. ○ ○ ○ ○ ○ ○ Write one more problem like this one and trade it with a classmate.	Place a multiplication sign to make a number sentence that is true. 63945 = 31,970 Write two more problems like this one and trade them with a classmate.	Which two numbers should you exchange so that the product of the numbers on each card is the same? 120 4 102 / 85 6 8 3 / 3 17 30 2 Write two more problems like this one and trade them with a classmate.
Make a collage of items that come in equal groups.	Interview a classmate about what he or she knows about multiplication. Find out as much as you can in three minutes. Write a report with suggestions for teaching.	Your friend solved a word problem by multiplying 3 by 24 and then subtracting 9. Write two interesting word problems that your friend could have solved this way.

Figure 7–7. *Multiplication Think Tac Toe* example for fourth-grade students.

RAFT

A RAFT is a strategy for differentiating learning that can also provide choice for students. The acronym stands for role, audience, format, and topic. To complete a RAFT activity, students create a product while being mindful of all four categories. For example, as a game designer (role) for children (audience), students might create a game (format) to practice basic facts (topic). Because there is a specific purpose for each suggestion in a RAFT, this instructional strategy also helps to emphasize the usefulness of mathematics and offers students an opportunity to think about how mathematics is used beyond the classroom.

Second Grade: *Telling Time RAFT*

A second-grade teacher decides to create a RAFT about telling time (Figure 7–8; also available as Reproducible 35). She identifies writing times and drawing clocks as key ideas. She tries to think about a variety of roles that might appeal to her students, and different products they could create. She pays special attention to thinking about formats that will match a variety of

Figure 7–8. A RAFT chart about time (available as Reproducible 35).

learning styles. She believes that her students who enjoy wordplay will like to create riddles, whereas her more artistic students will enjoy illustrating a book. Visual learners who are not interested in drawing may wish to make a collage. She thinks the opportunity to reflect on their favorite times of day will appeal to her introspective students.

Learning Stations

Learning stations can be used to augment a current unit or to maintain skills from a previous one. They are particularly helpful when there are not enough materials for the whole class to engage with at the same time. For example, a geometry learning station might include photographs of shapes in nature, items that most classrooms would not have in multiple copies. We think of a learning *station* as a temporary feature in the classroom. We choose to reserve the term *center* for permanent areas in the room, such as a computer or listening center. Many teachers, however, use these terms interchangeably, and that is fine.

For more on learning stations connected to multiple intelligences (including video), see "Tap Into Multiple Intelligences," page 158, Chapter 5.

> We think of a learning *station* as a temporary feature in the classroom. We choose to reserve the term *center* for permanent areas in the room, such as a computer or listening center.

Combination First and Second Grade: Measurement Station

In a combination first- and second-grade class, the teacher designs a new station for her students to use as they work on a measurement unit. She identifies the following three goals for the focus of the unit.

Measurement Unit Goals

1. Compare length measures.
2. Use standard and nonstandard measurements.
3. Select appropriate measurement tools.

From previous experience, the teacher knows that measurement is an enjoyable, although challenging, unit for this age group. She realizes that students need time and repeated opportunities to make the goals related to measurement salient. Her thought is to have a measurement station where students can explore activities introduced throughout the unit many times. She also recognizes that learning about measurement requires numerous materials that can make some activities difficult to manage with the whole class working at the same time. She wants to design a station where a small group

Lesson Idea!

Focus: Measure lengths

Domain: Measurement and data

Context: Learning stations that provide opportunities to measure

of students can work independently or collaboratively while additional learning opportunities are taking place in other areas of the classroom.

Step One: Designing Tasks for the Station

Selecting or designing appropriate tasks is the teacher's first step in setting up the measurement station. She wants the station to allow for a variety of measurement activities, but not be overwhelming for her students. She wants the tasks to be somewhat open-ended, but also self-sustaining, because she does not want to be called to the station too frequently while she is working with other groups. She also wants the activities to feel linked, not random, to her students, so that they can make connections as they build their understanding of measurement.

She decides to identify the following questions as a way to clarify the focus of the station and frame the different tasks that will be included there.

Clarifying Questions for Measurement Station Tasks

- Why do we measure things?
- What do we use when we measure?
- How tall are students in our class?
- Are parts of your body all the same distance around?
- How long is this ribbon?

The teacher prints all of these questions on sentence strips and posts them on the bulletin board nearest the table where the measurement station is located. She expects students to draw or write about their ideas. She plans to post their responses on the bulletin board beside each question.

***Station Task:* Measure Each Other's Height** For the *Measure Each Other's Height* task, the teacher posts a store-bought height chart in the bulletin board area and includes plastic measuring tapes. She expects that students will work in pairs to measure each other in inches. Because measuring themselves on the height chart is a one-time activity, the teacher tacks up a string tied to a pencil that students can use to mark their height and to add their initials on the chart. She also posts a class list nearby so that students can cross off their name when they complete the task. In this way, she can make sure that each child is included.

Station Task: **Compare the Distance Around Your Wrist, Knee, and Ankle** The teacher also includes an activity using yarn that asks students to compare the distance around different parts of their body. On a recording sheet she draws an outline of a person with arrows going around the wrist, knee, and ankle. The children are to find out how long a piece of yarn is needed to go around each of these parts of their body. Next, they are asked to place these lengths in order from shortest to longest and then tape them onto a strip of construction paper. They are also expected to complete one of the following sentence frames for each distance:

My _____ is _____ _____ around.

My _____ is _____ _____ longer around than my _____.

Station Task: **Measuring Ribbon Lengths** For the *Measuring Ribbon Lengths* activity, the teacher cuts twelve pieces of various lengths of 1-inch-wide ribbon. She labels each piece from *A* to *L*. Some lengths are shorter and other lengths are much longer to provide for different levels of readiness. Because the teacher wants students to explore measuring these ribbons using both nonstandard and standard units, she sets out containers of craft sticks, paper clips, and Unifix cubes, as well as rulers. Two types of rulers are included, those with demarcations of only an inch and ones with only centimeters. She looks forward to seeing how students use these units and tools to measure the ribbons. Will all students recognize that the same unit must be used when measuring to compare? What will they do if there are not enough of the units they have chosen to cover the length of one of the ribbons? She knows she will have many opportunities to learn about her students' measurement concepts and skills as they work with these tasks. Last, she provides a corresponding recording sheet that asks students to indicate which ribbons they chose, the estimated lengths, what they used for measuring, and how many they used. The teacher prints directions on posters for each activity. For example, the ribbon activity poster looks similar to the following.

Measuring Ribbon Lengths

Problem

How can you tell how long a piece of ribbon is?

Directions

1. Use any of the materials to help you.
2. Record your answers on the recording sheet.
3. Find the length of at least 3 ribbons.
4. You may work with a partner, but you each need to record your own work.

More Tasks? There are now many activities at the station, not to mention materials, and yet the teacher is still thinking about other possibilities. She could add new tasks if the original ones grow tiresome. She thinks about adding a task on time, because children do not think of time as a form of measurement. The ideas keep flowing until she realizes that she needs to stop. Although the possibilities seem endless, she knows to focus the station on only some of the goals established for the unit. She wants the station to be interesting, but not too complex. She decides that she can always add activities later; for now, she believes the station is ready.

Step Two: Introducing the Station Tasks

During math time the next day, the teacher spends a few minutes introducing the guiding questions for each task and the related materials. She wants her students to be aware of the purpose of the station and the goals for learning. She does not model how to complete the activities, but rather briefly describes each one, making a point to show the materials available and to set expectations around working with a partner and how to complete any recording sheets.

Step Three: Students Work on the Station Tasks

Throughout the course of the next three weeks, the students work diligently on the tasks at the station. The teacher finds that children ask to use the station throughout the day, not just during math time. As the days pass, she notices children working together and many ideas being challenged. One day she overhears this exchange.

Malcolm: How come you got so many more? [This is said while he looks at Stephanie's recording sheet for the same ribbon.]

Stephanie: How many did you get?

Malcolm: I got three.

Stephanie: I got eighteen.

Malcolm: But it's three.

Stephanie: What did you use?

Malcolm: What do you mean?

Stephanie: I used the interlocking cubes. Did you?

Malcolm: Oh! I used the sticks.

Stephanie: That's why I have more. They are bigger. I mean the cubes are smaller than the sticks, so they take more.

Stations such as this one take time to develop and organize, but the teacher knows her time was well spent when she hears students talking about the fact that a greater number of units is needed when the unit is smaller.

Managing Stations

Determining what is to happen at each station, and feeling confident that the activities are aligned to the curriculum, must always be in the forefront of your thoughts. Consider the following questions.

Key Questions for Managing Stations

- Who decides what materials or activity are available and when?
- Who decides if a student will engage in this work?
- How will time be managed? How long will students be given to complete a task?
- Who initiates what goes on at a center or station?
- How will activities at a center or station be assessed?

These questions are among a host of decisions that may be on your mind as you create and implement learning centers and stations, as well as the other instructional strategies for structuring choice presented in this chapter. Let's consider implications for each.

Who Decides What Materials or Activities Are Available and When?

After curriculum objectives are agreed on, teachers identify which materials are needed to help students meet the established goals. If the materials are new to students, the students need to learn how they are used and where they are stored. After the materials are familiar, however, many materials can be made available to students at all times to be used whenever needed. Of course, some materials, such as thermometers, may be kept in a safe place and made available only under adult supervision. In the spirit of choice, though, we recommend that students choose materials whenever that choice does not hinder safety or greatly reduce the likelihood that learning will be successful.

Ideally, station materials can be stored in a plastic tub or folder (without the related manipulatives) so that they are ready to be used again and again. Some teachers also need to store station materials in such ways all the time because they need the station to be portable. In this way, the station can be used in different parts of the room, or even be put away for a few days, if necessary. Ample space can be a rare commodity in many classrooms.

Who Decides If a Student Will Engage in This Work?

Often, teachers operate from a mind-set that all students should complete every activity. This stance may stem from their desire to support inclusive and equitable classrooms. Teachers need to balance this desire with the realization that, to be equitable, each student must get what he or she needs based on readiness, interest, and learning style. Clearly, there will be times when this is not exactly the same thing. All students do not need to complete every activity to support a classroom community. Also, teachers need to open their minds to the possibility that students themselves can participate in making these decisions. In fact, they can often be quite helpful. As one fifth grader explained to his teacher, "I need to work more on my division facts before I do problems like this." Conversely, sometimes a student might select a more difficult task from a RAFT option than the teacher would have assigned. When students are motivated and supported, they often can achieve and understand more than might be expected.

> Often we operate from a mind-set that all students should complete every activity . . . . We need to balance this desire with the realization that to be equitable, each student must get what he or she needs based on readiness, interest, and learning style.

How Will Time Be Managed? How Long Will Students Be Given to Complete a Task?

Every teacher in every classroom has an ongoing battle with the clock. Teachers can all agree that there is never enough time. Part of this dilemma stems from the fact that no two students seem to work at the same pace or learn at the same rate. Many teachers plan for an average amount of time it will take most students to complete a task and then are flexible for those students who finish early and those who require more time. Students who finish early can be encouraged to move on to another activity or station instead of waiting for everyone to be done. Stations can also be kept up for an indefinite amount of time, because they often only require a small percentage of space in the classroom. What is of most value is the recognition that students need different amounts of time at different points of learning.

Who Initiates What Goes on at a Center or Station?

This question of "Who initiates what goes on at a center or station?" begs the notion of the teachable moment. Certainly, teachers make initial plans for learning stations, but they always want to be open for ideas that students offer as a direction for learning. How they finesse these ideas, offer students permission to share their ideas, and give them time, space, and materials to follow their interests is an art. Unfortunately, this strategy seems to be in conflict with some current trends in educational practices. *Coverage* of material included in curriculum guides and standardized tests seems to be of major concern, and student questions that do not map immediately onto an easily recognizable curriculum objective are sometimes viewed as unnecessary tangents. This concern has increased as school systems have adopted pacing guides that teachers are expected to follow.

> "Certainly, teachers make initial plans for learning stations, but they always want to be open for ideas that students offer as a direction for learning."

Teachers do not want their students to think of school as a place where what they want to learn about is disregarded. Often, when teachers stop and think about how they can relate the topic of study to a current interest, a path can be found. For example, an interest in a lost tooth can lead to an investigation on how many teeth different animals have, and a table and related story problems can result.

How Will Activities at a Center or Station Be Assessed?

When an activity results in a product of some kind, teachers often feel that assessment is more manageable and they become more confident in their decision making. The review and reflection of student work samples is an important step in evaluating children's learning. So, too, is taking time to observe students in action and to engage students in conversations as their work unfolds. Keeping anecdotal records is a natural strategy for capturing these moments (for more on anecdotal records, see Chapter 2, page 39); a digital camera or video can be a wonderful way to document learning as well.

See CHAPTER 2

Assessments of activities at learning centers or stations come full circle, as do all assessments, to the learning goals that led to development of the center or station in the first place. Being mindful of your goals—and letting students know them—helps to focus assessment in any learning environment, whether there is a tangible product or a set of scenarios that tell the story of learning.

Answering the questions posed here can be difficult. They require that teachers make decisions that can be demanding of their time and effort. How to make any best decision is rooted in the context of your own school setting and your students' needs. Teachers must remember that these decisions are not set in stone. Flexibility is key; as you gather new information or learn new instructional strategies, you can revise your practice to meet more completely the growing needs of all of your students. As the following teacher reflection makes clear, making strategic decisions is ongoing as a teacher plans.

TEACHER REFLECTION

I have come to value the need for setting up, maintaining, and rotating learning stations in my classroom. They have helped me be able to offer more choices to my students. In my mind, this equates to more opportunities to practice and to learn. After a station is up and running, my goal is for it to be self-sustaining. I want to be able to engage with other students at their point of need or to have a chance to sit back a bit and observe. So, I try to design stations that do not require any teacher direction after the initial introduction.

Because I have been teaching for a few years, I have been able to reuse learning stations as a unit comes up for study in later years. Over time, I have been able to test out how self-sustaining an activity may be for the majority of my students. I know I always have to be open to different learning styles and preferences. I even have to consider if students are required to read or write to fulfill learning expectations at any given point in the year.

I also need to consider what I use to define the space for the station. Have I given ample room? Have I separated stations from other work areas so that

> Lately, my grade-level team has been working together. We each create a station and then we share them. It saves time and, because we each tend to do things somewhat differently, my students have access to a greater variety of experiences.

students are not unnecessarily distracted? Have I provided all the necessary materials for success? Do these materials need to be placed at the station or do my students know where to find them when they want them? I have to think about the best ways to juggle all of these things. To help, I have set an expectation that the students are the ones who know what they need at any point in time and are encouraged to act responsibly on that need.

Lately, my grade-level team has been working together. We each create a station and then we share them. It saves time and, because we each tend to do things somewhat differently, my students have access to a greater variety of experiences.

This teacher uses a word in her reflection that sounds familiar to all teachers—*juggle*. Juggling is part of the art and craft of teaching and learning.

Keeping Student Interest Alive

A final note: Along with empowering your students, providing choice in your classroom helps you tap into the interests of your students; but, just having choices available does not guarantee interest. Any parent who has heard the lament "There's nothing to do!" understands this well. Part of the excitement of making a choice is that it can lead to something new and exhilarating. Changing the materials made available to students on a regular basis adds a fresh look. Having a familiar material or activity disappear can pique curiosity or may even be a relief. Having it come back again in a few weeks or months can also be a welcome change. As one first grader told his teacher, "I wondered where the attribute blocks went. I like to play with them. I was hoping you didn't lose them."

Change the Format of Student Work

Changing the format of student work also adds an element of interest that can maintain enthusiasm. Cutting recording sheets so they are in the shape of a rocket or a mailbox breaks the expectation of the 8-by-11-inch sheet of paper. Multimedia presentations can also create new interest. For example, one teacher created a slideshow on her computer of different architectural styles and famous buildings as a way to illustrate the use of shape and form.

Viewing in pairs, students could take a virtual tour while describing elements of shapes they noticed.

Introduce Topics in Novel Ways

Introducing topics in novel ways also piques interest. Treasure maps to find a new activity, giant footprints across the ceiling to introduce a unit on measurement, or a set of clues to help students make guesses about a new topic adds intrigue to learning. Adding a little surprise to your classroom can be fun and helps students view mathematics in new ways, even when routines or materials are highly familiar.

Connecting the Chapter to Your Practice

1. In your classroom, do learners at all levels of readiness have the same opportunities for choice? Explain.

2. Of the various strategies for organizing choice presented, which ones are you most likely to incorporate in your teaching? Why?

3. What is challenging about individual accountability during choice time?

PART 3

An Environment for Differentiation

. . . .

Overview

These final two chapters focus on strategies for maintaining differentiated instruction. Specific management skills are needed to support a classroom with a focus on differentiated instruction. Ultimately, it is these skills that allow you to implement differentiation strategies successfully. Because you are key to this process, you, too, must have sources of support.

Chapter 8   Manage the Classroom

(continued)

Introduction

The role of a teacher has been compared with that of a coach or a conductor. Both lead a group of individuals with different talents and do not assume that those talents will be nurtured in the same manner. Coaches and conductors know how to motivate each member of their group and aim to develop all of the participants' strengths and work on weaknesses. Practices are held with the whole group, identified subgroups, and individuals. Each athlete or musician has slightly different tasks to perfect and yet, in the end, the goal is for everyone to work together to produce a unified and masterful performance on the field or in the concert hall.

Teachers also need to develop a sense of a unified classroom while addressing individual students' strengths and weaknesses. In a differentiated classroom, where students are more likely to be engaged in multiple tasks that support their different levels of learning readiness, learning styles, and interests, it can be challenging also to develop a mathematical learning community that comes together to build, discuss, and verify ideas; yet, this is a challenge teachers must address. Differentiated instruction is not the same thing as individualized instruction. We do not believe that students should learn mathematics in isolation or that they should be deprived of the joy of being an active member of a well-functioning community group.

> Differentiated instruction is not the same thing as individualized instruction. We do not believe that students should learn mathematics in isolation or that they should be deprived of the joy of being an active member of a well-functioning community group.

Teachers must also figure out how to manage different tasks going on at the same time. They need to distribute and collect materials in ways that do not require a lot of time and effort. They are challenged to find ways to have other students engaged in meaningful activities while they work uninterrupted with a small group. There is a necessity to create classroom spaces for noisy activities and quiet ones. Teachers need to think about the limitations of space, materials, and time as they make their plans. They must take the intricate components of classroom life and the complex needs of young learners and create a masterful learning environment.

Although we do not want to promote the idea that a teacher must create a masterpiece each day in the classroom, we do believe that a well-managed classroom that supports students' learning while maintaining a sense of community is a masterpiece, one that begins its composition the moment students walk in the door on the first day of school. Right from the beginning, values, routines, and expectations need to be established that will develop an environment conducive to learning in a differentiated classroom. In this chapter, we take a closer look at elements necessary to create a successful, differentiated classroom—from classroom space and respect for differences to routines, the grouping of students, time with individual students, ragged time and sponge activities, and whole-class work.

When Managing a Differentiated Classroom, Think About:

- classroom space,
- respect for differences,
- routines,
- the grouping of students,
- time with individual students,
- ragged time and sponge activities, and
- whole-class work.

Classroom Space

Ample space can be a rare commodity in many classrooms. Careful decisions need to be made about how the limited space is used so that a variety of groupings and activities can be supported. The following guidelines may be helpful.

Desks or Tables?

If you only have room for desks or tables, choose tables. In general, tables are more useful because they can accommodate individual or small-group learning and provide additional space for shared materials. Round tables are more conducive to small-group work because they allow each person's face to be seen more easily. If tables are not available, consider arranging desks in clusters to form a similar workspace to support collaboration and conversation.

Without desks, you will need to provide storage bins for students to keep their materials and belongings. Decisions need to be made about where to house these bins. Keeping them in clear sight and easily accessible from the various tables in the room are just two conditions to be considered. Establishing their function and any expectations for use, or boundaries around private versus communal space and supplies, are also matters of importance when making your plans. Fabric bags that slip over the back of a chair also help to organize personal materials that students use frequently, and their use keeps students from traveling back and forth to bins on a regular basis.

If you are asking your students to function without desks, think about doing the same yourself. Although you also need ample personal storage areas, removing the teacher's desk may allow you to add an extra learning station or private space in the classroom. This strategy may seem out of the question or unrealistic to you at first; however, if you allow yourself the chance to consider this option, you may discover new possibilities for the use of space in your classroom. It may also lead you to reflect on how space and arrangement may influence teaching and learning.

Traffic Patterns

Consider traffic patterns. Make sure that students can travel easily from one table to another, to and from the classroom door, and to and from the various mathematical supplies and manipulatives in the room. Make these pathways wide enough so that you and the students can move back and forth without having to ask other students to move or to interrupt their work.

Storage Space

Ample storage space is essential to helping classrooms be organized and efficient. Just as with your drawers and closets at home, too many materials in a small space results in disorganization. Think about storing materials that only are used occasionally or during specific units in a supply closet or in higher cabinets in the room.

Math manipulatives, games, and puzzles are certainly not the only tools used to learn mathematics. Along with these materials, designate a space for shared pencils, paper, scissors, glue, and myriad of other art materials such as markers, crayons, and colored pencils to support mathematical pursuits. Because these materials are used by all students throughout the day and across all subjects, think about where and how to organize them; this decision is key to classroom efficiency and effectiveness. In many schools, students are required to provide their own supplies of this nature. If this is the case where you teach, consider ways to make some or all of these materials more communal.

Designate space for other vital materials such as recording sheets or packets for student work, finished-work baskets, portfolios, or other assessment-related data. For example, think about the use of hanging file folders. Some teachers use them as a way to organize papers for newly assigned work. Teachers sometimes place all of the activity sheets related to a new unit in an open file box that is labeled so that students can get a new sheet easily without asking. Files of this sort can also be used for collecting student work. Many teachers put a hanging file or an open file box beside the place where they do their planning. In this way, teachers can access student work easily as they plan for the next day, prepare for student or parent conferences, or write report cards. They can also file students' work easily in portfolios or other data-type collectors.

A Whole-Class Discussion Area

If at all possible, designate an open area for whole-class discussions or meetings. A rug placed in the corner of a classroom can create this special space. The rug allows students to sit on the floor in a circle, rather than having to drag their chairs to a meeting place, and the corner placement helps some students to focus better. Sometimes, a long bench can be used to provide additional seating. It is important that the meeting area be attractive and inviting, and support students' sense of belonging to a community.

Matching Room Features to the Type of Work Being Done

Match features in the room to the type of work that will be done there. For example, place the classroom library near the rug area because students like to relax when they read and there won't be other groups working in that area. Conversely, keep art materials away from the rug area to avoid unnecessary stains. In terms of mathematics, it makes sense to place a table adjacent to the storage area for the math materials. This placement allows one group of students to work with the materials without having to carry them too far. It also allows you and the students to place bins on a nearby tabletop when further organization or distribution of the materials is necessary.

Second Grade: Private Offices

Although the previous guidelines can help you to think about the arrangement of your room, most teachers need to find creative solutions to provide enough space for both groups and individuals to work. Consider the story of Odessa.

Odessa is a second-grade teacher who just completed her first year of teaching. During the summer, she thought about what worked during the year and what changes she wanted to make for the following year. One of the factors was the layout of the classroom. She realized that she had ample open tables and work areas where students mostly worked together, but few spaces where students could work more privately and be less distracted by what was happening around them. She remembered hearing about a simple concept called a *private office*, where you overlap two manila folders and then staple the doubled center panel to make a trifold. The trifolds could stand up on desks or tables and provide private, separate spaces for students to work.

The following September, Odessa introduces this idea and the students are excited about having their own office. As Seth explains, "My mom has an office at home, but I don't. Now I have one, too!" The students decorate both the outside and the inside of the folders with things you would find in an office: monthly calendars, plants (made from construction paper), and pictures of families brought from home. One girl writes, *Math is cool!*, which reminds Odessa of how she puts inspirational quotes around her desk to keep her motivation high.

Sometimes she asks everyone in the class to go in to their private offices. For example, during an assessment task she has the students set up their office while they write word problems to share. She feels that this approach gives her a more accurate measure of what students are able to produce on their own. It also creates a bit of mystery and the students seem more excited about the problems they share. Spontaneously, some of the students begin to bring their "offices" to a table when they want to work independently without distractions. Throughout the course of the year, Odessa notices more variation in office use. A few of the students seem to use it quite often whereas some only do so under direction. She is comfortable with the variety and believes that students are making appropriate choices for their learning styles.

That spring, a staff developer who understands the importance of giving teachers opportunities to share their personal success stories leads a system-wide professional development meeting for elementary teachers. The agenda is: Come share your best idea that has made a difference in how students learned this year. Odessa is excited to share her idea about creating private working spaces in her classroom. When she does so, many of her peers express interest in the idea. Colleagues from first and third grade even ask Odessa if they can visit her classroom to see how the students use their offices.

Third Grade: Private Offices

Monica decides to plan a visit to Odessa's classroom. She is a third-grade teacher who is struggling with meeting her students' needs this year. The range of the students' ability levels seems broader than usual; she also has more students on individualized education plans (IEPs). She thinks the private office would help her students learn through different models and visual cues. For example, Monica knows that some of her students really need a hundreds chart on their desk to help them visualize relationships among numbers whereas other students have a strong preference for using a number line. Some of the students need support with vocabulary words, and the word

> Seth explains, "My mom has an office at home, but I don't. Now I have one, too!"

> Some of the students begin to bring their "offices" to a table when they want to work independently without distractions.

wall does not seem to be enough for them. She envisions them writing some words on sticky notes and posting them just as you might in a cubicle. One of her students still reverses the teen numbers and, with a private office, he could put up cues to prompt him on what to do. In their private offices, the students could make decisions about what they want to put in their spaces to support their learning. Monica can envision helping some students create sequence cards that they could hang in their office to remind them of specific steps that are required for success. Also, these offices are portable, allowing the students to bring their supportive tools (models and cues) with them wherever they work.

> In their private offices, the students could make decisions about what they want to put in their spaces to support their learning.

After the visit to Odessa's classroom, Monica is even more enthusiastic and decides to implement this idea. Her students are also excited about the opportunity to decorate their own spaces and, with some prompting, are able to make decisions about what learning tools and models to include as well. One student, Jessica, always forgets the words *numerator* and *denominator*, and feels that these words are important to put in her office. She draws a rectangular model of three-fourths and writes *3 = numerator* and *4 = denominator* below the figure. Some students even make similar offices to use when they are doing homework.

Monica encourages the students to tape tools to their folders. She wants them to be attached firmly, but she also wants tools that can be replaced as the students' learning evolves. If the students write directly on the folders, Monica believes her students will think of the tools as more permanent, as something they will always need, which may not be the case. The offices give the students privacy and encourage them to take ownership of their own learning. They also help Monica differentiate the scaffolding each student receives.

Respect for Differences

In order for differentiated classrooms to function well, all participants must know that respectful behavior is required. Everyone must respect others' learning needs and styles and realize that everyone has the right to have their needs met. Activities that identify and celebrate differences help students better understand why their classrooms are organized the way that they are. They also help students get to know themselves and each other better. This knowledge allows students to support each other individually and to feel more connected as a community of learners.

Kindergarten: *Self-Portraits*

In one kindergarten class, children draw pictures of themselves early in September. Placing these self-portraits up on the bulletin board to be shared helps these new students claim the classroom as their own. Under the title "Our Class," these pictures portray students' oneness, while honoring them as individuals. Throughout the course of the year, portraits are made again and serve as a way for students to compare their drawing skills and update their self-image. In spring, as more literacy skills are emerging, these students also draw themselves doing something. By completing the phrases "I am [who?]" and "I am [doing what?]" kindergartners add words to their portraits.

> Under the title "Our Class," these pictures portray students' oneness, while honoring them as individuals.

In one class, to connect with this literacy and self-discovery activity, the teacher asks students to think about themselves and what they are doing as they learn math. The students brainstorm words that describe what they do, then they each record an individual response—for example, working, making a pattern, drawing a shape, playing, reading, adding, counting, building, weighing, comparing, taking a survey, seeing shapes, cooking, matching, concentrating, measuring, seeing how much, and answering. One child added the word *growing*. He said, "I am growing, and when I get measured it shows." (See Figure 8–1.)

Figure 8–1. This child's drawing relates mathematics to growing taller.

Second Grade: *What Matches You?*

REPRODUCIBLE 36

A second-grade teacher has students complete a survey form sometime during the first week of school. The form is called *What Matches You?* and provides twenty-five different "I statements" for students to consider. (See Figure 8–2; also available as Reproducible 36.) Some of the items are general statements about learning, such as "I need quiet when I work." Other statements focus on mathematics, such as "I am better at addition than subtraction."

As you learn from the teacher's reflection on the next page, this form can spark conversations about learning and mathematics.

Reproducible 36

What Matches You?

Student name: _____

Try to find two classmates to fit each description. Have them write their initials in the box that matches. No one may initial more than 3 boxes on 1 sheet.

I learn best through hands-on experiences.	I like to solve problems.	I prefer to work alone.	I find it helpful to write about my mathematical ideas.	I sometimes get confused when others explain their thinking.
I like face clocks better than digital ones.	I like to measure things.	I use drawings to understand a problem.	I learn best when the teacher writes on the board.	I find Unifix cubes more helpful than base ten blocks.
I am better at subtraction than addition.	I like building things.	I need quiet when I work.	I find base ten blocks more helpful than Unifix cubes.	I prefer to work with others.
I know my basic facts well.	I like digital clocks better than face clocks.	I am better at addition than subtraction.	I like geometry.	I like to find different ways to solve problems.
I like to brainstorm ideas with a group and then follow up alone.	I like logic games and puzzles.	I want rules for solving problems.	I would like to use a calculator all of the time.	I like collecting data and making graphs.

Figure 8–2. A survey form for second graders: *What Matches You?* (available as Reproducible 36).

Fourth Grade: *Graph Your Intelligences*

See CHAPTER 5

One fourth-grade teacher uses the idea of multiple intelligences to help students realize that everyone has unique gifts and that they do not all learn the same way (see Chapter 5 for a closer look at multiple intelligences). First, students look up the definition of the word *intelligence* in the dictionary and then the students talk about ways people are intelligent. Students usually

For a couple of years I used a form like *What Matches You?* during the first day or two of school. It got students walking around and talking to each other and learning something about their classmates. I used to put in items such as "I like to play baseball" or "I like chocolate ice cream." This year I decided to focus more on learning. I decided that students would eventually find out about each other's recreational and food preferences, but that they might never talk about how they each learn. Also, I was hoping this activity might help students to gain an intuitive sense of why I strive to provide differentiated learning opportunities in our classroom.

The responses took somewhat longer to be formulated. They know right away whether they like chocolate, but deciding if they wanted rules for solving problems required some reflection. Some students were amazed to find that everybody didn't think a digital clock was better than a face clock, and others were pleased to find someone else who preferred to work alone.

After we did this activity, we talked about the differences in our classroom and how it was important to respect these different ways of learning. We made a list of what we learned.

Marcus said, "I have to be quiet sometimes so that Billy can think."

Jamie remarked, "I might want to try using base ten blocks."

Ellie noted, "It's good that we are different. Otherwise, it would be boring." It felt wonderful to hear the students articulate these ideas.

Immediately after this conversation, we began our first differentiated learning activity. I introduced it by saying, "Many times in our classroom we will be doing different activities from each other. Why do you think that is so?" Several hands popped up and I called on Ricardo, who said, "Because we are different." I couldn't have been more pleased.

> After we did this activity, we talked about the differences in our classroom and how it was important to respect these different ways of learning.

identify reading, math, and writing first, and then add ideas such as sports, drawing, and singing. The teacher tells them informally about Dr. Howard Gardner's research and writes the eight different intelligences on the board. The areas are named in terms the students can understand, for example, logical–mathematical is identified as *number smart*. Possible career choices related to each intelligence are discussed as well.

Next, the students reflect on themselves in relation to these areas. For each intelligence, they write about their abilities, score themselves on a scale of 1 to 10 points, and make a bar graph to display their ratings.

Alex writes, *Pretty good for word smart, but not that good. I can speak well but I don't no [sic] how to spell.*

Bernie records, *I will use numbers in my job, but I will not be an accountant, scientist, or computer programmer.*

For "self smart" Cassandra writes, *I don't like to work alone or be alone and I like to share my ideas not keep them to myself.* (See Figure 8–3.) The students are engaged throughout this process and it is clear that they are learning about themselves.

As Lorenzo explains, "I thought I just liked to draw, but now I know I have art and space intelligence!" They are also learning about each other.

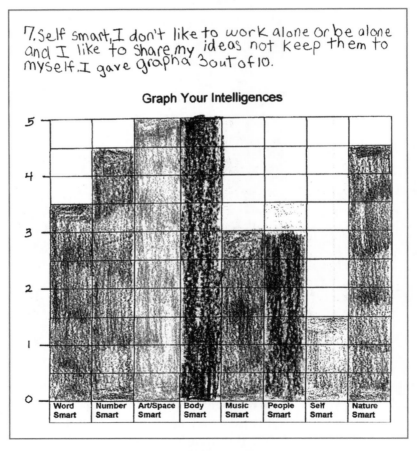

Figure 8–3. Cassandra's description and graph.

Leanna looks at her friend's work and exclaims, "I didn't know you liked nature. I've got a great place for us to explore sometime."

When the written work is completed, each student makes a self-portrait. Then, with the written work, graphs, and portraits in front of them, they each make a "brain collage." They do this by sketching an outline of their head and filling this space with pictures found in newspapers and magazines. The students choose pictures that represent their intelligences. They hang their work on the wall for Back-to-School Night. They staple their four pieces of work together; the collage is on top, then the graph, the written information, and the self-portraits. Parents are challenged to identify their children's work before they see the self-portraits. From the teacher's reflection that follows, you learn that not all parents do so successfully.

TEACHER REFLECTION

I started the *Graph Your Intelligences* activity a couple of years ago when I sensed an increase in the amount of name calling going on at recess. Too often, students who excelled in mathematics were being called *nerds* and those who were athletic were referred to as *jocks*. I wanted my students to view each other with more openness, to be interested in and get along with people who were different from them. I felt that if I could help them understand that there is more than one way of doing things, then the bullying and teasing would lessen. I also wanted them to understand their own learning styles better so that they could take more responsibility for their work and think about how they might expand their skills. I certainly didn't want them to view success with mathematics as a negative trait!

The students enjoy this activity and learn a lot. It definitely diminishes name calling and builds respect for differences. Parent's night is always interesting. The first year, I was surprised to find out how many parents could not identify their children after looking at the first three pages. Some of the parents who do recognize their children's work are still surprised by the specifics. It's not unusual to hear, "When did she learn to sew?" or "I didn't know he was so interested in people." After parent's night, we still keep the graphs on display. They provide us all with a visual reminder about our similarities and differences.

> "Too often, students who excelled in mathematics were being called *nerds* and those who were athletic were referred to as *jocks*."

Routines

Routines serve several purposes in a classroom. After students recognize ways to get into groups, distribute assignment papers, put away materials, get in line, and walk in the hallway, these activities will occur quickly and efficiently. Much of the first weeks of school are spent creating these routines and making sure that everyone can follow them. Although considerable time and effort is needed to get them launched, once established they are adhered to with minimal energy and teacher supervision. This is particularly important in a differentiated classroom in which students are expected to manage themselves more frequently and often for longer durations while the teacher is working with other students.

Routines also instill feelings of safety and security. When the same procedures are followed on a daily or weekly basis, students understand what is expected of them and can predict what will happen next. Such regularity helps students to feel emotionally safe in school and thus more able to participate in the learning process. Established routines also create community. As students identify and describe the ways in which their classroom runs, they are forming their understanding of the unique culture of their classroom.

> As students identify and describe the ways in which their classroom runs, they are forming their understanding of the unique culture of their classroom.

In differentiated mathematics instruction, each group of students may be working with different mathematical materials, but they need to gather and return the materials to the math storage area in the same manner. The importance of putting materials away in the same way you found them is stressed as one of the ways to respect all members of the class. Figuring out how to share materials is an important aspect of developing respect.

What happens when someone else is using a material a student desires or needs? Too often, young children grab without asking. This quickly leads to hurt feelings and destroyed work. Role-playing ways to acknowledge these types of conflicts and successful ways of resolving them is critical. Mathematically, it can also lead to new learning when a first-grade teacher asks, "If all of the hexagons in the pattern block set are being used, what else can you use to fill in the puzzle outline?" Although initially a child may not see selecting different blocks as a viable solution to either the math work or the social conflict, in time, seeing the relationships in the blocks can lead to exciting new opportunities for solving all kinds of problems.

Routines also provide common experiences that help create a sense of community. It seems all teachers, regardless of their students' age, have some beginning-of-the-day ritual. In many classes, morning work is used to help students transition smoothly into a new day. Such work provides the time to pick up from where students left off the day before, helps to frame or launch new challenges for the day, or provides additional practice in areas of need. While students dive in, the teacher can take care of greeting each student individually and performing any record keeping chores, such as taking attendance, getting a lunch count, and dealing with communications from home. Some teachers ask students to be responsible for several of these record keeping responsibilities.

After everyone has arrived, some classrooms hold a community meeting. Often there are several routines followed during a morning meeting, some of which are designed to build social skills and some to build academic ones. One fifth-grade class includes Numbers in the News in their morning routines. In addition to taking attendance and calling on students to share, two morning leaders are each responsible for telling their classmates about a number in the news. It is their teacher's hope that this routine exposes students to some current events as well as supports students' number sense.

Kindergarten: Calendar Routines

In one kindergarten classroom, the community calendar time is often done in song, as children sing the days of the week and then figure out the day and date for that day. In some classes, the teacher always conducts this part of the morning meeting; in other classes, being the calendar helper rotates each day.

Calendar Helper

Encouraging one child at a time to lead the class in community calendar time offers many opportunities for the teacher to differentiate the exercise for the calendar helper. For example, Ken is the calendar helper on January fourteenth. His teacher knows he has been working hard to recall the names of all the teen numbers. After he leads the class in song, Ken's teacher asks him to predict which number he will turn over on the calendar to reveal the number/date for the day. Ken begins to hesitate and looks up at his teacher. "How can you figure this out?" she asks. Ken's classmates are familiar with this type of question and do not try to chime in. Waiting is never easy, but it is a sign of respect. Ken points his finger at the 1 on the calendar and begins to count as he moves his finger along in the same manner he would read a book. "Eight, nine, ten, eleven, twelve, thirteen," he pauses. "Thirteen, thirteen, thirteen," he says more silently to himself. Some of Ken's classmates are just on the verge of shouting out, but the teacher puts her palm up in their direction. "Fourteen!" Ken exclaims and turns the card over and confirms his prediction.

Individual Calendars

The same kindergarten class also uses individual calendars as a way to learn more about the calendar and to give children additional opportunities to practice writing numbers. Each student is given a monthly calendar sheet. In September, the teacher chooses to have all of the numbers dotted for the dates Monday through Friday; the weekend days are filled in completely. Each day, the children trace the new number. As the months go on, fewer numbers are dotted or even shown at all on the grid. This supports the growth the children make in writing numbers and their familiarity with how a calendar works. The teacher can customize these calendars as she deems appropriate.

Calendar Questions

After children fill in the next number on the calendar, they then show their work to their teacher, who in turn asks them a calendar question. For the teacher, this additional step makes the learning opportunities even more child centered. She might ask a student such as Ken to count aloud the number of days on the calendar. She might ask another student to predict what number will come on a day later in the week or next week. Questions focus on number recognition, patterns, computation skills, and skip-counting; on concepts such as *today*, *tomorrow*, and *yesterday*; or on indicating when a special event might occur. In this way, the calendar can also begin to be seen as a representation of time passing.

Fourth Grade: Weekly Number Routines

Although some upper-elementary classes do not have a meeting each day, some teachers hold one on Mondays to help students transition back from the weekend. One fourth-grade teacher includes a number sense activity within this time block. From her reflection, you learn that she began this practice because she felt that students lost interest in numbers during their elementary school years.

The teacher writes *38,000* on the board and asks her students what this number could represent in baseball. A few suggestions are made such as the number of years baseball has existed and the total number of outs in a season. Finally, someone proposes the correct answer: the approximate number of fans that attend a game at Fenway Park in Boston, Massachusetts. The teacher explains to the students how knowing this number fact helps her to think about other numbers. For example, about 30,000 people live in her

As a parent, I noticed that when my children were younger they loved numbers. They would count all the time and I would often hear them sing songs about numbers. At age four, my son's favorite number was four. If I asked him how many cookies he wanted, he would respond with an attitude that suggested he couldn't imagine why anyone would want more or less than four. Four was the perfect number for him until, of course, he turned five. This passion for numbers existed for all of my children until around second grade, and then numbers became just ordinary and the passion no longer existed. When I started teaching fifth grade, I noticed this same lack of interest in numbers. Personally, I love numbers. I particularly love numbers as they apply to baseball. One of my favorite numbers is 38,000. I decided to use this number to launch a weekly number routine.

> "This passion for numbers existed for all of my children until around second grade, and then numbers became just ordinary and the passion no longer existed."

community. She can imagine all of those people being at Fenway Park and this gives her a visual image of what that number of people would look like.

Next, the teacher tells the students, "Each week a student is going to share at our Monday meeting a number that means something to him or her. We will call these numbers *landmark* or *benchmark numbers* because they help us to understand other numbers." She reminds Katley that she is meeting leader next week and that she should be sure to think of a number.

Katley's Number: 100

The following week, Katley says her number is 100 and that she heard the number on television. Many classmates offer suggestions as to what this number could represent, such as how much money someone got for his birthday, how much money someone lost, or how much money someone found. Katley then tells her classmates that it is the amount of money a personal trainer can make in an hour. Katley also shared that she thought this was a lot of money for one hour's work, and others agreed. This conversation led to other benchmark numbers that might be relevant here, such as the minimum wage and the average wage of a personal trainer. The teacher was pleased that the discussion led to a more realistic view of this career. Many of her students were of lower socioeconomic status and they were sometimes drawn to lifestyles that appeared glamorous on television.

Doreen's Number: 325

Doreen was responsible for the next week's number and she also identified a number related to money. Doreen's number was 325, the cost of a particular Coach purse. When this was identified, Jason said they should think about minimum wage again. The class figured out that if you were sixteen years old working for minimum wage, it would take about sixty hours to earn enough money to buy the purse. The purse no longer seemed such a necessity! The teacher was once again pleased at how mathematics was helping her students to develop number sense skills that could inform their choices and their understanding of the world.

Frank's Number: 218,000

As the year continues, the students' interest in this activity is maintained and they become more adapt at identifying questions related to the given numerical information. In March, Frank's number is 218,000, which is the approximate number of LED light bulbs in the historical Citgo sign outside of Fenway Park. This number fact leads students to want to know other numerical data, and they create the following list of questions:

- How many bulbs are replaced each year because they are hit by a baseball?
- How tall is the Citgo sign and who gets to change the light bulbs?
- How big are the light bulbs?
- How long does a light bulb last before it needs to be replaced?

Some students spend snack time or indoor recess looking up answers to these questions. Most important, they are engaged with numbers in ways that make sense to them, and community spirit is built through this routine.

Do-Now Routines

Many clasrooms have developed a Do-Now routine at the beginning of math instruction. A problem or task is identified for students to consider for, at most, five minutes. Such tasks provide a way to get a class started, activate prior knowledge, or preview a new topic. They also provide a quick way to assess readiness. The tasks are particularly effective when students are returning to the classroom from gym or lunch, or when students change teachers for math instruction.

VIDEO CLIP 8.1 ·

A Do-Now Routine

In this video clip we see Ms. Loguidice's fifth-grade class engaged in a Do-Now routine—a daily routine Ms. Loguidice plans for the first five minutes of each class.

Before watching the clip, solve 6,000 − 199. What strategies did you use?

As you watch the clip, consider:

1. Why would the teacher routinely plan a "Do Now" at the beginning of a math class?
2. What is the role of the student during the "Do Now"?
3. Can you think of lessons you teach where the students could benefit from the review of needed prerequisite skills that would then allow them better access to the math in the lesson?

The Grouping of Students

Another way to maximize learning is to think critically about group work. Although whole-group teaching can be very powerful and some teachers believe it promotes equality by ensuring that all students are taught the same lessons, it is not always the most effective way to learn. As you have explored throughout this resource, differentiation is focused on finding the most effective ways of meeting students' various needs. Organizing students into groups can promote individual learning.

Grouping for differentiated instruction is different than working in groups. Group work has been long recognized as a way to break up the whole-class instructional pattern, to engage students more actively in their learning, and to provide greater opportunities for communication and social interactions. Traditionally, each group may be completing the same task. The teacher rotates among the groups, supporting their work and informing their thinking. Although a useful instructional strategy, grouping for differentiated instruction is even more intentional.

Within differentiated instruction, grouping is flexible—that is, groups are formed with a specific focus and then reconfigured when a new purpose is identified. The formation of groups may be based on readiness, learning styles, or interests and can be heterogeneous or homogeneous. Groups may

> **Grouping for differentiated instruction is different than working in groups.**

be formed for a day, a week, or a few weeks. The flexible grouping keeps students from being labeled and allows them to work with a variety of their peers.

It takes time and thought to group students. Thinking about why you are grouping and whether groups will be designed around a specific learning goal, learning style, interest, product, or behavior is all part of the process. Identifying the appropriate size of the groups, the amount of time the group should work together, and the composition of the group are all decisions that need to be made. Teachers also need to think about how groups and their materials will be identified and organized.

Forming Groups at Random

Sometimes, groups are formed at random. Some teachers keep a deck of cards with stickers on them. If five groups are needed and there are twenty students in the class, five different kinds of stickers are used. The deck is shuffled and students select a card at random. All the like stickers form a new group. Sometimes these stickers correspond to tables or areas of the room and, as students pick a card, they know right away where to go to meet their new group.

Giving Students Group Choices

Sometimes, students choose their own groups or partnerships. Allowing students to make this choice is one of the ways you can share classroom authority. Many teachers find that they are most comfortable with this option when only dyads are being formed, when groups will be intact for a short period of time, or when partners or groups work together on the basis of interest.

Forming Groups Intentionally

More often, differentiated instruction requires teachers to form groups intentionally—that is, teachers match students specifically in ways to meet learning needs best. One teacher frequently changes student groups in her classroom. She keeps two large magnetic boards resting on the chalk tray to help her organize this process. For each board, she has a set of nametags backed with magnetic tape. When she plans an activity for which new groups are required, she moves the names on the board according to her criteria. As she explains, "I used to do this on paper. When the grouping was obvious, this worked fine. Sometimes, though, I find it challenging to make groups, and I change my mind several times. With the board, I can try out several formations easily. Then, when I am done, the list is already there for my students to see."

Many teachers keep a log of the groups that are formed during the first few weeks of school. The log serves as a place to keep notes about groups that function particularly well together or partnerships that seem to require more supervision. A teacher can also make sure that everyone has the opportunity to work with all the other classmates during these first weeks of community building. It is also worthwhile to note how the groups were formed so that, over time, students work according to readiness, learning styles, and interests.

Concern for Student Feelings

Although a student might become upset or feel isolated at any time, forming partners and groups can heighten such feelings. Some students may wonder why they are in one group versus another. Others may worry about being chosen or welcomed. Concern for isolation, safety, comfort, friendships, and working relationships must always be part of the grouping process. Whether in math or any other subject, it is essential to keep students' social–emotional development in mind.

Offering Math Clinics

Many students have heard of or have had the opportunity to attend a sports clinic. Such a clinic is shorter in duration than a camp and focuses on specific skills development. For example, a tennis clinic might focus on the backhand stroke. Players of all ability levels can take advantage of a clinic if they believe it is a skill on which they are ready to work to improve. In classrooms, math clinics provide students the chance to work in a similarly focused manner.

 VIDEO CLIP 8.2

A Math Clinic

In this video clip we see Mrs. Miller facilitating a division math clinic with a group of her fourth graders. These fourth graders have chosen to do this clinic.

As you watch the clip, consider:

1. What is the role of the teacher during the clinic?
2. What is the role of the students in the clinic?
3. In your own classroom, what content would be best taught in a clinic format?

Teachers can offer open clinics where students can drop in for extra help, assign students to start off at a clinic within a rotation of choices, or create a clinic of a combination of student-chosen and teacher-chosen participants. When successful, clinics become an expected instructional opportunity for all. There is no stigma for working in a clinic; in fact, a clinic could extend the challenge level. Ideally, participating students are viewed positively for recognizing their needs and taking proactive responsibility for their own learning. Teachers can help develop students' metacognitive awareness by interviewing them about areas in which they may want further instruction.

Time with Individual Students

There are times when teachers and students need and want to work one-on-one. Although some may consider this a luxury in a busy classroom, many teachers find such work to be one of the most enlightening aspects of their day. Working with an individual student can be a time for getting to know the student better, to assess a specific skill or competence, or just to dig deeper together on a problem. Sitting side-by-side can be rewarding and informative to both the student and teacher, and can help nourish the supportive, trusting relationship that is so necessary to teaching and learning.

By building expectations for different learning activities to occur simultaneously, differentiated instruction supports opportunities to work with individual students. Other students do not expect the teacher always to be available to them, and thus their ability to work independently from the teacher is developed. Teacher–student partnerships become just one of the various configurations in the classroom. Such acceptance also supports longer individual interactions, such as when interviews are conducted, tutoring is needed, or particular follow-up to a lesson or task is required.

The image of keeping several plates spinning in the air is one to which many teachers can relate. Teachers work tirelessly to keep every student engaged and learning. Sometimes, even with their best attempts, plates fall. During these moments, it is important to have time carved out in the day and classroom to work with individual students. Sometimes teachers can anticipate a falter, and a quick spin or adjustment will help the child get back on track. Sometimes, more intensive work is needed.

Fourth Grade: Riley and His Parallel Lines

In one fourth-grade class, for example, students were asked to complete the following task:

I have 4 sides.

Two of my sides are parallel.

My other 2 sides are not parallel.

Draw me.

Riley is convinced that this drawing is impossible. "This is a trick question," he complains. His teacher hears his frustration and invites him to join her at the small round table at the back of the room. The teacher asks Riley to begin the task. With reluctance, he agrees to do so and draws two parallel line segments:

_____

_____

"See," he begins to explain, "you can't connect these lines with anything but parallel lines. And it says they can't be."

The teacher isn't surprised by Riley's thinking; she knows many students may find this task challenging. She begins by asking him, "Is there another way you could draw that first set of lines?"

Riley nods yes and he draws the lines exactly the same, but in a vertical orientation. "It's still the same. This can't be done." The teacher believes a strong hint is needed and suggests that, this time, he make his lines different lengths. Riley draws the line segments shown here, but is unable to complete the drawing. Instead, he announces, "I can't use these lines. They aren't parallel."

_____

_____

After a few more questions to confirm, it becomes clear to his teacher that Riley thinks that parallel lines have to be the same length. The teacher understands the tendency for most of her students to begin this task by drawing two parallel line segments of the same length, but before this conversation, she never understood that they believed this to be a requirement. She checks with a couple of other students and finds that they, too, share this belief. She thinks about the illustrations shown in the curriculum materials and realizes that examples almost always show line segments that are congruent. After these conversations, she knows she needs to review the definition of parallel lines with the whole class and show them drawings that challenge their thinking. Without the time she spent individually with Riley, she never would have realized this misconception.

> "After a few more questions to confirm, it becomes clear to his teacher that Riley thinks that parallel lines have to be the same length."

Fifth Grade: Bryce and His Multiplication Algorithm

Sometimes, while they are at home looking at student work, teachers discover the need to meet individually with a student. Such was the case with a fifth-grade teacher who was examining three multiplication examples completed by Bryce, a new student in the class who had been taught the traditional algorithm for multiplication. As the teacher examines his work, she cannot diagnose his error. She isn't surprised that the first example is correct; no regrouping is required. She looks closer at the other two examples. The issue doesn't seem to be a basic fact error, nor does Bryce seem to be adding in the regrouped number before he multiplies, a systematic error with which she is familiar. The teacher recognizes that Bryce also only seems to have difficulty when he multiplies by the tens digit, but she can't figure out what he is doing. She places the paper with the other three samples that she has identified as needing follow-up conversations.

The teacher meets with Bryce the next day and asks him to talk aloud as he explains his work. He describes the first example clearly and she is eager to hear what he will say about the second example, shown in Figure 8–4. As she expects, he is fine until he comes to multiplying by the tens digit.

Bryce says, "I write the zero to show I am really multiplying by tens. Two times five is ten. I write the zero and trade the one. I can't multiply four numbers, but I know I have to multiply and then add, so you get eight and three and that's eleven."

The teacher tries to follow his thinking, but feels lost. "Where did you get the eight and three?" she asks.

"Easy," he replies. "Two times four is eight and three times one is three." The teacher thinks a bit and then looks at his last example. She sees the four numbers in his tens column and realizes he has followed the same procedure. He has multiplied each pair of numbers (5×2 and 6×4) and then added the results ($10 + 24$) to get thirty-four. (See Figure 8–4.)

The teacher knows she will have to spend more time with Bryce. His algorithm needs adjusting and she would like him to explore some alternative approaches as well as focus more on estimating products so that he can judge the reasonableness of his responses. But, she has learned that his error was systematic, which means he can follow a series of steps consistently. She is sure he will be fine with just a bit of time working with her or a peer tutor. When students have relatively simple procedural misconceptions, she finds that peers can be effective teachers. This peer support also gives her more

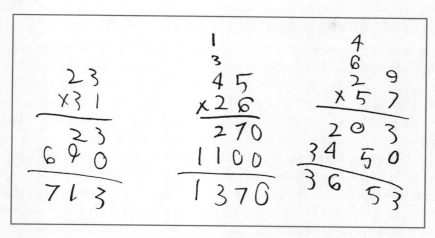

Figure 8–4. Bryce's written work.

time to assess other student difficulties or work with students whose errors are not systematic (for more on peer teaching, see Chapter 6, p. 194).

See CHAPTER 6

Soon, Bryce crosses off each regrouped number after he has used it and his work is basically error free. He can also connect his recordings to work with base ten blocks so that his procedural and conceptual knowledge are linked. When the teacher believes that Bryce is a bit more settled in his new class, she will explore alternative strategies with him; for now, however, she wants to validate his approach while helping to ensure its accuracy.

Ragged Time and Sponge Activities

When students are involved in different tasks and work at different rates, this creates what some educators refer to as *ragged time*. Helping each student transition to another appropriate activity when the assigned task is completed is not good use of a teacher's time, so it is important to have activities that students go to naturally. Such activities are sometimes known as *sponges*, because they soak up the extra time between early and late finishers. In the literacy curriculum, this often translates to free reading or journal writing. It is important to have similar choices within the mathematics curriculum. A number of options are possible and different choices may be available on different days or within different units.

> It is important to have activities that students go to naturally. Such activities are sometimes known as *sponges*, because they soak up the extra time between early and late finishers.

First Grade: Offering Two Unit-Based Activities

A first-grade teacher begins a fall mini-unit on facts to ten by giving pairs of students ten-frame cards and some counters. She notes that some pairs immediately start to order the cards, while others spread them randomly about their work area. She tells students to find the seven card and says, "How many chips do we need to make this card show ten? Hold up your fingers to show me your answer." She notes that some students place the chips to count, some tap their fingers on each empty place, and some immediately raise three fingers. She gives a few more examples and then students complete similar problems independently. The next day she displays ten-frames on her projector and asks the same type of questions. This time she records both an addition and a subtraction sentence to correspond to each example. For the next example, she has the students record the equations.

Once she is confident the students understand this activity, it is added to the math center table. A few days later she introduces the *Under the Cup* activity. She has ten beans and places some under the cup and some outside the cup. The task is for students to identify the number under the cup. For a couple of days, the students explore the activity again as a whole class, but she invites students to take her part in leading it. In this way, students are able to practice this role with support, before doing it alone. The students now have two unit-based activities between which they may choose when their work is finished.

Third Grade: A Jigsaw Puzzle

During a geometry unit, one third-grade teacher always sets up a jigsaw puzzle at a table in a corner of the room. Working on the puzzle is a choice during indoor recess or when their math work is completed. Over about three or four weeks, the puzzle is finished by many pairs of students placing a few pieces correctly each time they visit the table. Sometimes the teacher picks out a few pieces and places them strategically so that each student can contribute. The class feels a great sense of accomplishment when the puzzle is completed.

Fifth Grade: KenKen Puzzles

A fifth-grade teacher launches her discussion of proof with consideration of KenKen puzzles. She finds some examples online that are appropriate for her students. At first, many of her students respond, "I just think it should go there," when they explain the placement of a particular digit. During the course of the week, she uses these puzzles to help students understand what it means to prove that an identified digit, and only that digit, must be placed in a particular cell. Later, the teacher refers to this experience whenever she thinks her students need to be reminded about what it means to prove something. She also collects a group of puzzles that students can pursue when their work is finished. They are purposely color-coded by difficulty, and students are comfortable saying, "I'm taking a yellow one, because these puzzles are new to me."

Across Grade Ideas

Choosing to practice basic math facts during ragged time is supported in most classrooms. Students might work in pairs with flash cards or take advantage of computer software. Some teachers set out a collection of unit-related literature books when beginning a new topic. These books can be placed in a special location and explored when the day's specific math task is completed. The *Guinness Book of World Records* is a favorite to have in the upper-elementary classroom. Students may also be directed to problem decks, technology, menu choices, and stations. All sponge activities don't have to be related to the current topics; in fact, bringing back some favorite choices can be a way to maintain skills. What's important is that students know what to do when they finish their work, and that they continue to be involved in mathematical explorations throughout the time designated for mathematics.

Whole–Class Work

Whole-class lessons remain important. Often, the notion of all of the students working on the exact same thing at the same time seems contradictory to the notion of differentiated instruction. As you have seen throughout the stories shared from various classrooms, whole-class lessons are vital. They provide common experiences and expose students to a greater array of thinking. They help develop common vocabulary and a sense of community. They offer an efficient means for introducing new content that can then be continued later working in small groups, in pairs, or individually. There is a time and a place for each form of instruction; knowing your intent and figuring out the best way to meet your goals is what is critical.

Lesson Framework

During the lesson, the following are several things you can do to help it be more successful for diverse students.

Lesson Framework for Success

Start with a Do-Now *Problem*	Start with a *Do-Now* problem to introduce the content and, perhaps, an additional problem from the previous unit to keep that knowledge current. Although most students focus on this expectation, preteach vocabulary or review prerequisite skills with a few students.
Launch the Lesson as a Whole Group	Launch the lesson as a whole group. Include one or two quick think/pair/share times during the launch so students can stop and check their understanding or gain the support of a partner in a larger group setting.
Independent or Small-Group Work	Have students work independently or in small groups after the launch. Make sure this work time includes some form of differentiation. Make sure students understand what they are to do if they need support while you are working with another group or if they finish their work early. Listen as students work so you can idenify insights and misunderstandings that you want to address when the students come together again as a group.
Debrief as a Group	When you debrief as a whole group, wait for students to respond and encourage several students to contribute. Teach students how to connect their comments to those of the previous speaker. Consider having sentence stems visible as reminders, for example:

I agree with _____ and I would like to add _____.

I have a question about _____.

I disagree with _____ because _____.

Debriefing Differentiated Tasks

Although differentiated instruction emphasizes meeting individual needs, teachers must not lose sight of the importance of the collective experience during this process. Participation in a learning community is powerful. What students (and teachers!) learn together can far exceed what any one individual can learn alone or any single teacher can teach. Finding ways to bring a class of students together to share their experiences is an essential component of differentiated classrooms. Even when students are working on separate tasks, there needs to be designated times for students to gather and share their new knowledge, ideas, and strategies.

 **VIDEO CLIP** ·

Revisiting Video Clips 4.3, 7.1, and 7.2: Debriefing Differentiated Tasks

Let's revisit some of the clips we've presented up to this point in the resource. You may select one of the clips—4.3, 7.1, or 7.2—or choose to view them all. Specifically, watch the final section of each clip in which the teacher debriefs with the students about the lesson experience. This is the section with the transition screen labeled "Summarizing."

As you watch each clip, consider:

1. What do you notice about the strategies the teacher is using to focus the summary when students have completed different activities and/or problems?
2. In your classroom what is challenging about debriefing a lesson when the students have completed different activities and/or problems?

Whether in class meetings or summary sessions, students require time together to report findings, review ideas, and raise new questions. During these discussions, students can see how others take on new challenges and make sense of new material. When students have not worked on exactly the same task, sharing can seem less important to them and, to some, maybe even irrelevant or confusing. Teachers need to orchestrate these conversations in ways that build commonalities while respecting and celebrating differences.

A good place to start is to look for common ground. That's why teachers always identify the curriculum goal or standard before they design tasks, form groups, and make other decisions about customizing instruction (see Chapter 3). Refocusing students on the common threads of their individual learning experiences helps them to understand that it makes sense to share.

See CHAPTER 3

Sometimes, simply asking students to describe one new thing they learned today, this week, or during a current unit can both honor and link individual experiences. Recording personal responses in a concept web may unearth more similarity and common ground than first perceived (for more on concept webs, see Chapter 6, p. 199).

See CHAPTER 6

Class discussions can focus on process as well as content. Sometimes, talking about how you organize data, visualize a relationship, or represent thinking may be more informative than sharing an answer or a solution. Furthermore, as children learn more about each other's thinking, they are able to validate frustrations more authentically, make note of growth, and celebrate success.

Connecting the Chapter to Your Practice

1. How does your classroom environment support differentiated instruction?

2. How would you respond to a new teacher who asks, "What classroom routines should I establish during the first week of school?"

3. Describe a management technique that has proved valuable in allowing you time to meet with small groups or individual students.

4. On average, what do you think is the ideal percentage of instructional time students should spend working as a whole class, in a group, or individually? Why?

Chapter 9

Teach with the Goal of Differentiation: Ten Ways to Sustain Your Efforts

(continued)

Introduction

Hopefully, you, too, believe that it is essential to differentiate mathematical instruction and now have some additional ideas about what that means and how it might look in your classroom. Even with this recognition and vision, however, differentiated instruction is a long-term goal, and working toward and sustaining such a goal is often difficult. Just as you require encouragement, reminders, and support to meet other significant challenges in your life, you need to find ways to help your differentiation lens stay in focus and to find ways to meet students' readiness, learning styles, and interests. So what can you do to keep your spirit for differentiation high? In this chapter, we provide you with ten suggestions.

Suggestion 1: Identify Where You Already Provide Differentiation

It's important to remember that differentiation in mathematics is not brand new. You are already grouping students in some ways, working with students individually, and making modifications to meet students' needs. The idea is that now these decisions will be more preplanned and made with more specific needs in mind. Rather than making changes after a lesson has been problematic, you begin to make adjustments during the planning process. Sometimes, just tweaking a familiar activity allows the learning experience to be more on target, to be deeper and richer for each student.

Some teachers begin by thinking about the students who are the least successful with the curriculum as presented. Perhaps there are three or four students in your class who need much more support or challenge. Putting the effort into making lessons work for these students may take time, but the end result will be well worth it. As one teacher expressed, "Now I work more ahead of time, so I don't have to work so hard when I am teaching."

Don't lose sight of what you can do and, in fact, what you are doing already. Regardless of whether you make differentiated instruction in mathematics a priority, you still need to assess what students know and then align your curriculum to national, state, and local standards. These assessment and alignment processes can jump-start your goal of differentiation. It is valuable to do them anyway and they give you a secure foundation on which to base instructional decisions and to build activities that meet individual needs more effectively.

> "Don't lose sight of what you can do and, in fact, what you are doing already.

Be clear about what new work is needed and what is required already. As you learn from the following teacher reflection, this clarity is not always present.

> I sometimes start out new projects with a bit of pessimism. It's important for me to remember why I am doing something and to be clear about what the actual costs and benefits are.

I spent all day Saturday getting ready for these new mathematics activities I wanted to try. I had been to a workshop on differentiated instruction and decided to do some things differently in the measurement unit we were about to begin. I had given my students a preassessment on Friday and spent much of Saturday morning looking at their work and rereading my school's curriculum along with a few other resources. It was a beautiful day and my husband and children were headed out for a hike. I wanted to go with them and I was feeling grouchy that my schoolwork kept me from joining them. I was beginning to wish that I had never started this work. I complained to my husband who said, "But you always spend a Saturday working on stuff before you start a new unit. Is this like the house cleaning?"

I had to laugh at myself then. Just last week I had been complaining about how much work it was to have his parents to dinner. At noon we had cleaned the house and gone food shopping, and I hadn't even started to cook yet. My husband had been clear then, too. He reminded me that we always went food shopping and cleaned the house on Saturday mornings regardless of whether his parents were coming to dinner. How did I forget that? When I looked at it that way, the additional time I spent on Saturday wasn't that long and it turned out to be a lovely evening. I sometimes start out new projects with a bit of pessimism. It's important for me to remember why I am doing something and to be clear about what the actual costs and benefits are.

Suggestion 2: Recognize Where You Are Along the Journey

Many teachers provide an assessment task in September that students complete again sometime in November or December. The comparison of these work samples provides students and parents with concrete examples of growth. Such evidence can boost morale, particularly for students who struggled initially or who may not realize how their abilities have changed. Just as initial benchmarks help students appreciate what they have gained, teachers also benefit from learning how their teaching abilities have adapted, sharpened, broadened, or transformed. So, before you begin or renew your commitment to differentiated mathematics instruction, you might want to self-assess your current level of differentiation in mathematics.

> Just as initial benchmarks help students appreciate what they have gained, teachers also benefit from learning how their teaching abilities have adapted, sharpened, broadened, or transformed.

We encourage you to make a copy of the Self-Assessment of Differentiation Practices form. (See Figure 9–1; also available as Reproducible 37.)

REPRODUCIBLE 37

Reproducible 37

Self-Assessment of Differentiation Practices

Rate your agreement with each of the following statements using the scale provided here:

1–disagree strongly, 2–disagree somewhat, 3–agree somewhat, 4–agree strongly

I feel confident in my ability to facilitate the learning of mathematics at my grade level.	1 2 3 4
I can challenge my most mathematically able students.	1 2 3 4
I know how to support my least mathematically able students.	1 2 3 4
I can meet students' individual needs in mathematics as well as or better than I can in literacy.	1 2 3 4
I have enough knowledge of mathematics to support a variety of models, representations, and procedures in my classroom.	1 2 3 4

Rate the likelihood of the following activities occurring within a week of mathematical instruction using the scale presented here:

1–very unlikely, 2–somewhat unlikely, 3–somewhat likely, 4–very likely

I work with students individually.	1 2 3 4
Students are grouped by readiness.	1 2 3 4
Students are grouped by interest.	1 2 3 4
Students are grouped by learning preferences.	1 2 3 4
Different students are working with different materials and tasks.	1 2 3 4

Check off each instructional strategy that you have tried in your teaching of mathematics. Give yourself 2 points for each checkmark.

☐ Transformation of tasks to make them more open-ended
☐ RAFT
☐ Learning station

☐ Menu
☐ Think Tac Toe
☐ Compacting
☐ Tiered task

Total score: _____

Scores range from 10 to 54 points.

Are you comfortable with where you are on this continuum of change? What next steps do you want to take?

Figure 9–1. *Self-Assessment of Differentiation Practices* form (available as Reproducible 37).

Complete Reproducible 37 now and put it in a place where you can find it at a later date. If you keep a personal calendar, mark a date two to three months from now when you will complete this form for a second time. (You may also want to note where you are putting your original response!) Most teachers who make this comparison find that there are significant differences between their responses. For some teachers, just knowing they are going to complete the form again encourages them to try some new instructional strategies.

Suggestion 3: Start Small and Build up Your Differentiation Muscles

Once teachers recognize the need for differentiated instruction, they sometimes feel as if they have to differentiate every lesson for every student. This would be an overwhelming task, especially if differentiated mathematics instruction is a new practice for you. Just as if you were starting a new exercise program, it's best to start slowly and extend your goals as you build your skills and experience success. Exercising too much, too soon, can result in injuries, frustration, and a sense of failure. These repercussions cause many who make an initial commitment to fitness to conclude, "Exercise just isn't right for me." So, begin slowly and increase the differentiation in your mathematics teaching as your skills and confidence grow.

One way to start is to begin with the content standard you believe you know the best or the one that would benefit the most from differentiation strategies. For most teachers, operations and algebraic thinking or numbers and operations in base ten are good starting points. These are the topics that get the greatest attention during the elementary grades and, if you have been teaching for a few years, the ones for which you probably have the greatest number of supplementary resources. After you have selected a cluster or standard, you can narrow your focus to a unit, a series of lessons, or a particular outcome, such as add and subtract fluently within one hundred (National Governors Association Center for Best Practices and the Council of Chief State School Officers 2010, 36). Work with numbers and operations often yields the widest range of abilities among students. Perhaps because the skill set is so familiar to most teachers, student abilities are often apparent quickly and can be challenging to address within the same activity. This difficulty is in contrast, for example, to the way student differences seem to be addressed more easily within the measurement and data domain.

Most elementary teachers find that all students can be engaged easily with the same task of measuring if choice is given about what they are measuring and, perhaps, whether they would like to measure alone or with a partner. Interest will sustain their efforts to be accurate. Readiness will affect how they engage with the measurement tools. Are they able to use different types of tools to measure? Can they measure using more than one unit of measure? Learning preferences may influence how students like to record their measurement. If they are measuring an item that needs for them to measure beyond a ruler, do they use multiple rulers to keep track or do they use the one ruler and keep track every time they measure to the end? Readiness, learning styles, and interests may inform how the information is recorded and what conclusions are drawn. Most important, these differences occur naturally and do not require much teacher intervention. This is less likely to be the case with numbers and operations. The following reflection shows how choosing a familiar strategy and topic can be a positive way to begin.

> **Choosing a familiar strategy and topic can be a positive way to begin.**

TEACHER REFLECTION

I decided that I would try to incorporate some of the instructional strategies I use in reading in my mathematics program. I often select books with a similar theme that span a wide range of reading levels. In this way, I feel like I can place the right book in the hands of every student, books that will challenge their levels of comprehension while being well within the instructional range of their skill levels for reading. At the same time, we can have a class discussion about themes that emerge in each story and students can be regrouped to share with those who may not have read the same book. There is usually enough commonality to sustain a dynamic conversation. If I have selected

I decided that I would try to incorporate some of the instructional strategies I use in reading in my mathematics program. I often select books with a similar theme that span a wide range of reading levels. In this way, I feel like I can place the right book in the hands of every student, books that will challenge their levels of comprehension while being well within the instructional range of their skill levels for reading. At the same time, we can have a class discussion about themes that emerge in each story and students can be regrouped to share with those who may not have read the same book. There is usually enough commonality to sustain a dynamic conversation. If I have selected nonfiction material,

(continued)

students can compare details and share facts, thus allowing everyone to benefit by the different books read.

Trying to set up a similar dynamic for math has not been as straight-forward, but I wanted to give it a try. Focusing on numbers and operations, I selected a word problem and then created three versions of it. The structure of each problem was the same. I created a story around a set of twins who each earned an allowance for doing chores. Within the three versions of the problem, I differentiated the amount of money each child earned, the number of times each chore was completed, and how the problem was worded. I predetermined which students would answer each problem. Students initially worked alone and then I paired them with other students who were working on the same problem. When I thought everyone had solved and compared with at least one other classmate, I grouped children in triads, with one student representing each type of problem.

Using this new configuration, students were asked to share their problems, answers, and solution strategies. My hope was that each student would act as the expert for the problem they were presenting to the group. When everyone had familiarized themselves with the three problems, I wanted them to discuss what was the same or different in each problem. This seemed to work well. Students made comments such as, "In your problem, Julio and Rita each did the chores a lot more times." "Rita earned more money than Julio in my problem." "We all used division to get the answers."

This was a small step for me, but it was one that really worked. I could see doing something like this about once a week without too much trouble. The students were successful with their individual problems, but also were exposed to other levels of thinking. Maybe next time I could change problem settings as well, choosing contexts that I knew would appeal to different students' interests.

> "This was a small step for me, but it was one that really worked.

Suggestion 4: Anticipate

Teachers are often thinking about what happens next. Sometimes this anticipation can be to their benefit; sometimes it can lead to trouble. You need to think about how to use anticipation to your best advantage.

On the positive side, being able to anticipate the time and resources a specific activity requires is very helpful. Haven't teachers all started a lesson only to realize that there weren't enough copies of the activity packet, or that there really wasn't enough time to complete a new lesson because it took much longer to launch than expected? Decisions that avoid situations like these come with experience, although even the most seasoned veteran makes similar errors in judgment from time to time. Not having quite the right resources can derail a potentially successful differentiated lesson, so it's important to make sure that manipulatives, worksheets or packets, directions and pieces for games, and any supplies or tools required are readily available. You have to consider purpose and quantity, need for replacement during completion of the task, and the mathematical implications of the types of manipulatives or technology you offer your students. Asking yourself, "Is this the right tool to support this standard in mathematics?" will allow for students to visualize the concept at hand more completely.

Visualizing a future event is part of anticipation. It is important to think about how you envision a lesson unfolding. Keep in mind your goals, where a given lesson falls in the learning progression, and the current levels of your students' understanding.

> **Visualizing a future event is part of anticipation. It is important to think about how you envision a lesson unfolding.**

- What responses might you anticipate?
- What leaps in students' understanding might occur?
- What questions might the students ask?
- What possible errors might students make and what misconceptions might they have?

Draw on your knowledge and past experiences to help you anticipate your responses to new insights, questions, errors, and incomplete understandings that arise. Consider what distractions or diversions might come up, and identify key questions to ask. Determine the ways to scaffold learning (see Chapter 6) and plan groups that work well together and support the students in their pursuits. Basically, by trying to do as much work up front as possible, teachers reduce potential roadblocks to learning and increase the likelihood that they are available to work with a small group or to support individual students after a learning activity has begun.

See CHAPTER 6

Establish blocks of uninterrupted time so that students can really dig in to a task. Check your schedule. Many teachers comment that any time they want to start a new unit or are planning a debriefing session, they want all students present. Some students receive support outside of class and it is important to be mindful of what is happening for each student as you prepare new lessons and set a schedule. Also, build in extra time for students to explore any new materials in the lesson. Captivating models and tools such as pattern blocks, geoboards, and real coins are distracting when they are first introduced.

As you anticipate, you need to be fresh and ready for new challenges and possibilities. One way that anticipation can lead you into trouble is the overanticipation of behavior. It is only natural for teachers to want to set up the most positive learning environment for students. Keeping everyone's behavior in check can be part of this mind-set. Sadly, most teachers can describe a time in their classroom when a student's behavior overshadowed or impeded learning. To avoid this happening, many teachers overly anticipate how a specific student might respond and then provide unnecessary scaffolding. Although this is a natural instinct, this form of anticipation can be shortsighted and can limit student potential. As you strive for differentiation in your math class, realize that part of your goal is to support students in all areas of their development. Many teachers find that when they create tailor-made assignments, negative behavior is diminished. So, for example, under new and more comfortable learning conditions, students may no longer need supportive prompts or a separate space to work. Also, even students who have had difficulty working together in the past may learn to appreciate more about each other's strengths.

> As you strive for differentiation in your math class, realize that part of your goal is to support students in all areas of their development.

Many teachers lament about how impossible it is to differentiate mathematics instruction. This attitude and worry can defeat them before they even begin. Part of anticipation is looking forward. Try and visualize how you want your students to succeed, and how you want them to develop a rich understanding of and appreciation for mathematics while gaining self-confidence in their abilities. Can you see your students taking more ownership for their own learning as their interest level increases? Get excited about the possibilities and visualize yourself as the key ingredient in making this happen. Change is scary and risky, and can be problematic. It can also be exciting, rewarding, and fun.

Suggestion 5: Expect Surprises

Throughout this resource we have presented classroom vignettes and videos that contained surprises. Sometimes students didn't use the materials in quite the way the teacher expected, or they experienced unexpected difficulty with a representation. This happened even though experienced teachers took time to plan lessons carefully and anticipate students' needs and reactions. However, instead of halting the students' work or getting frustrated, these teachers appreciated the opportunities to learn more about their students' thinking.

Sometimes teachers are surprised to find out that a student knows more than they thought or exhibits a more positive attitude toward mathematics than they believed possible. When choice is involved and mathematics is connected to students' interests, students are often able to make mathematical connections in new ways. For example, as one student, Jalissa, explained, "Once I learned that it takes four quarters to make a dollar, I remember that my music teacher told me about quarter notes and that it's the same. Fractions are everywhere. Even when you bake cookies you need a quarter of a cup."

Parents can also be the source of surprises. Teachers have found that when parents understand how much differentiated instruction helps their children, many ask more questions about mathematics and offer more help. They no longer make statements such as "Well, I wasn't very good at mathematics either; that's just the way it is," and recognize that their children can succeed under the right circumstances.

Teachers remark that they have been surprised to learn that making plans for differentiated instruction is time-consuming at first, but in fact saves time in the long run. Another surprise teachers have expressed is that when they differentiate instruction, they feel more creative and empowered as decision makers. Teachers are also surprised at the amount of mathematics they are learning. For example, when one student asked, "So why can't you divide by zero?" his teacher realized he needed to find out.

Surprises are part of the joyful mystery of teaching. They keep educators interested and help them learn. They are stimulating and can help sustain commitment to differentiated instruction.

> When choice is involved and mathematics is connected to students' interests, students are often able to make mathematical connections in new ways.

Suggestion 6: Let Students Help

Classrooms require significant management of people and materials. Differentiated instruction often requires even more organization and record-keeping skills. You will be more successful if you let your students take some of the responsibility. The following list presents tasks that students can manage successfully.

Tasks for Students to Manage

- Organize and distribute materials.
- Review one another's work.
- Keep track of their own choices and work.
- Make sure a partner understands an assigned task.

(continued)

- Lead a routine or familiar game.
- Answer peer questions when you are working with a group.

When you encourage your students to take more responsibility for the operation of the classroom, you are fostering their confidence and helping them to be more independent. Their involvement may also increase the likelihood that differentiated activities will succeed.

Jeanette's Story: A Math Game Library

Sometimes, the summer months provide teachers with time to tackle projects that never seem to get accomplished during the year. One summer, Jeanette decided to create a math game library. Throughout the years, Jeanette came to recognize that most of her students would benefit from more practice with basic facts and mental arithmetic than she felt she had time for during the week. She decided that offering math games they could play during the weekend would give her students extra practice as well as involve their families in their learning.

Jeanette identified six basic games and then designed three levels of each game by changing a few rules or the specific numbers involved. She wrote directions for each of these eighteen game versions and collected the materials, such as cards and dice, that were needed. She wanted four copies of each game so four students could take home the same activity. She decided to store the games in sealed plastic bags that would protect the games as they were carried back and forth to school. In each bag she put a direction sheet, a materials list, the needed supplies, and a reflection sheet that posed the questions: How did this game help you learn the mathematics? What new questions do you have?

In the fall, she organized a storage area for the games and made additional copies of the directions, materials lists, and reflection forms for replacement. She also stored some extra packs of cards and dice in this area. She had a student teacher that fall who was given the responsibility for distributing the games on Friday afternoons and checking them back in on Monday mornings. The morning process involved collecting the reflection slips, following up on any missing materials, inserting new reflection sheets, and putting the games away. Students were eager to get their "weekend game," and Jeanette noted a marked improvement in their skills.

After the winter break, Jeanette's student teacher returned to his college campus and Jeanette took over support of this activity. She was surprised at how difficult it was to accomplish this process at the same time that so many students seemed to need her. After the second Monday morning, she was certain that this ritual would need to end; she just couldn't support it. She shared her disappointment with the school's math coach who responded, "Could your students be assigned the job?"

Jeanette had to admit that she hadn't thought of this and, at first, didn't believe that it would work. As she thought about it throughout the day, she decided it was worth a try. To her surprise the students became quite adept at taking over this responsibility. Students assigned to this task were listed on the class chore board along with those who were slated to complete other classroom chores. Students were given this task for two weeks. The first week they served as assistants, so that they could learn what was expected of them. During the second week they were the "math game librarians" in charge of distributing and checking in the materials, as well as training new assistants. Jeanette remarked, "I am so glad this was suggested to me. Instead of being frustrated with having to give this up, my students have taken over and it really works!"

It's worth thinking about some of the clerical and custodial tasks that you are performing. Could your students take more responsibility for them? Are there more important things you could accomplish with this time?

Suggestion 7: Work with Parents

 VIDEO CLIP 9.1

Student and Parent Interviews

In this video clip, we first see Ms. Corpas meet with one of her kindergarten students, Aurora. After the school day, Ms. Corpas then meets with Aurora's mom.

As you watch the clip, consider:

1. What are the pros and cons of asking for parent input?
2. What have you learned about your students' math abilities by working with parents that you wouldn't have known from working with the student in class?
3. How has parent input informed your instruction and allowed you to better differentiate lessons?

> For examples of the questionnaires the teacher is using in these interviews, see Reproducibles 2 and 4.

See CHAPTER 2

As you know, parental support can make the difference between success and failure, so it is important that your students' parents understand how your classroom works. Ask parents to help you know their children better, perhaps by completing surveys or by talking with you informally before or after school (see Chapter 2). Most parents support efforts to make sure their children's individual needs are met, after they believe that this is really going to be the case. The first Back-to-School Night in the fall is also an opportunity to gain parental understanding and support.

When one teacher was on an errand, she started to think about the ways she met her own children's needs. She was buying her three children socks; one child wanted high basketball socks, one wanted tennis socks so low you could hardly see them, and her youngest wanted tube socks because, as he explained, "The seams hurt my feet when I have shoes on." She chuckled as she thought about how not having the "right socks" could ruin a morning for the entire family. She decided to share these thoughts at Back-to-School Night and to ask the parents some additional questions such as: Do each of your children need the same amount of sleep? Enjoy the same activities? Want to eat the same food? In what ways do you adjust to meet these individual needs and interests? She found parents enjoyed talking about these differences with others who were also trying to meet children's needs that didn't always match. It was simple to then help the parents understand that these same differences existed in the classroom and must be addressed there as well.

Evidence of their children's growth is often the most persuasive argument. Collect early work so that it can be compared with later samples at the first parent–teacher conference. Help parents see the specific concepts and skills their children have gained. Let them know how differentiated instructional strategies supported this improvement. Conferences can also be a time to address their particular concerns about the way you are teaching. Be prepared to help parents understand that:

- all learning activities are tied directly to curriculum goals and standards,
- differentiated instruction is not a secret method for tracking the students (groups change often and for a variety of reasons), and
- they are always welcome to visit the classroom and participate in the learning activities.

Then, follow up the initial meetings with continued communication. Many teachers create their own Web sites or blogs that offer parents examples of how math is being learned in the classroom. Some teachers prefer newsletters, especially for the start of a new unit, outlining the highlighted standards with examples of how parents can support this learning at home. Also, an occasional note or e-mail reinforces how each student is engaging in learning mathematics in unique ways.

Sometimes, talking about their child's particular learning strengths and challenges reminds parents of their own learning profiles. Parents may also have had their own struggles in school because their learning needs weren't met. Many teachers find that when they share observations with parents about their child's learning profiles, the parents sometimes ask questions that suggest they identify with what they have just heard. Comments such as "I wonder what kind of learning disability they might find for me if I were just starting out in school today?" or "I loved math class because I didn't have to read as much. But I'm worried about how much more reading my son needs to do in math class. It seems to be turning him off."

Parents' feelings are strong and their insights about their child's learning are often profound. It is not always easy for parents to open up about their school experiences, but they often do so after a level of trust has been established with the teacher. About a month after a conference in which a teacher shared with a father that his daughter was struggling to learn the names of numbers and that perhaps this was what was making her development in counting so labored and frustrating for her, the father emailed the teacher. The parent's note appears in the following Parent Reflection.

> It is not always easy for parents to open up about their school experiences, but they often do so after a level of trust has been established with the teacher.

PARENT REFLECTION

I had an interesting conversation with my daughter last night that I think is informative concerning her counting abilities. Lately, while playing games like hide-and-seek with her, I have been trying things such as having her start at fifteen when she counts. She tends to hang up at the transitions between twenty to thirty to forty, and so on, and she becomes very upset at this, which has resulted in several teary and frustrated breakdowns. Last night, I asked her how she felt about it and she confided to me that she was ashamed and upset. She went on to say that she experiences a lot of stress at school trying to hide these defects from her peers and teachers. These are my words, but her feelings. I am fairly confident that it is an accurate portrayal.

(continued)

I also want you to know that I had similar learning difficulties as a child and I still have been unable to memorize half of the multiplication table. Perhaps my little one has inherited some of the same mental challenges.

Specific to counting, it is my opinion that Beth understands the number system conceptually, but that she just can't recall in a timely fashion the words that represent the numbers. I'm curious if this fits in with your current understanding of the situation. My game plan has been to integrate counting into as many activities as possible during our free time together to provide repetition, but I will downplay the errors so that she doesn't become overly upset. I also have a large repertoire of mental tricks that I have accumulated to help me with these issues and I am trying to pass them on to her. She was visibly relieved the first time I confided to her that I, too, had problems like hers. As I am sure you are aware, she is a terribly proud child and I think her discomfort with needing help has caused her to avoid the very things that need more attention.

> "As I am sure you are aware, she is a terribly proud child and I think her discomfort with needing help has caused her to avoid the very things that need more attention."

Beth's teacher was honored to receive this missive and knew that this parent's trust was a wonderful gift, one that would help ensure that his daughter's needs would be better met.

Suggestion 8: Find Sources of Professional Development

Ideally, you are working with colleagues as you strive to differentiate your mathematics instruction further, and your school system has provided you with coaches, consultants, time, and resources. Such circumstances are increasingly rare, however, and so it is more than likely that you will need to find some ways to support your efforts. Sometimes just finding one other teacher that will work with you is sufficient. Here are some activities that other teachers have engaged in with one or more colleagues:

Visit other classrooms	Use planning time or arrange coverage for your class so you can visit each other's classroom. It will help you understand how things are currently working and the challenges each of you face.
Attend conferences	Attend mathematics conferences in the local area to gain new ideas and connect with a wider group of teachers.
Watch videos	Return to watching the video clips included with this resource. Choose a clip you remember as being of particular interest or pick one randomly. In addition, search the Web for videos of mathematics or the general practice of differentiated instruction that you could watch alone or with a colleague.
Work with specialists	Work more closely with any instructional specialists in your school system. Many specialists are eager to work with teachers who want to transform their practice.
Exchange ideas online	Follow a blog or read posts from other educators who are also committed to differentiating instruction in their classrooms. *Pinterest.com* is an active site where teachers exchange and collect fresh ideas on electronic pinboards.
Explore the National Council of Teachers of Mathematics (NCTM)	Find out whether your school system has a membership in the NCTM, and read its journal, *Teaching Children Mathematics*, if it is available. In addition, explore the NCTM Web site and lesson exemplars.
Seek out funding	Talk with your principal to determine the support that might be available to fund attendance at conferences or purchases of resource materials.
Debrief with others	Engage in instructional debriefing with one another about what is happening during math time. In addition, look at student work with colleagues. This is a practice that often leads to a deeper understanding of your students' mathematical needs and furthers opportunities to differentiate instruction.

Suggestion 9: Reflect on Your Journey

When teachers reflect on their teaching they take the time to deliberate actively about what is working and what needs additional attention. Perhaps during the evening you might sift through what happened that day, and may even replay conversations with your students. Sometimes you uncover something that you didn't know was bothering you; sometimes you develop new insights and ideas. Over time, reflecting on what happens in your classroom can help you transform as well as reaffirm aspects of your teaching habits and beliefs. Although reflecting on your teaching is always important, it is particularly helpful when you are adjusting your practice.

Some teachers reflect with others about their teaching; some spend their commute time mulling over the day. A few teachers reflect more intentionally, by keeping a journal. If you record your reflections, you have documentation that you can return to and reread—information that can help you identify patterns and note your changes over time. One teacher reserves Wednesday afternoon for journal writing. Let's take a look at her reflection about this tradition.

TEACHER REFLECTION

> Now when I return to my desk on Wednesdays, I immediately take out my journal and set a timer for fifteen minutes.

Early on in my career, I found that, by Wednesday, I needed to spend a bit more time working after school. By then, school plans made during the previous weekend needed more attention, and my desk was a bit disorganized. Also, like many, I think of Wednesday as "hump day," so working a bit longer on that day made sense to me.

At first, it took me a while to get started after I returned from walking my students to the bus and pickup area. I'd come back to my desk and collapse in my chair, and maybe check my e-mail. Sometimes it would take me an hour to get back up to speed. Then I learned about journaling and how that can give you energy, help you focus. I decided to try it on Wednesdays and it really worked for me. Now when I return to my desk on Wednesdays, I immediately take out my journal and set a timer for fifteen minutes. It might take me a minute or two to start writing, but soon the words just begin to flow and I'm often amazed by what I write. I get so focused that I'm usually surprised when the timer goes off. Maybe it's the quiet, the focus, or the introspection, but after writing I have the energy to tackle the other things I need to do.

Some teachers prefer to take notes rather than write in prose. One teacher has a daily writing practice. She makes notes on a file card about two questions each day: How did I address individual needs today? and What did I learn about my students today that will inform what I do tomorrow? When she comes in the next morning, she rereads the notes to help her focus on the new day. Some teachers follow a similar process, but record these notes in their plan books so that they are maintained over time. Other questions that may help you to think about your practice of differentiation follow.

Questions to Guide Your Thinking About Differentiation

- Did the pace of today's mathematics instruction work? For whom? Why? Why not?
- Are all students being challenged mathematically?
- How did I address students' interests this week? Did I learn anything new about an interest a student has?
- How were different types of learning styles addressed today?
- Are there students I want to meet with individually tomorrow?
- Is there a student I am worried about in terms of mathematics?
- Would some of my students be more successful using different mathematical manipulatives, representations, or recording systems?

Suggestion 10: Keep the Vision

There will no doubt be times when you question the goal of differentiated mathematics instruction, or at least its viability or sustainability. Perhaps a principal will express reservations about your instructional style, a parent will complain about his or her child not doing the same work as the neighbor's child, or a colleague will suggest that you are making too much work for yourself. At these times it's important to remember the significance of the goal and the good sense it makes. Focus on what is working well in your classroom and what is best for your students. Remember that differentiated instruction is a long quest, a journey that never truly ends. It serves as a lens to remind you to focus on how you can best support the individual differences among your students, and provides you with a vision of how you want your classroom to be organized and your curriculum to be implemented. It takes courage and passion to sustain your efforts toward the goal of differentiated instruction, and the vision of all of your students becoming successful learners of mathematics.

> It takes courage and passion to sustain your efforts toward the goal of differentiated instruction.

 **VIDEO CLIP 9.2** ·

Sustaining Your Differentiation Efforts

In this final video clip, we hear authors Linda Dacey and Jayne Bamford Lynch share some advice to support you in continuing to sustain your differentiation efforts.

As you watch this clip, consider:

1. When the authors describe the benefits of collaborating with colleagues, what do you agree with?
2. What would you suggest as an additional benefit?
3. What is your next step in sustaining your differentiation efforts?

· ·

Connecting the Chapter to Your Practice

1. In terms of differentiation, where would you place yourself along the continuum of novice to expert? Why?

2. How can you influence parents' understanding of the benefits of differentiated instruction?

3. Are there opportunities to increase students' responsibilities in your classroom? Explain.

4. Who in your school system is most likely to help you identify worthwhile professional development opportunities?

Reproducibles

Differentiation Planning Chart

	CONTENT	PROCESS	PRODUCT
Readiness			
Interests			
Learning Profile			

Narrative–Style Parent or Guardian Questionnaire

Distribute to parents at the beginning of the school year.

Student name: _____

Dear Parent or Guardian:

I am always so excited about the start of the school year and a roomful of eager students. I am looking forward to getting to know each and every one of them, as well as their families. Because no one knows your child as well as you do, I am hoping that you will have the time to answer these few questions. There are no right or wrong answers, just responses that will help me to meet your child's needs more completely when he or she is learning math. I am very interested in helping children realize that math is an important part of the world, and is exciting to learn. I believe that by connecting the learning of math to other important aspects of your child's life, I can make it more relevant and exciting. Please feel free to call me if you have any questions. Thank you.

1. What are your child's favorite hobbies, interests, pastimes, books?

2. In what ways is mathematics part of your child's life at home?

3. What, if any, concerns do you have about your child's knowledge of mathematics?

4. What is a mathematical strength that you see in your child?

5. Describe your child's experience with math homework.

Survey–Style Parent or Guardian Questionnaire

Distribute to parents at the beginning of the school year.

Dear Parent or Guardian:

This first day has been a wonderful start to the school year. I am excited about getting to know each of my new students. I hope that you will help me by completing this questionnaire about mathematics. There are no right or wrong answers! Please feel free to call me if you have any questions. Thank you.

Student name: _____

Please circle the number next to the statement that corresponds to the number key listed here:

1 = agree
2 = somewhat agree
3 = somewhat disagree
4 = disagree

My child will stick with a math problem, even when it is difficult.	1 2 3 4
My child lacks confidence in mathematics.	1 2 3 4
My child has strong computational skills.	1 2 3 4
My child's favorite subject is mathematics.	1 2 3 4
My child becomes frustrated solving math problems.	1 2 3 4
My child does math homework independently.	1 2 3 4
As a caregiver, it is my job to help my child with math homework.	1 2 3 4
Math is talked about at home and is part of our everyday life.	1 2 3 4
I do not always understand the way my child thinks about math problems.	1 2 3 4
Math is taught better today than when I was in school.	1 2 3 4

Comments:

What Interests You? Questionnaire

Distribute to students early during the school year. For younger children, ask the parent or guardian to complete this questionnaire at home, with the adult reading and recording the information given by the child.

Student name: _____

What Interests You?

1. What activities do you like to do after school?

2. What are your favorite sports or games?

3. What do you like to do during indoor recess?

4. If you could plan a field trip, where would you want to go?

5. Who is your favorite character from a book or a video?

6. In the following list, place a 1 next to the things you like the most. Place a 2 next to the things you like second best.

    ____ music   ____ reading

    ____ sports   ____ nature walks

    ____ acting   ____ drawing or art projects

    ____ being with friends   ____ building things

    ____ science experiments   ____ field trips to historical places

Who Are You as a Learner? Questionnaire

Distribute to students early during the school year. For younger children, ask the parent or guardian to complete this questionnaire at home, with the adult reading and recording the information given by the child.

Student name: _____

Who Are You as a Learner?

1. If you could learn about anything at school, what would you choose?

2. What do you know a lot about?

3. How do you work best in school (check all that describe you)?

____ alone   ____ partner   ____ small group   ____ large group

4. Where do you like to work at school (check all that describe you)?

____ desk   ____ table   ____ hallway   ____ floor   ____ library area   ____ other

5. You learn best when your classroom is (check all that describe you)

____ quiet   ____ somewhat quiet   ____ somewhat noisy   ____ noisy

6. Do you like schoolwork to be (check all that describe you)

____ easy   ____ somewhat easy   ____ somewhat hard   ____ hard

7. What else helps you to learn?

8. What makes it hard for you to learn?

What Do You Think About Mathematics? Questionnaire

Distribute to students early during the school year. For younger children, ask the parent or guardian to complete this questionnaire at home, with the adult reading and recording the information given by the child.

Directions: Complete these sentence starters.

Student name: _____

What Do You Think About Mathematics?

1. Math is important to learn because . . .

2. When I am learning math I feel . . .

3. One thing I am good at in math is . . .

4. One thing I am not good at yet in math is . . .

5. This year in math I want to learn about . . .

A Mathematics Autobiography

Student name: _____

My Mathematics Autobiography

Directions: Write an autobiography that focuses on your experiences with mathematics. Use the following questions to guide your thinking. Be sure to explain your answers. You don't need to answer every question, but comment on at least 5 of them.

1. How do you feel about yourself in math class?

2. What is your first memory of using mathematics?

3. What do you remember about learning to count or using numbers?

4. What kinds of things have your math teachers done to help you enjoy math?

5. What is your favorite area in mathematics (geometry, computation, logic, problem solving)?

6. What kind of math equipment, tools, or games do you like to use when learning mathematics? Why?

7. What are 2 examples of when you have used math outside of school?

8. When solving problems, do you prefer working alone or in a group? Why?

9. What area of math is a strength for you?

10. What area of math do you find the most challenging?

Sums Investigation: Red

Getting Started

- Write the numbers 3, 6, 8, and 10 on the blank cards clipped to this sheet. Write one number on each card.

- Put your number cards in the bag and shake it.

To Play

- Pull out two cards. Record the numbers and their sum.

- Return the cards to the bag and take another turn.

- Do this at least fifteen times.

Stop and Think

- List all the sums you get.

What Did You Learn?

- Do you think you have all the different sums that can be made by adding two of your numbers at a time?

- Talk together about why you think you have all the possibilities.

Sums Investigation: Blue

Getting Started

- Write the numbers 4, 5, 11, and 17 on the blank cards clipped to this sheet. Write one number on each card.

- Put your number cards in the bag and shake it.

To Play

- Pull out two cards. Record the numbers and their sum.

- Return the cards to the bag and take another turn.

- Do this several more times.

Stop and Think

- Make a list of all the sums you could get when using these four number cards.

- Continue to play.

What Did You Learn?

- Make a list showing all the sums you made.

- Do you think you have them all?

- Talk together about why you think you have all the possibilities.

From *How to Differentiate Your Math Instruction: Lessons, Ideas, and Videos with Common Core Support, Grades K–5: A Multimedia Professional Learning Resource* by Linda Dacey, Jayne Bamford Lynch, and Rebeka Eston Salemi. © 2013 by Scholastic Inc. Permission granted to photocopy for nonprofit use in a classroom or similar place dedicated to face-to-face educational purposes. Downloadable at *www.mathsolutions.com/howtodifferentiatereproducible*.

Sums Investigation: **Green**

Getting Started

- Write the numbers 12, 15, 19, and 24 on the blank cards clipped to this sheet.

- Put your number cards in the bag and shake it.

To Play

- Pull out two cards. Record the numbers and their sum.

- Return the cards to the bag and take another turn.

- Do this a few times.

Stop and Think

- How many different sums do you get when you pull two of these number cards from the bag?

- How do you know you have all the possibilities?

What Did You Learn?

- Write about your thinking.

Shape Puzzler Card: Red

These are sops.

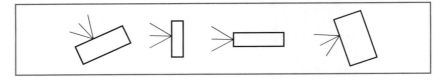

These are not sops.

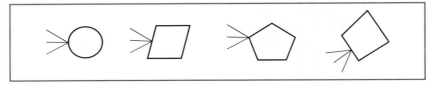

Which one of these is a sop?

Talk with a partner about what makes a sop.

From *How to Differentiate Your Math Instruction: Lessons, Ideas, and Videos with Common Core Support, Grades K–5: A Multimedia Professional Learning Resource* by Linda Dacey, Jayne Bamford Lynch, and Rebeka Eston Salemi. © 2013 by Scholastic Inc. Permission granted to photocopy for nonprofit use in a classroom or similar place dedicated to face-to-face educational purposes. Downloadable at *www.mathsolutions.com/howtodifferentiatereproducible*.

Shape Puzzler **Card: Blue**

These are mips.

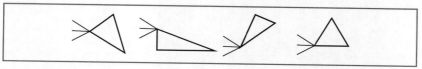

These are not mips.

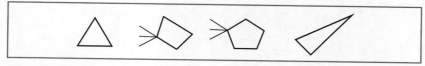

Which ones of these are mips?

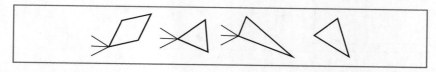

Draw a new example of a mip.

Shape Puzzler Card: Green

These are reps.

These are not reps.

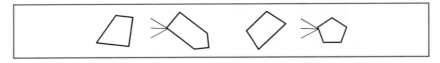

Which ones of these are reps?

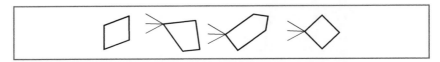

Make your own *Shape Puzzler*.

Directions

Write the name in the blanks.

Draw the missing pictures.

These are _____.

These are not _____.

Which of these are _____?

Talk with a partner about your *Shape Puzzler*.

From *How to Differentiate Your Math Instruction: Lessons, Ideas, and Videos with Common Core Support, Grades K–5: A Multimedia Professional Learning Resource* by Linda Dacey, Jayne Bamford Lynch, and Rebeka Eston Salemi. © 2013 by Scholastic Inc. Permission granted to photocopy for nonprofit use in a classroom or similar place dedicated to face-to-face educational purposes. Downloadable at *www.mathsolutions.com/howtodifferentiatereproducible*.

Addition Facts: **Red**

Materials

shuffled ten-frames for 0 to 9

Directions

1. Turn the frames facedown.

2. Look at the ten-frame on top.

3. Copy this: _____ + _____ = 10

4. Write the number shown on the frame in a blank.

5. Talk with a partner about how to find the missing number.

6. Write the number in the blank that makes the equation true.

7. Put this ten-frame aside.

8. Repeat Steps 2 through 7 four times.

Addition Facts: **Blue**

Materials

2 sets of shuffled ten-frames for 0 to 9

Directions

1. Turn each set facedown.

2. Look at the top ten-frame in each set.

3. Talk with a partner about how to use the ten-frames to find the sum.

4. Write an equation to show the sum.

5. Put these two frames aside.

6. Write another equation for this sum.

7. Repeat Steps 2 through 6 four times.

Addition Facts: Green

Materials

2 sets of shuffled number cards 5 to 9

Directions

1. Turn each set facedown.

2. Look at the top card in each set.

3. Write an equation to show the sum.

4. Put these two cards aside.

5. Use different numbers to write three more equations for this sum.

6. Repeat Steps 2 through 5 four times.

7. Talk with a partner about how to find other equations with the same sums.

Ten-Frame

Number Cards 1 to 10

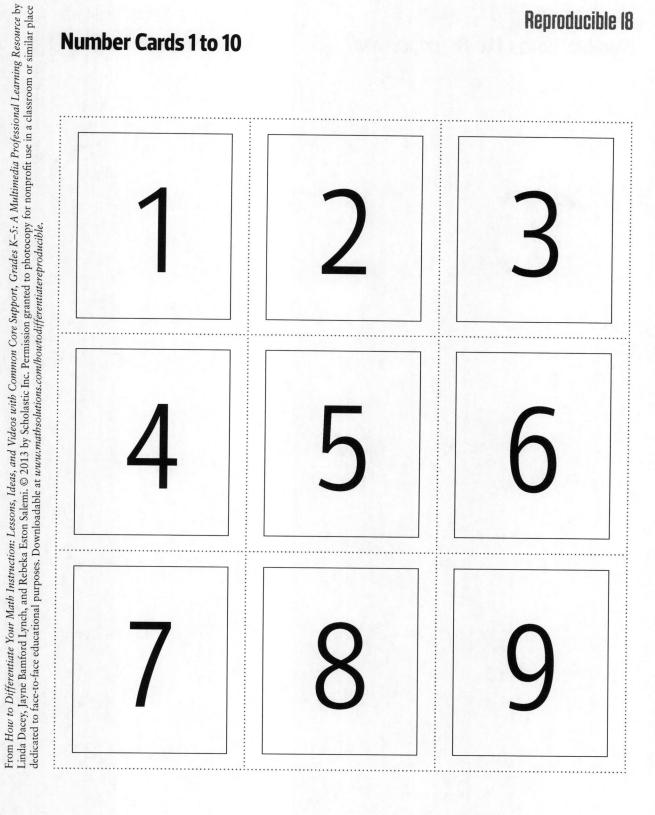

Number Cards 1 to 10 *(continued)*

10

Finish the Story: Red

1	7:25	20	7:05	2

Dani woke up at _____ a.m. She was ready to run _____

minutes later, at _____ a.m. She ran for _____ miles.

She drank _____ liter of water as soon as she got home.

Directions

1. Fill in each blank so the story makes sense.

2. Explain in writing how you decided what to write in the first blank.

Finish the Story: **Blue**

18	280	6:23	8	6:41

Lisa got home from work at _____ p.m. and, _____ minutes later, at _____ p.m., she and her dog Max went out for a walk. Max weighs _____ kilograms and eats about _____ grams of food each day.

Directions

1. Fill in each blank so the story makes sense.

2. Explain in writing how you decided the number of kilograms that made sense.

3. What time do you think Lisa and Max got back from their walk? Write the time and explain your thinking.

Finish the Story: Green

| 12:24 | 30 | 12:34 | 4 | 150 | 11:09 | 75 |

Cam and Andi went to the gym at _____ a.m. and completed their

workout _____ minutes later, at _____ p.m. They both

lifted _____ kilograms with each arm to strengthen their biceps. At

_____ p.m., they each ate an apple that weighed about _____

grams. They were home _____ minutes later.

Directions

1. Fill in each blank so the story makes sense.

2. Write about the hardest number for you to place.

3. Add a sentence to the story. Make sure a measurement of kilograms or grams is in the sentence.

Hopping Robots: **Red**

Imagine a robot that make hops along a number line.

A 5-hopper robot starts at 0 and makes 15 hops.

1. On what numbers will the robot land when it hops?

2. Write the numbers.

3. Make a list of the patterns you see in the numbers.

4. Think about:

    *   patterns in the ones place,

    *   patterns in the tens place, and

    *   even and odd number patterns.

Start the robot at a different number.

5. On what numbers will the robot land when it makes fifteen hops?

6. Which patterns stay the same?

7. Which patterns change?

Hopping Robots: **Blue**

Imagine a robot that make hops along a number line.

The five-hopper robot is going for a walk.

1. Pick the number on the line where the robot starts.

2. List the numbers on which the robot lands when it makes fifteen hops.

3. Pick a different start number.

4. List the numbers on which the robot lands when it makes fifteen hops.

5. Write equations that would let you find the 20th numbers in each list.

6. Write about four patterns you find in your lists.

Hopping Robots: Green

Imagine a robot that make hops along a number line.

You have a two-hopper robot and a five-hopper robot.

1. Pick the number on the line where the robots will start.

2. List the numbers on which the robots land when they make fifteen hops.

3. Pick a different start number.

4. List the numbers on which robots land when they make fifteen hops.

5. Write equations that would let you find the 20th numbers in each list.

6. Write about patterns you find in your lists.

7. What changes a pattern more: the hopper or the start number? Explain your thinking.

8. Predict how many hops a four-hopper robot must make for the pattern in the ones place to repeat. Explain your thinking and then check your prediction.

Real–World Connections: Red

Plan a Class Field Trip

1. Survey your classmates to find out the type of field trip they would like to take. The choices are a science museum, a historic tour, an art museum, or an aquarium.

2. Prepare a report of what you learn. In your report include:

   - the choices each person made,

   - a table of your data,

   - a bar graph of your data, and

   - your recommendation for a class trip.

3. Consider the cost of the class trip. Your jobs are to:

   - brainstorm possible costs (remember to include four parent helpers),

   - use the computer or make calls to collect data,

   - find the total cost.

Real–World Connections: Blue

Consult to a Business

The local athletic store wants to know more about students' preferences for sneakers. The owners are interested in learning more about the number, color, size, and type of sneaker that they should keep in stock. You are to collect the data for our classroom and prepare a report.

1. Make sure to include the choices each person made using tables and graphs in your report, as well as your recommendations.

2. Investigate prices of sneakers. Based on your data, how much do you think your classmates will spend on sneakers this year?

Real–World Connections: Green

Plan a Lunch Party

We are going to have lunch with our kindergarten reading buddies. Use supermarket fly–ers to prepare possible choices.

1. Collect data about lunch preferences and activities for both classes. Make sure to include choices students made, using tables and graphs in your report, as well as your recommendations.

2. Analyze your menu. Use references to estimate total calories and sodium content.

3. Make a shopping list. Use the flyers to find the price of the items we need to buy. Explain how to use the information to estimate the total cost of the lunch.

Mystery Puzzles

RED

$$\nabla + \Diamond + \Diamond = 110$$

$$\Diamond + 30 = 35$$

$$\nabla = \underline{\hspace{2cm}}$$

$$\Diamond = \underline{\hspace{2cm}}$$

Explain how you solved this problem.

BLUE

$$\Diamond + \Diamond + \nabla + \nabla + \nabla = 236$$

$$\Diamond - \nabla = 88$$

$$\Diamond = \underline{\hspace{2cm}}$$

$$\nabla = \underline{\hspace{2cm}}$$

Explain how you solved this problem.

GREEN

$$\otimes + \otimes + \Lambda + \Lambda = 522$$

$$\otimes + \Lambda = 261$$

$$\otimes = \underline{\hspace{2cm}}$$

$$\Lambda = \underline{\hspace{2cm}}$$

Explain how you solved this problem. Can you find more than two solutions? Prove it!

Vocabulary Sheet

New word: _____

My definition: _____

_____

_____

_____

Examples

Used in a sentence:

_____

_____

A Project Contract

Student name: _____

1. Due date:

    The topic for my mathematical project is:

    This is what I want to learn:

    I will use these materials and resources:

    This is what I will create to show what I learned about mathematics:

2. Due date:

    This is what I have accomplished so far:

    This is what I still have to do:

3. Due date:

    My project is complete. The three most important things I learned about mathematics are:

    The best part of this project was:

    The most challenging part of this project was:

From *How to Differentiate Your Math Instruction: Lessons, Ideas, and Videos with Common Core Support, Grades K–5: A Multimedia Professional Learning Resource* by Linda Dacey, Jayne Bamford Lynch, and Rebeka Eston Salemi. © 2013 by Scholastic Inc. Permission granted to photocopy for nonprofit use in a classroom or similar place dedicated to face-to-face educational purposes. Downloadable at *www.mathsolutions.com/howtodifferentiatereproducible.*

Geometry Menu

Student name: _____

Make a check mark (✓) to show what you chose.

	MONDAY	TUESDAY	WEDNESDAY	THURSDAY	FRIDAY
Feely Box					
Art Project					
Books					
Sorting					
Block Area					

Measurement Menu

Student name: _____

20 points

- Get a flyer from a supermarket or a sports store. Cut out items that list a measure in liters, grams, or kilograms and make a collage.

- Measure the lengths of 5 items in your classroom that are shorter than $6\frac{1}{2}$ inches. Measure to the nearest half-inch. Make a list of the items and their measures.

30 points

- Write two story problems about liters, grams, or kilograms.

- Measure the lengths of 5 items in your classroom that are between $4\frac{1}{4}$ inches and $8\frac{1}{2}$ inches long. Measure to the nearest quarter-inch. Work with a partner to create a line plot using the lengths of all the items you each measured.

50 points

- Go through your kitchen or visit a supermarket. Make a guide that shows examples of items with their measures given in liters, grams, or kilograms that would be helpful to use as benchmarks. Use drawings and words to show how to use these items to estimate other masses or liquid volumes.

- Write a story about a scientist or designer who has to measure the perimeters of items very carefully. Include the measures of 5 real items in your story.

Menu: Math All Around Us

Student name: _____

Main Course *(You must do each one.)*

- For 1 week, keep a list of all the ways you use mathematics outside of school.

- Interview 2 adult neighbors or relatives about the ways they use mathematics when they are at work. Share your information with your team. Together, make a visual summary of your combined data.

- Create your own character. Write and illustrate your own version of *Math Curse.* Make sure your story contains at least 10 math problems, and attach an answer key.

Side Orders *(Complete two.)*

- Write about how mathematics is used in your favorite sport.

- Read 3 stories in the newspaper. Make notes about the ways mathematics is used in the articles or how knowing mathematics helps you to understand the articles.

- Reread *Math Curse* and solve 6 of the problems in the story.

- Make a photo display of geometry in our world.

- Choose 1 of the real-world math Web sites that have been saved as favorites and write 4 problems to put in our real-world problem box.

Desserts *(Do one or more if you are interested.)*

- Read a biography of author Jon Scieszka and coauthor/illustrator Lane Smith at www.kidsreads.com/series/series-warp-author.asp.

- Make up a song called "These Are a Few of My Favorite Uses of Math."

Counting Think Tac Toe

Student name: _____

Choose and complete one activity in each row.

Play *Count to 120*. 	Talk with a partner about what someone needs to know and do to be a good counter.	Complete 3 number clue cards.
Count the number of doors there are in our hallway. Write the number. 	Count the number of steps you take to get from our classroom to the office. Write the number. 	Does it take more steps to walk from the cafeteria to the nurse's office or the gym to the nurse's office?
Ask an adult to tell you all the things he or she counted today.	Count to find the total number of letters in the first names of all the members of your family.	Keep track of how many times you turn off the bathroom light on a Saturday. 

From *How to Differentiate Your Math Instruction: Lessons, Ideas, and Videos with Common Core Support, Grades K–5: A Multimedia Professional Learning Resource* by Linda Dacey, Jayne Bamford Lynch, and Rebeka Eston Salemi. © 2013 by Scholastic Inc. Permission granted to photocopy for nonprofit use in a classroom or similar place dedicated to face-to-face educational purposes. Downloadable at *www.mathsolutions.com/howtodifferentiatereproducible*.

RAFT: *Telling Time*

Student name: _____

ROLE	AUDIENCE	FORMAT	TOPIC
Teacher	Our class	Riddles (with clues and clock pictures)	What Time Is It?
Writer/illustrator	Second graders	Illustrated children's book	All About Time
Camp counselor	Campers	Schedule with activities and times	First Day of Camp
Self	Parents	Analog clock with explanation	This Is the Time I Like the Best!
Self	Classmates	Collage of clocks with written times and activities	How I Spend Saturdays

What Matches You?

Student name: _____

Try to find two classmates to fit each description. Have them write their initials in the box that matches. No one may initial more than 3 boxes on 1 sheet.

I learn best through hands-on experiences.	I like to solve problems.	I prefer to work alone.	I find it helpful to write about my mathematical ideas.	I sometimes get confused when others explain their thinking.
I like face clocks better than digital ones.	I like to measure things.	I use drawings to understand a problem.	I learn best when the teacher writes on the board.	I find Unifix cubes more helpful than base ten blocks.
I am better at subtraction than addition.	I like building things.	I need quiet when I work.	I find base ten blocks more helpful than Unifix cubes.	I prefer to work with others.
I know my basic facts well.	I like digital clocks better than face clocks.	I am better at addition than subtraction.	I like geometry.	I like to find different ways to solve problems.
I like to brainstorm ideas with a group and then follow up alone.	I like logic games and puzzles.	I want rules for solving problems.	I would like to use a calculator all of the time.	I like collecting data and making graphs.

From *How to Differentiate Your Math Instruction: Lessons, Ideas, and Videos with Common Core Support, Grades K–5: A Multimedia Professional Learning Resource* by Linda Dacey, Jayne Bamford Lynch, and Rebeka Eston Salemi. © 2013 by Scholastic Inc. Permission granted to photocopy for nonprofit use in a classroom or similar place dedicated to face-to-face educational purposes. Downloadable at *www.mathsolutions.com/howtodifferentiatereproducible*

Self–Assessment of Differentiation Practices

Rate your agreement with each of the following statements using the scale provided here:

1—disagree strongly, 2—disagree somewhat, 3—agree somewhat, 4—agree strongly

I feel confident in my ability to facilitate the learning of mathematics at my grade level.	1 2 3 4
I can challenge my most mathematically able students.	1 2 3 4
I know how to support my least mathematically able students.	1 2 3 4
I can meet students' individual needs in mathematics as well as or better than I can in literacy.	1 2 3 4
I have enough knowledge of mathematics to support a variety of models, representations, and procedures in my classroom.	1 2 3 4

Rate the likelihood of the following activities occurring within a week of mathematical instruction using the scale presented here:

1—very unlikely, 2—somewhat unlikely, 3—somewhat likely, 4—very likely

I work with students individually.	1 2 3 4
Students are grouped by readiness.	1 2 3 4
Students are grouped by interest.	1 2 3 4
Students are grouped by learning preferences.	1 2 3 4
Different students are working with different materials and tasks.	1 2 3 4

Check off each instructional strategy that you have tried in your teaching of mathematics. Give yourself 2 points for each checkmark.

☐ Transformation of tasks to make them more open-ended ☐ Menu

☐ RAFT ☐ Think Tac Toe

☐ Learning station ☐ Compacting

☐ Tiered task

Total score: _____

Scores range from 10 to 54 points.

Are you comfortable with where you are on this continuum of change? What next steps do you want to take?

References

Abedi, J., and C. Lord. 2001. "The Language Factor in Mathematics Tests." *Applied Measurement in Education* 14:219–34.

Anderson, L., and D. Krathwohl, eds. 2001. *Taxonomy for Learning, Teaching, and Assessing: A Revision of Bloom's Taxonomy of Educational Objectives.* New York: Addison Wesley Longman.

Barger, R. 2009. "Gifted, and Talented, and High Achieving." *Teaching Children Mathematics* 16:154–61.

Beilock, S., E. Gunderson, G. Ramirez, and S. Levine. 2010. *Female Teachers' Mathematical Anxiety Impact Girls' Math Achievement.* http://cas.uchicago.edu/workshops/education/files/2010/01/.

Bloom, B., ed. 1984. *Taxonomy of Educational Objectives: Book 1 Cognitive Domain.* Reading, MA: Addison-Wesley.

Bressor, R., K. Melanese, and C. Sphar. 2008. *Supporting English Language Learners in Math Class.* Sausalito, CA: Math Solutions.

Carolan, J., and A. Guinn. 2007. "Differentiation: Lessons from Master Teachers." *Improving Instruction for Students with Learning Needs* 64:44–47.

Chiu, L.-H., and L. Henry. 1990. "Development and Validation of the Mathematics Anxiety Scale for Children." *Measurement and Evaluation in Counseling and Development* 23:121–27.

Christaldi, K. 1996. *Even Steven and Odd Todd.* New York: Scholastic.

Conklin, M. 2010. *It Makes Sense! Using the Ten-Frames to Build Number Sense.* Sausalito, CA: Math Solutions.

Conklin, M., and S. Sheffield. 2012. *It Makes Sense! Using the Hundreds Chart to Build Number Sense.* Sausalito, CA: Math Solutions.

Connolly, A. 2008a. *KeyMath–3 Diagnostic Assessment.* Minneapolis, MN: Pearson.

———. 2008b. *KeyMath–3 Essential Resources.* Minneapolis, MN: Pearson.

Cooper, H., J. Civey Robinson, and E. Patall. 2006. "Does Homework Improve Academic Achievement? A Synthesis of Research, 1987–2003." *Review of Educational Research* 76:1–62.

Dacey, L., and D. Perry. 2012. "Common Core State Standards for Mathematics: The Big Picture." *Teaching Children Mathematics* 18:378–83.

Diezmann, C., and N. McCosker. 2011. "Reading Students' Representations." *Teaching Children Mathematics* 18:162–69.

Dunn, K., and S. Mulvenon. 2009. "A Critical Review of Research on Formative Assessment: The Limited Scientific Evidence of the Impact of Formative Assessment in Education." *Practice Assessment, Research & Evaluation* 14.

Fernandes, A., C. Anhalt, and M. Civil. 2010. "Mathematical Interviews to Assess Latino Students." *Teaching Children Mathematics* 16:162–69.

Gardner, H. 1999. *Frames of Mind: The Theory of Multiple Intelligences*, 3rd ed. New York: Basic Books.

Geist, E. 2010. *The Anti-Anxiety Curriculum: Combating Math Anxiety in the Classroom*. http://web.ebscohost.com.ezproxyles .flo.org/ehost/pdfviewer/pdfviewer?vid=4&hid=126&sid=500f 84c9-1fe3-4354-bbc6-148bbb6608c3%40sessionmgr111.

Gillies, R., and M. Haynes. 2011. "Increasing Explanatory Behavior, Problem-Solving, and Reasoning Within Classes Using Cooperative Group Work." *Instructional Science* 39:349–66.

Gomez, C. 2010. "Teaching with Cognates." *Teaching Children Mathematics* 16:470–74.

Holton, D., and D. Clark. 2006. "Scaffolding and Metacognition." *International Journal of Mathematical Education in Science and Technology* 37:127–43.

Individuals with Disabilities Education Improvement Act of 2004. 20 U.S.C. 33 Section 1400 *et seq.* www.ed.gov/policy/apeced/guid/ idea2004.html.

Islas, D. 2011. *How to Assess While You Teach Math: Formative Assessment Practice and Lessons, Grades K–2*. Sausalito, CA: Math Solutions.

Joyner, J., and M. Muri. 2011. *INFORMative Assessment: Formative Assessment to Improve Math Achievement, Grades K–6*. Sausalito, CA: Math Solutions.

Kilpatrick, J., J. Swafford, and B. Findell, eds. 2001. *Adding It Up: Helping Children Learn Mathematics*. Washington, DC: National Academies.

Konold, K., S. Miller, and K. Konold. 2004. "Using Teacher Feedback to Enhance Student Learning." *Teaching Exceptional Children* 36:64–69.

McCombs, B. L. 2006. Learner-Centered Practices: Providing the Context for Positive Learner Development, Motivation, and Achievement. In *Handbook of Research on Schools, Schooling, and Human Development*, eds. J. Meece and J. Eccles, 60–74. Mahwah, NJ: Erlbaum.

National Clearinghouse for English Language Acquisition. 2011. The Growing Numbers of English Language Learner Students, 1998/99–2008/09. February.

National Governors Association Center for Best Practices and the Council of Chief State School Officers. 2010. *Common Core State Standards Initiative: Common Core State Standards for Mathematics*. Washington, DC. www.corestandards.org/assets/ccssi-introduction.pdf.

No Child Left Behind Act. 2002. U.S. Department of Education. Washington, DC.

Otis, N., F. Grouzet, and L. Pelletier. 2005. "Latent Motivational Change in an Academic Setting: A 3-Year Longitudinal Study." *Journal of Educational Psychology,* 97(2):170–83.

Popham, W. J. 2008. *Transformative Assessment*. Alexandria, VA: Association for Supervision and Curriculum Development.

Reid, M., and S. Chamberlain. 1990. *The Button Box*. New York: Penguin Books.

Richardson, K. 2003. *Assessing Math Concepts*. Bellingham, WA: Math Perspectives.

Russell, S. J. 2012. CCSS: "Keeping Teaching and Learning Strong." *Teaching Children Mathematics* 19:50–55.

Saye, J., and T. Brush. 2002. "Scaffolding Critical Reasoning About History and Social Issues in Multimedia-Supported Learning Environment." *Educational Technology Research and Development* 50:77–96.

Scieszka, J., and L. Smith. 1995. *Math Curse*. New York: Penguin.

Shaughnessy, M. 2011. "Identify Fractions and Decimals on a Number Line." *Teaching Children Mathematics* 17:428–34.

Siemens, G. 2005. Connectivism: A Learning Theory for the Digital Age. *International Journal of Instructional Technology & Distance Learning*. Retrieved from www.itdl.org/Journal/Jan_05/article01.htm